W9-ANU-656

From the Cradle to the Grave

Classic Essays on Coming of Age and Aging

Janet Marting

The University of Akron

NTC *Publishing Group*
a *division of* NTC/CONTEMPORARY PUBLISHING COMPANY
Lincolnwood, Illinois USA

Executive Editor: Marisa L. L'Heureux
Development Editor: Lisa A. De Mol
Project Editor: Heidi L. Hedstrom
Cover and interior design: Ophelia M. Chambliss
Cover art: Celia Johnson/Gerald & Cullen Rapp, Inc.
Production Manager: Margo Goia

Acknowledgments begin on page 291, which is to be considered an extension of this copyright page.

ISBN: 0-8442-5305-7 (student text)
ISBN: 0-8442-5306-5 (instructor's edition)

Library of Congress Cataloging-in-Publication Data

From the cradle to the grave : classic essays on coming of age and
    aging / [compiled by] Janet Marting.
        p.   cm. — (NTC's library of classic essays)
    Includes index.
    Summary: Includes essays on every age in the life cycle beginning
with childhood as well as biographical headnotes about each writer,
discussion questions, and writing assignments.
        ISBN 0-8442-5305-7 (pbk.)
        1. Aging—Literary collection. 2. Youth—Literary collections.
    3. Life cycle, Human—Literary collections.   [1. Aging. 2. Youth.
    3. Life cycle, Human.]   I. Marting, Janet. II. Series.
    PN6071.A48F76   1997
    808.8'49354—dc21   97-350
                                                                    CIP
    7 8 9 VP 0 9 8 7 6 5 4 3 2 1   AC

Contents

Classic Essays on Early Adulthood   97

Classic Essays on Middle Age   157

Classic Essays on Aging and Old Age   201

Classic Essays on Death and Dying   247

Preface

NTC's Library of Classic Essays

This is a six-volume collection of some of the finest essays ever written, providing a broad yet in-depth overview of the development and scope of the genre. In essence, an essay is a short prose composition, usually exploring one subject and often presenting the personal view of the author. An essay may take a variety of forms (from narration to description to autobiography) and may reflect any number of moods (from critical to reflective to whimsical).

Although we recognize a few early works by Plato, Aristotle, and others as essays, it was really Michel de Montaigne, a French philosopher and writer, who substantially defined the form when he published two volumes of his own essays under the title *Essais* in 1580. Montaigne considered himself to be representative of humankind in general: thus, his essays, though they are to be read as general treatises on the human condition, are largely reflective of Montaigne's own attitudes and experiences.

The essay proved to be a most adaptable form. In the eighteenth century, both journalists and philosophers in England and pamphleteers and patriots in the American colonies quickly discovered the power of a well-crafted and provocative essay. By the middle of the nineteenth century, the essay was the form of choice for such brilliant writers as the American Ralph Waldo Emerson and the British George Eliot. In the twentieth century, the essay has become the most widely read genre—from personal essays in periodicals to scholarly essays in scientific journals to argumentative essays on the editorial pages of newspapers worldwide.

From the Cradle to the Grave:
Classic Essays on Coming of Age and Aging

This volume contains thirty-three classic essays that illustrate the growth and self-discovery that people experience at various stages of their lives. Organized chronologically, these essays explore the maturation process—physical, mental, and emotional—typical of all people, across time and space. If, however, one of your favorites is not included here, it may well be in one of the other volumes: *The Family Tree: Classic Essays on Family and Ancestors; Plato's Heirs: Classic Essays; Daughters of the Revolution: Classic Essays by Women; Diverse Identities: Classic Multicultural Essays;* or *Of Bunsen Burners, Bones, and Belles Lettres: Classic Essays across the Curriculum.*

This volume brings you essays that explore how writers think and write about the people and the events that affected them in diverse ways throughout their lives. It is our hope that this collection will allow you to examine who you are and better enable you to explore your place—and the place of others—in the universe.

CLASSIC ESSAYS
ON

Childhood

On Being Found Out

WILLIAM MAKEPEACE THACKERAY

William Makepeace Thackeray (1811–1863) was born in Calcutta, India, but lived the majority of his life in England. He received his education at Trinity College, Cambridge University from 1829 to 1830. Thackeray studied law briefly before he turned to writing full-time when he was unable to sustain an interest in formal education. His first publications were short articles and satires, but he later wrote serials and longer works of fiction. The author of the novels *Pendennis* (1850), *Henry Esmond* (1852), and *The Newcomes* (1855), Thackeray is most famous for *Vanity Fair* (1848). His other writing includes *The Book of Snobs* (1848), eight volumes of *Miscellanies: Prose and Verse* (1849–1857), *A Shabby Genteel Story and Other Writings* (1852), *Men's Wives* (1852), *Ballads* (1856), *Lovel the Widower* (1860), *Denis Duval* (1864), and *Loose Sketches, an Eastern Adventure, Etc.* (1894). A prolific writer, Thackeray is also the author of a collection of essays, *The Roundabout Papers* (1863), originally published in *Cornhill Magazine*, which he edited from 1860 to 1862. A Victorian novelist, Thackeray was particularly adept at creating memorable characters such as Becky Sharp and Amelia Sedley in *Vanity Fair*. In the following selection, which first appeared in *Cornhill*

Magazine, Thackeray recalls an incident from his childhood when, as the title reveals, he was "found out."

1   At the close (let us say) of Queen Anne's reign, when I was a boy at a private and preparatory school for young gentlemen, I remember the wiseacre of a master ordering us all, one night, to march into a little garden at the back of the house, and thence to proceed one by one into a tool or hen house (I was but a tender little thing just put into short clothes, and can't exactly say whether the house was for tools or hens), and in that house to put our hands into a sack which stood on a bench, a candle burning beside it. I put my hand into the sack. My hand came out quite black. I went and joined the other boys in the schoolroom; and all their hands were black too.

2   By reason of my tender age (and there are some critics who, I hope, will be satisfied by my acknowledging that I am a hundred and fifty-six next birthday) I could not understand what was the meaning of this night excursion—this candle, this toolhouse, this bag of soot. I think we little boys were taken out of our sleep to be brought to the ordeal. We came, then, and showed our little hands to the master; washed them or not—most probably, I should say, not—and so went bewildered back to bed.

3   Something had been stolen in the school that day; and Mr. Wiseacre having read in a book of an ingenious method of finding out a thief by making him put his hand into a sack (which, if guilty, the rogue would shirk from doing), all we boys were subjected to the trial. Goodness knows what the lost object was, or who stole it. We all had black hands to show the master. And the thief, whoever he was, was not Found Out that time.

4   I wonder if the rascal is alive—an elderly scoundrel he must be by this time; and a hoary old hypocrite to whom an old schoolfellow presents his kindest regards—parenthetically remarking what a dreadful place that private school was; cold, chillblains, bad dinners, not enough victuals, and caning awful!—Are you alive still, I say, you nameless villain, who escaped discovery on that day of crime? I hope you have escaped often since, old sinner. Ah, what a lucky thing it is, for you and

me, my man, that we are *not* found out in all our peccadilloes; and that our backs can slip away from the master and the cane!

5 Just consider what life would be, if every rouge was found out, and flogged *coram populo*! What a butchery, what an indecency, what an endless swishing of the rod! Don't cry out about my misanthropy. My good friend Mealymouth, I will trouble you to tell me, do you go to church? When there, do you say, or do you not, that you are a miserable sinner? and saying so do you believe or disbelieve it? If you are a M. S., don't you deserve correction, and aren't you grateful if you are to be let off? I say again, what a blessed thing it is that we are not all found out!

6 Just picture to yourself everybody who does wrong being found out, and punished accordingly. Fancy all the boys in all the schools being whipped; and then the assistants, and then the headmaster (Dr. Badford let us call him). Fancy the provost-marshal being tied up, having previously superintended the correction of the whole army. After the young gentlemen have had their turn for the faulty exercises, fancy Dr. Lincolnsinn being taken up for certain faults in *his* Essay and Review. After the clergyman has cried his peccavi, suppose we hoist up a bishop, and give him a couple of dozen! (I see my Lord Bishop of Double-Gloucester sitting in a very uneasy posture on his right reverend bench.) After we have cast off the bishop, what are we to say to the Minister who appointed him? My Lord Cinqwarden, it is painful to have to use personal correction to a boy of your age; but really *Siste tandem, carnifex!* The butchery is too horrible. The hand drops powerless, appalled at the quantity of birch which it must cut and brandish. I am glad we are not all found out, I say again; and protest, my dear brethren, against our having our deserts.

7 To fancy all men found out and punished is bad enough; but imagine all women found out in the distinguished social circle in which you and I have the honor to move. Is it not a mercy that a many of these fair criminals remain unpunished and undiscovered! There is Mrs. Longbow, who is forever practising, and who shoots poisoned arrows, too; when you meet her you don't call her a liar, and charge her with the wickedness she has done and is doing. There is Mrs. Painter, who passes for a most respectable woman, and a model in society. There is no use in saying what you really know regarding her and her goings on. There is Diana Hunter—what a little haughty prude it is; and yet *we* know stories about her which

are not altogether edifying. I say it is best, for the sake of the good, that the bad should not all be found out. You don't want your children to know the history of that lady in the next box, who is so handsome, and whom they admire so. Ah me, what would life be if we were all found out, and punished for all our faults? Jack Ketch would be in permanence; and then who would hang Jack Ketch?

They talk of murderers being pretty certainly found out. Psha! I have heard an authority awfully competent vow and declare that scores and hundreds of murders are committed, and nobody is the wiser. That terrible man mentioned one or two ways of committing murder, which he maintained were quite common, and were scarcely ever found out. A man, for instance, comes home to his wife, and— but I pause—I know that this Magazine has a very large circulation. Hundreds and hundreds of thousands—why not say a million of people at once?—well, say a million, read it. And amongst these countless readers, I might be teaching some monster how to make away with his wife without being found out, some fiend of a woman how to destroy her dear husband. I will *not* then tell this easy and simple way of murder, as communicated to me by a most respectable party in the confidence of private intercourse. Suppose some gentle reader were to try this most simple and easy receipt—it seems to me almost infallible—and come to grief in consequence, and be found out and hanged? Should I ever pardon myself for having been the means of doing injury to a single one of our esteemed subscribers? The prescription whereof I speak—that is to say, whereof I *don't* speak—shall be buried in this bosom. No, I am a humane man. I am not one of your Bluebeards to go and say to my wife, "My dear! I am going away for a few days to Brighton. Here are all the keys of the house. You may open every door and closet, except the one at the end of the oak-room opposite the fireplace, with the little bronze Shakespeare on the mantel-piece (or what not)." I don't say this to a woman—unless, to be sure, I want to get rid of her—because, after such a caution, I know she'll peep into the closet. I say nothing about the closet at all. I keep the key in my pocket, and a being whom I love, but who, as I know, has many weaknesses, out of harm's way. You toss up your head, dear angel, drub on the ground with your lovely little feet, on the table with your sweet rosy fingers, and cry, "Oh, sneerer! You don't know the depth of woman's feeling, the lofty scorn of all deceit, the entire absence of mean curiosity in the sex, or never, never would you libel us so!" Ah, Delia! dear, dear Delia! It is because I fancy I *do* know something about you (not all, mind—no, no; no man knows that)—Ah, my bride, my ringdove, my rose, my poppet—choose, in fact, whatever name you like—bulbul of my grove, fountain of my desert, sunshine of my darkling life, and joy of my dungeoned existence, it is because I *do* know a little about you that I conclude to say nothing of that private closet, and keep my key in my pocket. You take away that closet-key then, and the house-key. You lock Delia in. You keep her out of harm's way and gadding, and so she never *can* be found out.

9   And yet by little strange accidents and coincidences how we are being found out every day. You remember that old story of the Abbé Kakatoes, who told the company at supper one night how the first confession he ever received was—from a murderer let us say. Presently enters to supper the Marquis de Croquemitaine. "Palsambleu, Abbé!" says the brilliant marquis, taking a pinch of snuff, "are you here? Gentlemen and ladies! I was the abbé's first penitent, and I made him a confession, which I promise you astonished him."

10   To be sure how queerly things are found out! Here is an instance. Only the other day I was writing in these "Roundabout Papers" about a certain man, whom I facetiously called Baggs, and who had abused me to my friends, who of course told me. Shortly after that paper was published another friend—Sacks let us call him—scowls fiercely at me as I am sitting in perfect good-humor at the club, and passes on without speaking. A cut. A quarrel. Sacks thinks it is about him that I was writing: whereas, upon my honor and conscience, I never had him once in my mind, and was pointing my moral from quite another man. But don't you see, by this wrath of the guilty-conscienced Sacks, that he had been abusing me too? He has owned himself guilty, never having been accused. He has winced when nobody thought of hitting him. I did but put the cap out, and madly butting and chafing, behold my friend rushes out to put his head into it! Never mind, Sacks, you are found out; but I bear you no malice, my man.

11   And yet to be found out, I know from my own experience, must be painful and odious, and cruelly mortifying to the inward vanity. Suppose I am a poltroon, let us say. With fierce mustache, loud talk, plentiful oaths, and an immense stick, I keep up nevertheless a character for courage. I swear fearfully at cabmen and women; brandish my bludgeon, and perhaps knock down a little man or two with

it: brag of the images which I break at the shooting-gallery, and pass amongst my friends for a whiskery fire-eater, afraid of neither man nor dragon. Ah me! Suppose some brisk little chap steps up and gives me a caning in St. James's Street, with all the heads of my friends looking out all the club windows. My reputation is gone, I frighten no man more. My nose is pulled by whipper-snappers, who jump up on a chair to reach it. I am found out. And in the days of my triumphs, when people were yet afraid of me, and were taken in by my swagger, I always knew that I was a lily-liver, and expected that I should be found out some day.

12   That certainty of being found out must haunt and depress many a bold braggadocio spirit. Let us say it is a clergyman, who can pump copious floods of tears out of his own eyes and those of his audience. He thinks to himself, "I am but a poor swindling, chattering rogue. My bills are unpaid. I have jilted several women whom I have promised to marry. I don't know whether I believe what I preach, and I know I have stolen the very sermon over which I have been snivelling. Have they found me out?" says he, as his head drops down on the cushion.

13   Then your writer, poet, historian, novelist, or what not? The "Beacon" says that "Jones's work is one of the first order." The "Lamp" declares that "Jones's tragedy surpasses every work since the days of Him of Avon." The "Comet" asserts that "J's 'Life of Goody Twoshoes' is a κτῆμα ἐζ ἀεὶ, a noble and enduring monument to the fame of that admirable Englishwoman," and so forth. But then Jones knows that he has lent the critic of the "Beacon" five pounds; that his publisher has a half-share in the "Lamp;" and that the "Comet" comes repeatedly to dine with him. It is all very well. Jones is immortal until he is found out; and then down comes the extinguisher, and the immortal is dead and buried. The idea (*dies iræ!*) of discovery must haunt many a man, and make him uneasy, as the trumpets are puffing in his triumph. Brown, who has a higher place than he deserves, cowers before Smith, who has found him out. What is a chorus of critics shouting "Bravo?"—a public clapping hands and flinging garlands? Brown knows that Smith has found him out. Puff, trumpets! Wave, banners! Huzza, boys, for the immortal Brown! "This is all very well," B. thinks (bowing the while, smiling, laying his hand to his heart); "but there stands Smith at the window: *he* has measured me; and some day the others will find me out too." It is a very curious sensation to sit by a man who has found you out,

and who, as you know, has found you out; or *vice versâ*, to sit with a man whom *you* have found out. His talent? Bah! His virtue? We know a little story or two about his virtue, and he knows we know it. We are thinking over friend Robinson's antecedents, as we grin, bow and talk; and we are both humbugs together. Robinson a good fellow, is he? You know how he behaved to Hicks? A good-natured man, is he? Pray do you remember that little story of Mrs. Robinson's black eye? How men have to work, to talk, to smile, to go to bed, and try and sleep, with this dread of being found out on their consciences! Bardolph, who has robbed a church, and Nym, who has taken a purse, go to their usual haunts, and smoke their pipes with their companions. Mr. Detective Bullseye appears, and says, "Oh, Bardolph! I want you about that there pyx business!" Mr. Bardolph knocks the ashes out of his pipe, puts out his hands to the little steel cuffs, and walks away quite meekly. He is found out. He must go. "Good-by, Doll Tearsheet! Good-by, Mrs. Quickly, Ma'am!" The other gentlemen and ladies *de la société* look on and exchange mute adieux with the departing friends. And an assured time will come when the other gentlemen and ladies will be found out too.

14   What a wonderful and beautiful provision of nature it has been that, for the most part, our womankind are not endowed with the faculty of finding us out! *They* don't doubt, and probe, and weigh, and take your measure. Lay down this paper, my benevolent friend and reader, go into your drawing-room now, and utter a joke ever so old, and I wager sixpence the ladies there will all begin to laugh. Go to Brown's house, and tell Mrs. Brown and the young ladies what you think of him, and see what a welcome you will get! In like manner, let him come to your house, and tell *your* good lady his candid opinion of you, and fancy how she will receive him! Would you have your wife and children know you exactly for what you are, and esteem you precisely at your worth? If so, my friend, you will live in a dreary house, and you will have but a chilly fireside. Do you suppose the people round it don't see your homely face as under a glamour, and, as it were, with a halo of love round it? You don't fancy you *are*, as you seem to them? No such thing, my man. Put away that monstrous conceit, and be thankful that *they* have not found you out.

From *Roundabout Papers*, 1863.

Discussion Questions

1. In paragraph 5, why does Thackeray say "what a blessed thing it is that we are not all found out"? Discuss your reasons for agreeing or disagreeing with him.
2. In small groups, discuss why Thackeray's feelings when he was ordered to put his hand in the sack were typical or atypical of children his age.
3. Explain Thackeray's parenthetical remark in paragraph 2.
4. What does Thackeray imply about women's ability in "finding men out"?
5. What kinds of people (or what sorts of crimes) do you think should be "found out" and what kinds should not be? Explain.
6. What purpose is served by Thackeray's asking a number of rhetorical questions in the last paragraph?
7. What do you learn about Thackeray from his essay? What implications does the essay have on your own life?

Writing Assignments

1. Write an essay describing a time in which you were "found out." Be sure to detail not only what happened but also your feelings about the incident.
2. Write a letter to someone in authority (for example, a parent or a school official) explaining from a young person's perspective why children disobey rules.
3. To what extent is being "found out" a rite of passage, that is, an event in people's lives that signals their growing maturity? Write an essay in which you address this question and discuss the importance of such rites of passage.
4. Write an essay describing the many rites of passage children go through before becoming young adults. Are there any that symbolize your generation?
5. Do you think that boys experience more difficulty with rites of passage than girls (or vice versa)? Examine this question in an essay that explores the ethics of concealing secrets and being found out.

from Reveries over Childhood and Youth

WILLIAM BUTLER YEATS

William Butler Yeats (1865–1939) was born in Dublin, Ireland. From 1874 until 1883, the Yeatses lived in London. Yeats began his education at the School of Art in Dublin but turned to writing at the age of twenty-one. First writing plays, including *The Countess Cathleen* (1892) and *Cathleen ni Houlihan* (1902), Yeats is most known for his poetry. His first published poem appeared in the *Dublin University Review* in 1885, and, in 1891, he became one of the founders of the Pre-Raphaelite Rhymer's Club. His volumes of poetry include *In the Seven Woods* (1904), *The Green Helmet and Other Poems* (1910), *The Tower* (1928), and *The Winding Stair* (1929). *Essays* (1924) is Yeats's collection of nonfiction, and *Essays and Introductions* was published posthumously in 1961. In 1923, he was awarded the Nobel Prize in literature for his poetry. Yeats's experiments with rhyme, his use of symbols, and his diverse styles have made him one of the greatest twentieth-century poets of the English language. The following selection is from *The Autobiography of William Butler Yeats* (1927) and represents Yeats's deliberate, lyrical, and reflective writing style.

1   At length when I was eight or nine an aunt said to me, "You are
going to London. Here you are somebody. There you will be nobody
at all." I knew at the time that her words were a blow at my father
not at me, but it was some years before I knew her reason. She
thought so able a man as my father could have found out some way
of painting more popular pictures if he had set his mind to it and
that it was wrong of him "to spend every evening at his club."
She had mistaken, for what she would have considered a place of
wantonness Heatherley's Art School.

2   My mother and brother and sister were at Sligo perhaps when I
was sent to England, for my father and I and a group of landscape
painters lodged at Burnham Beeches with an old Mr. and Mrs. Earle.
My father was painting the first big pond you come to if you have
driven from Slough through Farnham Royal. He began it in spring
and painted all through the year, the picture changing with the
seasons, and gave it up unfinished when he had painted the snow
upon the heath-covered banks. He is never satisfied and can never
make himself say that any picture is finished. In the evening he heard
me recite my lessons or read me some novel of Fenimore Cooper's.
I found delightful adventures in the woods—one day a blind worm
and an adder fighting in a green hollow, and sometimes Mrs. Earle
would be afraid to tidy the room because I had put a bottle full of
newts on the mantelpiece. Now and then a boy from a farm on the
other side of the road threw a pebble at my window at daybreak,
and he and I went fishing in the big second pond. Now and then
another farmer's boy and I shot sparrows with an old pepper-box
revolver and the boy would roast them on a string. There was an
old horse one of the painters called the scaffolding, and sometimes
a son of old Earle's drove with me to Slough and once to Windsor,
and at Windsor we made our lunch of cold sausages bought from a
public-house. I did not know what it was to be alone, for I could
wander in pleasant alarm through the enclosed parts of the Beeches,
then very large, or round some pond imagining ships going in and
out among the reeds and thinking of Sligo or of strange sea-faring
adventures in the fine ship I should launch when I grew up. I had
always a lesson to learn before night and that was a continual misery,
for I could very rarely, with so much to remember, set my thoughts
upon it and then only in fear. One day my father told me that a
painter had said I was very thick-skinned and did not mind what was

said to me, and I could not understand how anybody could be so unjust. It made me wretched to be idle but one could not help it. I was once surprised and shocked. All but my father and myself had been to London, and Kennedy and Farrar and Page, I remember the names vaguely, arrived laughing and talking. One of them had carried off a card of texts from the waiting-room of the station and hung it up on the wall. I thought "he had stolen it," but my father and all made it a theme of merry conversation.

3   Then I returned to Sligo for a few weeks as I was to do once or twice in every year for years, and after that we settled in London. Perhaps my mother and the other children had been there all the time, for I remember my father now and again going to London. The first house we lived in was close to Burne Jones's house at North End, but we moved after a year or two to Bedford Park. At North End we had a pear tree in the garden and plenty of pears, but the pears used to be full of maggots, and almost opposite lived a schoolmaster called O'Neill, and when a little boy told me that the schoolmaster's great-grandfather had been a king I did not doubt it. I was sitting against the hedge and iron railing of some villa-garden there, when I heard one boy say to another it was something wrong with my liver that gave me such a dark complexion and that I could not live more than a year. I said to myself a year is a very long time, one can do such a lot of things in a year, and put it out of my head. When my father gave me a holiday and later when I had a holiday from school I took my schooner boat to the round pond sailing it very commonly against the two cutter yachts of an old naval officer. He would sometimes look at the ducks and say, "I would like to take that fellow home for my dinner," and he sang me a sailor's song about a "coffin ship" which left Sligo after the great famine, that made me feel very important. The servants at Sligo had told me the story. When she was moved from the berth she had lain in, an unknown dead man's body had floated up, a very evil omen; and my grandfather, who was Lloyd's agent, had condemned her, but she slipped out in the night. The pond had its own legends; and a boy who had seen a certain model steamer "burned to the water's edge" was greatly valued as a friend. There was a little boy I was kind to because I knew his father had done something disgraceful though I did not know what. It was years before I discovered that his father was but the maker of certain popular statues, many of

which are now in public places. I had heard my father's friends speak of him. Sometimes my sister came with me, and we would look into all the sweet shops and toy shops on our way home, especially into one opposite Holland House because there was a cutter yacht made of sugar in the window, and we drank at all the fountains. Once a stranger spoke to us and bought us sweets and came with us almost to our door. We asked him to come in and told him our father's name. He would not come in, but laughed and said, "Oh, that is the painter who scrapes out every day what he painted the day before." A poignant memory came upon me the other day while I was passing the drinking-fountain near Holland Park, for there I and my sister had spoken together of our longing for Sligo and our hatred of London. I know we were both very close to tears and remember with wonder, for I had never known any one that cared for such mementoes, that I longed for a sod of earth from some field I knew, something of Sligo to hold in my hand. It was some old race instinct like that of a savage, for we had been brought up to laugh at all display of emotion. Yet it was our mother, who would have thought its display a vulgarity, who kept alive that love. She would spend hours listening to stories or telling stories of the pilots and fishing people of Rosses Point, or of her own Sligo girlhood, and it was always assumed between her and us that Sligo was more beautiful than other places. I can see now that she had great depth of feeling, that she was her father's daughter. My memory of what she was like in those days has grown very dim, but I think her sense of personality, her desire of any life of her own, had disappeared in her care for us and in much anxiety about money. I always see her sewing or knitting in spectacles and wearing some plain dress. Yet ten years ago when I was in San Francisco, an old cripple came to see me who had left Sligo before her marriage; he came to tell me, he said, that my mother "had been the most beautiful girl in Sligo."

4   The only lessons I had ever learned were those my father taught me, for he terrified me by descriptions of my moral degradation and he humiliated me by my likeness to disagreeable people; but presently I was sent to school at Hammersmith. It was a Gothic building of yellow brick: a large hall full of desks, some small class-rooms and a separate house for boarders, all built perhaps in 1860 or 1870. I thought it an ancient building and that it had belonged to the founder of the school, Lord Godolphin, who was romantic to me because

there was a novel about him. I never read the novel, but I thought only romantic people were put in books. On one side, there was a piano factory of yellow brick , upon two sides half-finished rows of little shops and villas all yellow brick, and on the fourth side, outside the wall of our playing field, a brick-field of cinders and piles of half-burned yellow bricks. All the names and faces of my schoolfellows have faded from me except one name without a face and the face and name of one friend, mainly no doubt because it was all so long ago, but partly because I only seem to remember things dramatic in themselves or that are somehow associated with unforgettable places.

5   For some days as I walked homeward along, the Hammersmith Road, I told myself that whatever I most cared for had been taken away. I had found a small, green-covered book given to my father by a Dublin man of science; it gave an account of the strange sea creatures the man of science had discovered among the rocks at Howth or dredged out of Dublin Bay. It had long been my favourite book; and when I read it I believed that I was growing very wise, but now I should have no time for it nor for my own thoughts. Every moment would be taken up learning or saying lessons, or in walking between school and home four times a day for I came home in the middle of the day for dinner. But presently I forgot my trouble, absorbed in two things I had never known, companionship and enmity. After my first day's lesson, a circle of boys had got around me in a playing field and asked me questions, "Who's your father?" "What does he do?" "How much money has he?" Presently a boy said something insulting. I had never struck anybody or been struck, and now all in a minute, without any intention upon my side, but as if I had been a doll moved by a string, I was hitting at the boys within reach and being hit. After that I was called names for being Irish, and had many fights and never, for years, got the better in any one of them; for I was delicate and had no muscles. Sometimes, however, I found means of retaliation, even of aggression. There was a boy with a big stride, much feared by little boys, and finding him alone in the playing field, I went up to him and said, "Rise upon Sugaun and sink upon Gad." "What does that mean?" he said. "Rise upon hay-leg and sink upon straw," I answered and told him that in Ireland the sergeant tied straw and hay to the ankles of a stupid recruit to show him the difference between his legs. My ears were

boxed, and when I complained to my friends, they said I had brought it upon myself, and that I deserved all I got. I probably dared myself to other feats of a like sort, for I did not think English people intelligent or well-behaved unless they were artists. Every one I knew well in Sligo despised Nationalists and Catholics, but all disliked England with a prejudice that had come down perhaps from the days of the Irish Parliament. I knew stories to the discredit of England, and took them all seriously. My mother had met some English woman who did not like Dublin because the legs of the men were too straight, and at Sligo, as everybody knew, an Englishman had once said to a car-driver, "If you people were not so lazy, you would pull down the mountain and spread it out over the sand and that would give you acres of good fields." At Sligo there is a wide river mouth and at ebb tide most of it is dry sand, but all Sligo knew that in some way I cannot remember it was the spreading of the tide over the sand that left the narrow channel fit for shipping. At any rate the carman had gone chuckling all over Sligo with his tale. People would tell it to prove that Englishmen were always grumbling. "They grumble about their dinners and everything—there was an Englishman who wanted to pull down Knocknarea" and so on. My mother had shown them to me kissing at railway stations, and taught me to feel disgust at their lack of reserve, and my father told how my grandfather, William Yeats, who had died before I was born, when he came home to his Rectory in County Down from an English visit, spoke of some man he had met on a coach road who "Englishman-like" told him all his affairs. My father explained that an Englishman generally believed that his private affairs did him credit, while an Irishman, being poor and probably in debt, had no such confidence. I, however, did not believe in this explanation. My Sligo nurses, who had in all likelihood the Irish Catholic political hatred, had never spoken well of any Englishman. Once when walking in the town of Sligo I had turned to look after an English man and woman whose clothes attracted me. The man I remember had grey clothes and knee-breeches and the woman a grey dress, and my nurse had said contemptuously, "Tow-rows"—perhaps before my time, there had been some English song with the burden "tow row row"— and everybody had told me that English people ate skates and even dog-fish, and I myself had only just arrived in England when I saw an old man put marmalade in his porridge.

6   I was divided from all those boys, not merely by the anecdotes that are everywhere perhaps a chief expression of the distrust of races, but because our mental images were different. I read their boy's books and they excited me, but if I read of some English victory, I did not believe that I read of my own people. They thought of Cressy and Agincourt and the Union Jack and were all very patriotic, and I, without those memories of Limerick and the Yellow Ford that would have strengthened an Irish Catholic, thought of mountain and lake, of my grandfather and of ships. Anti-Irish feeling was running high, for the Land League had been founded and landlords had been shot, and I, who had no politics, was yet full of pride, for it is romantic to live in a dangerous country.

7   I daresay I thought the rough manners of a cheap school, as my grandfather Yeats had those of a chance companion, typical of all England. At any rate I had a harassed life and got many a black eye and had many outbursts of grief and rage. Once a boy, the son of a great Bohemian glass-maker, who was older than the rest of us, and had been sent out of his country because of a love affair, beat a boy for me because we were "both foreigners." And a boy, who grew to be the school athlete and my chief friend, beat a great many. His are the face and name that I remember—his name was of Huguenot origin and his face like his gaunt and lithe body had something of the American Indian in colour and lineament.

8   I was very much afraid of the other boys, and that made me doubt myself for the first time. When I had gathered pieces of wood in the corner for my great ship, I was confident that I could keep calm among the storms and die fighting when the great battle came. But now I was ashamed of my lack of courage; for I wanted to be like my grandfather who thought so little of danger that he had jumped overboard in the Bay of Biscay after an old hat. I was very much afraid of physical pain, and one day when I had made some noise in class, my friend the athlete was accused and I allowed him to get two strokes of the cane before I gave myself up. He had held out his hands without flinching and had not rubbed them on his sides afterwards. I was not caned, but was made to stand up for the rest of the lesson. I suffered very much afterwards when the thought came to me, but he did not reproach me.

9   I had been some years at school before I had my last fight. My friend, the athlete, had given me many months of peace, but at last

refused to beat any more and said I must learn to box, and not go near the other boys till I knew how. I went home with him every day and boxed in his room, and the bouts had always the same ending. My excitability gave me an advantage at first and I would drive him across the room, and then he would drive me across and it would end very commonly with my nose bleeding. One day his father, an elderly banker, brought us out into the garden and tried to make us box in a cold-blooded, courteous way, but it was no use. At last he said I might go near the boys again and I was no sooner inside the gate of the playing field than a boy flung a handful of mud and cried out, "Mad Irishman." I hit him several times on the face without being hit, till the boys round said we should make friends. I held out my hand in fear; for I knew if we went on I should be beaten, and he took it sullenly. I had so poor a reputation as a fighter that it was a great disgrace to him, and even the masters made fun of his swollen face; and though some little boys came in a deputation to ask me to lick a boy they named, I had never another fight with a school-fellow. We had a great many fights with the street boys and the boys of a neighbouring charity school. We had always the better because we were not allowed to fling stones, and that compelled us to close or do our best to close. The monitors had been told to report any boy who fought in the street, but they only reported those who flung stones. I always ran at the athlete's heels, but I never hit any one. My father considered these fights absurd, and even that they were an English absurdity, and so I could not get angry enough to like hitting and being hit; and then too my friend drove the enemy before him. He had no doubts or speculations to lighten his fist upon an enemy, that, being of low behaviour, should be beaten as often as possible, and there were real wrongs to avenge: one of our boys had been killed by the blow of a stone hid in a snowball. Sometimes we on our side got into trouble with the parents of boys. There was a quarrel between the athlete and an old German who had a barber's shop we passed every day on our way home, and one day he spat through the window and hit the German on his bald head—the monitors had not forbidden spitting. The German ran after us, but when the athlete squared up he went away. Now, though I knew it was not right to spit at people, my admiration for my friend arose to a great height. I spread his fame over the school, and next day there was a fine stir when somebody saw the old German going up the gravel walk to the head-master's room. Presently there was such a noise in the passage that even the master had to listen. It was the head-master's red-haired brother turning the old German out and shouting to the manservant, "See that he doesn't steal the topcoats." We heard afterwards that he had asked the names of the two boys who passed his window every day and had been told the names of the two head boys who passed also but were notoriously gentlemanly in their manners. Yet my friend was timid also and that restored my confidence in myself. He would often ask me to buy the sweets or the ginger-beer because he was afraid sometimes when speaking to a stranger.

10   I had one reputation that I valued. At first when I went to the Hammersmith swimming-baths with the other boys, I was afraid to plunge in until I had gone so far down the ladder that the water came up to my thighs; but one day when I was alone I fell from the spring-board which was five or six feet above the water. After that I would dive from a greater height than the others and I practised swimming under water and pretending not to be out of breath when I came up. And then if I ran a race, I took care not to pant or show any sign of strain. And in this I had an advantage even over the athlete, for though he could run faster and was harder to tire than anybody else he grew very pale; and I was often paid compliments. I used to run with my friend when he was training to keep him in company. He would give me a long start and soon overtake me.

11   I followed the career of a certain professional runner for months, buying papers that would tell me if he had won or lost. I had seen him described as "the bright particular star of American athletics", and the wonderful phrase had thrown enchantment over him. Had he been called the particular bright star, I should have cared nothing for him. I did not understand the symptom for years after. I was nursing my own dream, my form of the common schoolboy dream, though I was no longer gathering the little pieces of broken and rotting wood. Often instead of learning my lesson, I covered the white squares of the chessboard on my little table with pen and ink pictures of myself, doing all kinds of courageous things. One day my father said, "There was a man in Nelson's ship at the battle of Trafalgar, a ship's purser, whose hair turned white; what a sensitive temperament; that man should have achieved something!" I was

vexed and bewildered, and am still bewildered and still vexed, finding
it a poor and crazy thing that we who have imagined so many noble
persons cannot bring our flesh to heel.

Discussion Questions

1. In the first paragraph, Yeats admits, "Because I had found it hard
   to attend to anything less interesting than my thoughts, I was
   difficult to teach." Have you ever had similar feelings? Explain
   your answer.
2. Explain how Yeats's family affected the development of his character.
3. From whom did Yeats acquire the "only lesson I [he] had ever
   learned"? From whom did you learn important lessons?
4. In small groups, generate a list of Yeats's reflections that are
   common for youths his age.
5. Characterize Yeats from what he recounts in his essay. Identify
   specific passages that lead you to your answer.

Writing Assignments

1. Write a journal entry detailing your first memories of learning in
   school.
2. Write a letter to specific family members that describes the effect
   or influence they had on you growing up.
3. Recall a realization you had that was a turning point in your life.
   In an essay, describe it so that others can understand not only
   what happened but also your feelings and thoughts about the
   incident.

The Little Store

EUDORA WELTY

Eudora Welty was born in Mississippi in 1909 and received her education at the University of Wisconsin and the Columbia Business School. She began her career as a journalist and copywriter, and, during the Great Depression, she worked for the Works Progress Administration as a writer and photographer. She later wrote stories and novels about the people she met in Mississippi during the Depression. The recipient of a Pulitzer Prize, a PEN/Malamud Award, and the National Endowment for the Humanities Frankel Prize, Welty is the author of the novels *The Robber Bridegroom* (1942), *Delta Wedding* (1946), and *The Optimist's Daughter* (1972). Her stories are collected in *Thirteen Stories* (1965) and in *The Collected Stories of Eudora Welty* (1980). Welty's evocative portrayal of characters and the Southern experience has earned her the reputation as one of the leading contemporary American fiction writers of the South. In *One Writer's Beginnings* (1984), she details the people and events that influenced her life as a writer. Welty's nonfiction pieces are reminiscent of her stories: they often use narration as a way to present her ideas. The following essay from *The Eye of the Story* (1978) is an example of Welty's literary nonfiction. This selection, like many of her other pieces, addresses a common childhood preoccupation: an attempt to understand her place in the world, especially in the small southern town of Jackson, Mississippi.

1   Two blocks away from the Mississippi Sate Capitol, and on the same street with it, where our house was when I was a child growing up in Jackson, it was possible to have a little pasture behind your backyard where you could keep a Jersey cow, which we did. My mother herself milked her. A thrifty homemaker, wife, mother of three, she also did all her own cooking. And as far as I can recall, she never set foot inside a grocery store. It wasn't necessary.

2   For her regular needs, she stood at the telephone in our front hall and consulted with Mr. Lemly, of Lemly's Market and Grocery downtown, who took her order and sent it out on his next delivery. And since Jackson at the heart of it was still within very near reach of the open country, the blackberry lady clanged on her bucket with a quart measure at your front door in June without fail, the watermelon man rolled up to your house exactly on time for the Fourth of July, and down through the summer, the quiet of the early-morning streets was pierced by the calls of farmers driving in with their plenty. One brought his with a song, so plaintive we would sing it with him.

>   Milk, milk,
>   Buttermilk
>   Snap beans—butterbeans—
>   Tender okra—fresh greens. . .
>   and buttermilk.

3   My mother considered herself pretty well prepared in her kitchen and pantry for any emergency that, in her words, might choose to present itself. But if she should, all of a sudden, need another lemon or find she was out of bread, all she had to do was call out, "Quick! Who'd like to run to the Little Store for me?"

4   I would.

5   She'd count out the change into my hand, and I was away. I'll bet the nickel that would be left over that all over the country, for those of my day, the neighborhood grocery played a similar part in our growing up.

6   Our store had its name—it was that of the grocer who owned it, whom I'll call Mr. Sessions—but "the Little Store" is what we called it at home. It was a block down our street toward the capitol and a half a block further, around the corner, toward the cemetery. I knew

even the sidewalk to it as well as I knew my own skin. I'd skipped my jumping-rope up and down it, hopped its length through mazes of hopscotch, played jacks in its islands of shade, serpentined along it on my Princess bicycle, skated it backward and forward. In the twilight I had dragged my steamboat by its string (this was homemade out of every new shoebox, with candle in the bottom lighted and shining through colored tissue paper pasted over windows scissored out in the shapes of the sun, moon, and stars) across every crack of the walk without letting it bump or catch fire. I'd "played out" on this street after supper with my brothers and friends as long as "first-dark" lasted; I'd caught its lightning bugs. On the first Armistice Day (and this will set the time I'm speaking of) we made our own parade down that walk on a single velocipede—my brother pedaling, our little brother riding the handlebars, and myself standing on the back, all with arms wide, flying flags in each hand. (My father snapped that picture as we raced by. It came out blurred.)

7   As I set forth for the Little Store, a tune would float toward me from the house where there lived three sisters, girls in their teens, who ratted their hair over their ears, wore headbands like gladiators, and were considered to be very popular. They practiced for this in the daytime; they'd wind up the Victrola, leave the same record on they'd played before, and you'd see them bobbing past their dining-room windows while they danced with each other. Being three, they could go all day, cutting in:

> Everybody ought to know-oh
> How to do the Tickle-Toe
> (how to do the Tickle-Toe)—

they sang it and danced to it, and as I went by to the same song, I believed it.

8   A little further on, across the street, was the house where the principal of our grade school lived—lived on, even while we were having vacation. What if she would come out? She would halt me in my tracks—she had a very carrying and well-known voice in Jackson, where she'd taught almost everybody—saying "Eudora Alice Welty, spell OBLIGE." OBLIGE was the word that she of course knew had kept me from making 100 on my spelling exam. She'd make me miss it again now, by boring her eyes through me from across

the street. This was my vacation fantasy, one good way to scare myself on the way to the store.

9   Down near the corner waited the house of a little boy named Lindsey. The sidewalk here was old brick, which the roots of a giant chinaberry tree had humped up and tilted this way and that. On skates, you took it fast, in a series of skittering hops, trying not to touch the ground anywhere. If the chinaberries had fallen and rolled in the cracks, it was like skating through a whole shooting match of marbles. I crossed my fingers that Lindsey wouldn't be looking.

10   During the big flu epidemic he and I, as it happened, were being nursed through our sieges at the same time. I'd hear my father and mother murmuring to each other, at the end of a long day, "And I wonder how poor little *Lindsey* got along today?" Just as, down the street, he no doubt would have to hear his family saying, "And I wonder how is poor *Eudora* by now?" I got the idea that a choice was going to be made soon between poor little Lindsey and poor Eudora, and I came up with a funny poem. I wasn't prepared for it when my father told me it wasn't funny and my mother cried that if I couldn't be ashamed for myself, she'd have to be ashamed for me:

> There was a little boy and his name was Lindsey,
> He went to heaven with the influinzy.

He didn't, he survived it, poem and all, the same as I did. But his chinaberries could have brought me down in my skates in a flying act of contrition before his eyes, looking pretty funny myself, right in front of his house.

11   Setting out in this world, a child feels so indelible. He only comes to find out later that it's all the others along his way who are making themselves indelible to him.

12   Our Little Store rose right out from the sidewalk; standing in a street of family houses, it alone hadn't any yard in front, any tree or flowerbed. It was a plain frame building covered over with brick. Above the door, a little railed porch ran across on an upstairs level and four windows with shades were looking out. But I didn't catch on to those.

13   Running in out of the sun, you met what seemed total obscurity inside. There were almost tangible smells—licorice recently sucked

in a child's cheek, dill-pickle brine that had leaked through a paper sack in a fresh trail across the wooden floor, ammonia-loaded ice that had been hoisted from wet croker sacks and slammed into the icebox with its sweet butter at the door, and perhaps the smell of still-untrapped mice.

14 Then through the motes of cracker dust, cornmeal dust, the Gold Dust of the Gold Dust Twins that the floor had been swept out with, the realities emerged. Shelves climbed to high reach all the way around, set out with not too much of any one thing but a lot of things—lard, molasses, vinegar, starch, matches, kerosene, Octagon soap (about a year's worth of octagon-shaped coupons cut out and saved brought a signet ring addressed to you in the mail. Furthermore, when the postman arrived at your door, he blew a whistle). It was up to you to remember what you came for, while your eye traveled from cans of sardines to ice cream salt to harmonicas to flypaper (over your head, batting around on a thread beneath the blades of the ceiling fan, stuck with its testimonial catch).

15 Its confusion may have been in the eye of its beholder. Enchantment is cast upon you by all those things you weren't supposed to have need for, it lures you close to wooden tops you'd outgrown, boy's marbles and agates in little net pouches, small rubber balls that wouldn't bounce straight, frazzly kite-string, clay bubble-pipes that would snap off in your teeth, the stiffest scissors. You could contemplate those long narrow boxes of sparklers gathering dust while you waited for it to be the Fourth of July or Christmas, and noisemakers in the shape of tin frogs for somebody's birthday party you hadn't been invited to yet, and see that they were all marvelous.

16 You might not have even looked for Mr. Sessions when he came around his store cheese (as big as a doll's house) and in front of the counter looking for you. When you'd finally asked him for, and received from him in its paper bag, whatever single thing it was that you had been sent for, the nickel that was left over was yours to spend.

17 Down at a child's eye level, inside those glass jars with mouths in their sides through which the grocer could run his scoop or a child's hand might be invited to reach for a choice, were wineballs, all-day suckers, gumdrops, peppermints. Making a row under the glass of a counter were the Tootsie Rolls, Hershey Bars, Goo-Goo Clusters, Baby Ruths. And whatever was the name of those pastilles that came

stacked in a cardboard cylinder with a cardboard lid? They were thin and dry, about the size of tiddly-winks, and in the shape of twisted rosettes. A kind of chocolate dust came out with them when you shook them out in your hand. Were they chocolate? I'd say rather they were brown. They didn't taste of anything at all, unless it was wood. Their attraction was the number you got for a nickel.

18   Making up your mind, you circled the store around and around, around the pickle barrel, around the tower of Cracker Jack boxes; Mr. Sessions had built it for us himself on top of a packing case, like a house of cards.

19   If it seemed too hot for Cracker Jacks, I might get a cold drink. Mr. Sessions might have already stationed himself by the cold-drinks barrel, like a mind reader. Deep in ice water that looked black as ink, murky shapes that would come up as Coca-Colas, Orange Crushes, and various flavors of pop were all swimming around together. When you gave the word, Mr. Sessions plunged his bare arm in to the elbow and fished out your choice, first try. I favored a locally bottled concoction called Lake's Celery. (What else could it be called? It was made by a Mr. Lake out of celery. It was a popular drink here for years but was not known universally, as I found out when I arrived in New York and ordered one in the Astor bar.) You drank on the premises, with feet set wide apart to miss the drip, and gave him back his bottle.

20   But he didn't hurry you off. A standing scales was by the door, with a stack of iron weights and a brass slide on the balance arm, that would weigh you up to three hundred pounds. Mr. Sessions, whose hands were gentle and smelled of carbolic, would lift you up and set your feet on the platform, hold your loaf of bread for you, and taking his time while you stood still for him, he would make certain of what you weighed today. He could even remember what you weighed last time, so you could subtract and announce how much you'd gained. That was goodbye.

21   Is there always a hard way to go home? From the Little Store, you could go partway through the sewer. If your brothers had called you a scarecat, then across the next street beyond the Little Store, it was possible to enter this sewer by passing through a private hedge, climbing down into the bed of a creek, and going into its mouth on your knees. The sewer—it might have been no more than a "storm sewer"—came out and emptied here, where Town Creek, a

sandy, most often shallow little stream that ambled through Jackson on its way to the Pearl River, ran along the edge of the cemetery. You could go in darkness through this tunnel to where you next saw light (if you ever did) and climb out through the culvert at your own street corner.

22 I was a scarecat, all right, but I was a reader with my own refuge in storybooks. Making my way under the sidewalk, under the street and the street-car track, under the Little Store, down there in the wet dark by myself, I could be Persephone entering into my six-month sojourn underground—though I didn't suppose Persephone had to crawl, hanging onto a loaf of bread, and come out through the teeth of an iron grating. Mother Ceres would indeed be wondering where she could find me, and mad when she knew. "Now am I going to have to start marching to the Little Store for *myself?*"

23 I couldn't picture it. Indeed I'm unable today to picture the Little Store with a grown person in it, except for Mr. Sessions and the lady who helped him, who belonged there. We children thought it was ours. The happiness of errands was in part that of running for the moment away from home, a free spirit. I believed the Little Store to be a center of the outside world, and hence of happiness—as I believed what I found in the Cracker Jack box to be a genuine prize, which was as simply as I believed in the Golden Fleece.

24 But a day came when I ran to the store to discover, sitting on the front step, a grown person, after all—more than a grown person. It was the Monkey Man, together with his monkey. His grinding-organ was lowered to the step beside him. In my whole life so far, I must have laid eyes on the Monkey Man no more than five or six times. An itinerant of rare and wayward appearances, he was not punctual like the Gipsies, who every year with the first cool days of fall showed up in the aisles of Woolworth's. You never knew when the Monkey Man might decide to favor Jackson, or which way he'd go. Sometimes you heard him as close as the next street, and then he didn't come up yours.

25 But now I saw the Monkey Man at the Little Store, where I'd never seen him before. I'd never seen him sitting down. Low on that familiar doorstep, he was not the same any longer, and neither was his monkey. They looked just like an old man and an old friend of his that wore a fez, meeting quietly together, tired, and resting with their eyes fixed on some place far away, and not the same place.

Yet their romance for me didn't have it in its power to waver. I wavered. I simply didn't know how to step around them, to proceed on into the Little Store for my mother's emergency as if nothing had happened. If I could have gone in there after it, whatever it was, I would have given it to them—putting it into the monkey's cool little fingers. I would have given them the Little Store itself.

26   In my memory they are still attached to the store—so are all the others. Everyone I saw on my way seemed to me then part of my errand, and in a way they were. As I myself, the free spirit, was part of it too.

27   All the years we lived in that house where we children were born, the same people lived in the other houses on our street too. People changed through the arithmetic of birth, marriage, and death, but not by going away. So families just accrued stories, which through the fullness of time, in those times, their own lives made. And I grew up in those.

28   But I didn't know there'd ever been a story at the Little Store, one that was going on while I was there. Of course, all the time the Sessions family had been living right overhead there, in the upstairs rooms behind the little railed porch and the shaded windows; but I think we children never thought of that. Did I fail to see them as a family because they weren't living in an ordinary house? Because I so seldom saw them close together, or having anything to say to each other? She sat in the back of the store, her pencil over a ledger, while he stood and waited on children to make up their minds. They worked in twin black eyeshades, held on their gray heads by elastic bands. It may be harder to recognize kindness—or unkindness either—in a face whose eyes are in shadow. His face underneath his shade was as round as the little wooden wheels in the Tinker Toy box. So was her face. I didn't know, perhaps, didn't even wonder: were they husband and wife or brother and sister? Were they father and mother? There were a few other persons of various ages, wandering singly in by the back door and out. But none of their relationships could I imagine, when I'd never seen them sitting down together around their own table.

29   The possibility that they had any other life at all, anything beyond what we could see within the four walls of the Little Store, occurred to me only when tragedy struck their family. There was some act of violence. The shock to the neighborhood traveled to the children, of course; but I couldn't find out from my parents what had hap-

pened. They held it back from me, as they'd already held back many
things, "until the time comes for you to know."

30   You could find out some of these things by looking in the
unabridged dictionary and the encyclopedia—kept to hand in our dining room—but you couldn't find out there what had happened to the
family who for all the years of your life had lived upstairs over the Little
Store, which had never been anything but patient and kind to you,
who never once had sent you away. All I ever knew was its aftermath:
they were the only people ever known to me who simply vanished. At
the point where their life overlapped into ours, the story broke off.

31   We weren't being sent to the neighborhood grocery for facts of life,
or death. But of course those are what we were on the track of, anyway.
With the loaf of bread and the Cracker Jack prize, I was bringing home
the intimations of pride and disgrace, and rumors and early news of
people coming to hurt one another, while others practiced for joy—
storing up a portion for myself of the human mystery.

Discussion Questions

1. List the specific details in Welty's essay that you find most memo-
    rable. Explain why they stood out in your mind.
2. In small groups, discuss Welty's observations in paragraph 11,
    and recount your own experiences that confirm Welty's thinking.
3. Throughout the essay, why do you think Welty shifts from the
    past tense to the present, from first-person singular *I* to second
    person *you*, and from a child's perspective to an adult's?
4. What effect does Welty create by using the narrative form in her
    essay? Explain.
5. What does Welty mean in paragraph 28 when she states, "It may
    be harder to recognize kindness—or unkindness either—in a face
    whose eyes are in shadow"?
6. What did Welty bring home from the store that was unexpected?
    Why is this important to the essay?
7. What is Welty's main point in this narrative?
8. What do you know about Welty's character from her essay?
    Explain.

Writing Assignments

1. Identify some "things you weren't supposed to have need for" as a child and write a journal entry examining your fascination with them—as a way to recover the mind of a child.
2. Write an essay in which you describe a childhood ritual (such as Welty's going to the store or choosing what to buy with her nickel) that reveals the perspective you had as a child versus the one you developed as you became older.
3. In an essay, recount a childhood mystery, an incident that people kept secret from you. In what ways, if any, did it alter your perception of people, places, or things?

The Day Language Came into My Life

HELEN KELLER

Helen Keller (1880–1968) was born in Alabama. At the age of
nineteen months, she was afflicted with a disease that left her
deaf and blind. In 1887, Anne Sullivan Macy, a teacher of the
blind, took charge of training Keller, who soon after learned how
to read and speak, and, eventually, to write. Macy was Keller's
teacher until 1936. Keller graduated *cum laude* from Radcliffe
College in 1904 and was later awarded numerous honorary degrees
by universities worldwide. Beginning in the 1920s, she lectured
widely on behalf of the blind. In 1964, she was awarded the
Presidential Medal of Freedom, one of many awards that she
received. Keller's accounts of her experiences are found in *The
Story of My Life* (1902), *The World I Live In* (1908), *Out of the
Dark* (1913), *My Religion* (1927), and *Teacher, Anne Sullivan
Macy* (1955). Keller's life is chronicled in several movies and plays,
among them *The Unconquered* (1954) and the most famous *The
Miracle Worker* (1959), which dramatizes Keller learning language
from Macy. In the following essay, from *The Story of My Life,*
Keller reflects on one of the most monumental days in her life.
Portraying a classic tale of courage conquering fear, this essay has
been inspirational to people both with and without sight.

31

1   The most important day I remember in all my life is the one on
which my teacher, Anne Mansfield Sullivan, came to me. I am filled
with wonder when I consider the immeasurable contrast between
the two lives which it connects. It was the third of March 1887,
three months before I was seven years old.

2   On the afternoon of that eventful day, I stood on the porch,
dumb, expectant. I guessed vaguely from my mother's signs and
from the hurrying to and fro in the house that something unusual
was about to happen, so I went to the door and waited on the steps.
The afternoon sun penetrated the mass of honeysuckle that covered
the porch and fell on my upturned face. My fingers lingered almost
unconsciously on the familiar leaves and blossoms which had just
come forth to greet the sweet southern spring. I did not know what
the future held of marvel or surprise for me. Anger and bitterness
had preyed upon me continually for weeks and a deep languor had
succeeded this passionate struggle.

3   Have you ever been at sea in a dense fog, when it seemed as if a
tangible white darkness shut you in, and the great ship, tense and
anxious, groped her way toward the shore with plummet and sounding-line, and you waited with beating heart for something to happen?
I was like that ship before my education began, only I was without
compass or sounding-line and had no way of knowing how near the
harbor was. "Light! give me light!" was the wordless cry of my soul,
and the light of love shone on me in that very hour.

4   I felt approaching footsteps. I stretched out my hand as I supposed
to my mother. Someone took it, and I was caught up and held close
in the arms of her who had come to reveal all things to me, and,
more than all things else, to love me.

5   The morning after my teacher came she led me into her room
and gave me a doll. The little blind children at the Perkins Institute
had sent it and Laura Bridgman had dressed it; but I did not know
this until afterward. When I had played with it a little while, Miss
Sullivan slowly spelled into my hand the word "d-o-l-l." I was at
once interested in this finger play and tried to imitate it. When I
finally succeeded in making the letters correctly I was flushed with
childish pleasure and pride. Running downstairs to my mother I held
up my hand and made the letters for doll. I did not know that I was
spelling a word or even that words existed; I was simply making my
fingers go in monkeylike imitation. In that days that followed I

learned to spell in this uncomprehending way a great many words, among them *pin, hat, cup* and a few verbs like *sit, stand* and *walk*. But my teacher had been with me several weeks before I understood that everything has a name.

6   One day, while I was playing with my new doll, Miss Sullivan put my big rag doll into my lap also, spelled "d-o-l-l" and tried to make me understand that "d-o-l-l" applied to both. Earlier in the day we had had a tussle over the words "m-u-g" and "w-a-t-e-r." Miss Sullivan had tried to impress it upon me that "m-u-g" is *mug* and that "w-a-t-e-r" is *water*, but I persisted in confounding the two. In despair she had dropped the subject for the time, only to renew it at the first opportunity. I became impatient at her repeated attempts and, seizing the new doll, I dashed it upon the floor. I was keenly delighted when I felt the fragments of the broken doll at my feet. Neither sorrow nor regret followed my passionate outburst. I had not loved the doll. In the still, dark world in which I lived there was no strong sentiment or tenderness. I felt my teacher sweep the fragments to one side of the hearth, and I had a sense of satisfaction that the cause of my discomfort was removed. She brought me my hat, and I knew I was going out into the warm sunshine. This thought, if a wordless sensation may be called a thought, made me hop and skip with pleasure.

7   We walked down the path to the well-house, attracted by the fragrance of the honeysuckle with which it was covered. Some one was drawing water and my teacher placed my hand under the spout. As the cool stream gushed over one hand she spelled into the other the word *water*, first slowly, the rapidly. I stood still, my whole attention fixed upon the motions of her fingers. Suddenly I felt a misty consciousness as of something forgotten—a thrill of returning thought; and somehow the mystery of language was revealed to me. I knew then that "w-a-t-e-r" meant the wonderful cool something that was flowing over my hand. The living word awakened my soul, gave it light, hope, joy, set it free! There were barriers still, it is true, but barriers that could in time be swept away.

8   I left the well-house eager to learn. Everything had a name, and each name gave birth to a new thought. As we returned to the house every object which I touched seemed to quiver with life. That was because I saw everything with the strange, new sight that had come to me. On entering the door I remembered the doll I had broken,

I felt my way to the hearth and picked up the pieces. I tried vainly to put them together. Then my eyes filled with tears; for I realized what I had done, and for the first time I felt repentance and sorrow.

9   I learned a great many new words that day. I do not remember what they all were; but I do know that *mother, father, sister, teacher* were among them—words that were to make the world blossom for me, "like Aaron's rod, with flowers." It would have been difficult to find a happier child than I was as I lay in my crib at the close of that eventful day and lived over the joys it had brought me, and for the first time longed for a new day to come.

Discussion Questions

1. What does Keller mean in paragraph 1 by the "two lives" that her most important day connected for her?
2. Given that Keller was blind and deaf at the age of nineteen months, how can you account for her asking readers in paragraph 3 to imagine being in a "dense fog . . . as if a tangible white darkness shut you in"?
3. In paragraph 8, after Keller has learned language, Keller reports feeling "repentance and sorrow" over having previously broken a doll. What is the role of language in her emotions?
4. Do you think the sense of sight allows people to experience life fully? Explain your answer.
5. What senses replaced seeing and hearing in Keller?
6. In small groups, discuss what Keller can teach people who are neither blind nor deaf.
7. Explain the importance that learning had for Keller.

Writing Assignments

1. Despite the many negative adages about language (for example, talk is cheap, a picture is worth a thousand words, and so forth), language holds a special significance in our lives. Write a journal entry that examines *why* we take language for granted and why we should not do so.

2. Recall your "most important" day ever. Describe it so your readers can grasp not only what happened but also its significance to you.

3. Write an essay examining a moment in which you learned something that had previously eluded you. Be sure to discuss this lesson's importance to your life.

4. Mark Twain once wrote that "the difference between the *almost-right* word and the *right* word is really the difference between the lightning bug and the lightning." Choose some words that exemplify this idea, and write an essay that supports the need for precise language use.

The Achievement of Desire

RICHARD RODRIGUEZ

Richard Rodriguez (b. 1944) was born in San Francisco, the son of working-class Mexican parents. Spanish was his first language, and he barely spoke English when he started school at the age of five. He holds a B.A. from Stanford University, an M.A. from Columbia University, and a Ph.D. from the University of California at Berkeley. Along with serving as editor at Pacific News Services in San Francisco, being a contributing editor at *Harper's* magazine, and lecturing throughout the country on issues concerning affirmative action, Rodriguez is a full-time writer. He is the author of a series of autobiographical essays, *Hunger of Memory: The Education of Richard Rodriguez* (1982) and *Days of Obligation: An Argument with My Mexican Father* (1992). Rodriguez has established himself as a critic of affirmative action programs and writes about the dangers of bilingual education programs. Rodriguez's thoughtful, honest, and courageous exploration of the issues surrounding bilingual education in the United States has made him one of the leading figures in the field. In the following essay from *Hunger of Memory*, he examines his dilemma between assimilating into America culture and pleasing his parents.

36

1   I stand in the ghetto classroom—"the guest speaker"—
attempting to lecture on the mystery of the sounds of our words to
rows of diffident students. "Don't you hear it? Listen! The music
of our words. *'Sumer is icumen in . . .'* And songs on the car radio.
We need Aretha Franklin's voice to fill plain words with music—her
life." In the face of their empty stares, I try to create an enthusiasm.
But the girls in the back row turn to watch some boy passing outside.
There are flutters of smiles, waves. And someone's mouth elongates
heavy, silent words through the barrier of glass. Silent words—the
lips straining to shape each voiceless syllable: *"Meet meee late errr."*
By the door, the instructor smiles at me, apparently hoping that I
will be able to spark some enthusiasm in the class. But only one
student seems to be listening. A girl, maybe fourteen. In this gray
room her eyes shine with ambition. She keeps nodding and nodding
at all that I say; she even takes notes. And each time I ask a question,
she jerks up and down in her desk like a marionette, while her hand
waves over the bowed heads of her classmates. It is myself (as a boy)
I see as she faces me now (a man in my thirties).

2   The boy who first entered a classroom barely able to speak English,
twenty years later concluded his studies in the stately quiet of the
reading room in the British Museum. Thus with one sentence I can
summarize my academic career. It will be harder to summarize what
sort of life connects the boy to the man.

3   With every award, each graduation from one level of education
to the next, people I'd meet would congratulate me. Their refrain
always the same: "Your parents must be very proud." Sometimes
then they'd ask me how I managed it—my "success." (How?) After
a while, I had several quick answers to give in reply. I'd admit, for
one thing, that I went to an excellent grammar school. (My earliest
teachers, the nuns, made my success their ambition.) And my brother
and both my sisters were very good students. (They often brought
home the shiny school trophies I came to want.) And my mother
and father always encouraged me. (At every graduation they were
behind the stunning flash of the camera when I turned to look at
the crowd.)

4   As important as these factors were, however, they account inade-
quately for my academic advance. Nor do they suggest what an odd
success I managed. For although I was a very good student, I was
also a very bad student. I was a "scholarship boy," a certain kind of

scholarship boy. Always successful, I was always unconfident. Exhila-
rated by my progress. Sad. I became the prized student—anxious
and eager to learn. Too eager, too anxious—an imitative and unorigi-
nal pupil. My brother and two sisters enjoyed the advantages I did,
and they grew to be as successful as I, but none of them ever seemed
so anxious about their schooling. A second-grade student, I was the
one who came home and corrected the "simple" grammatical
mistakes of our parents. ("Two negatives make a positive.") Proudly
I announced—to my family's startled silence—that a teacher had said
I was losing all trace of a Spanish accent. I was oddly annoyed when
I was unable to get parental help with a homework assignment. The
night my father tried to help me with an arithmetic exercise, he kept
reading the instructions, each time more deliberately, until I pried
the textbook out of his hands, saying, "I'll try to figure it out some
more by myself."

5   When I reached the third grade, I outgrew such behavior. I became
more tactful, careful to keep separate the two very different worlds
of my day. But then, with ever-increasing intensity, I devoted myself
to my studies. I became bookish, puzzling to all my family. Ambition
set me apart. When my brother saw me struggling home with stacks
of library books, he would laugh, shouting: "Hey, Four Eyes!" My
father opened a closet one day and was startled to find me inside,
reading a novel. My mother would find me reading when I was
supposed to be asleep or helping around the house or playing outside.
In a voice angry or worried or just curious, she'd ask: "What do you
see in your books?" It became the family's joke. When I was called
and wouldn't reply, someone would say I must be hiding under my
bed with a book.

6   (How did I manage my success?)

7   What I am about to say to you has taken me more than twenty
years to admit: *A primary reason for my success in the classroom was
that I couldn't forget that schooling was changing me and separating
me from the life I enjoyed before becoming a student.* That simple
realization! For years I never spoke to anyone about it. Never mentioned a thing to my family or my teachers or classmates. From a
very early age, I understood enough, just enough about my classroom
experiences to keep what I knew repressed, hidden beneath layers
of embarrassment. Not until my last months as a graduate student,
nearly thirty years old, was it possible for me to think much about

the reasons for my academic success. Only then. At the end of my schooling, I needed to determine how far I had moved from my past. The adult finally confronted, and now must publicly say, what the child shuddered from knowing and could never admit to himself or to those many faces that smiled at his every success. ("Your parents must be very proud. . . .")

I

8   At the end, in the British Museum (too distracted to finish my dissertation) for weeks I read, speed-read, books by modern educational theorists, only to find infrequent and slight mention of students like me. (Much more is written about the more typical case, the lower-class student who barely is helped by his schooling.) Then one day, leafing through Richard Hoggart's *The Uses of Litaracy*, I found, in his description of the scholarship boy, myself. For the first time I realized that there were other students like me, and so I was able to frame the meaning to my academic success, its consequent price—the loss.

9   Hoggart's description is distinguished, at least initially, by deep understanding. What he grasps very well is that the scholarship boy must move between environments, his home and the classroom, which are at cultural extremes, opposed. With his family, the boy has the intense pleasure of intimacy, the family's consolation in feeling public alienation. Lavish emotions texture home life. *Then*, at school, the instruction bids him to trust lonely reason primarily. Immediate needs set the pace of his parents' lives. From his mother and father the boy learns to trust spontaneity and nonrational ways of knowing. *Then*, at school, there is mental calm. Teachers emphasize the value of a reflectiveness that opens a space between thinking and immediate action.

10   Years of schooling must pass before the boy will be able to sketch the cultural differences in his day as abstractly as this. But he senses those differences early. Perhaps as early as the night he brings home an assignment from school and finds the house too noisy for study.

> He has to be more and more alone, if he is going
> to "get on." He will have, probably unconsciously,
> to oppose the ethos of the hearth, the intense gre-

gariousness of the working-class family group. Since
everything centres upon the living-room, there is
unlikely to be a room of his own; the bedrooms are
cold and inhospitable, and to warm them or the
front room, if there is one, would not only be expensive, but would require an imaginative leap—out of
the tradition—which most families are not capable
of making. There is a corner of the living-room
table. On the other side Mother is ironing, the
wireless is on, someone is singing a snatch of song
or Father says intermittently whatever comes into
his head. The boy has to cut himself off mentally,
so as to do his homework, as well as he can.

The next day, the lesson is as apparent at school. There are even
rows of desks. Discussion is ordered. The boy must rehearse his
thoughts and raise his hand before speaking out in a loud voice to
an audience of classmates. And there is time enough, and silence, to
think about ideas (big ideas) never considered at home by his parents.

11   Not for the working-class child alone is adjustment to the classroom difficult. Good schooling requires that any student alter early
childhood habits. But the working-class child is usually least prepared
for the change. And, unlike many middle-class children, he goes
home and sees in his parents a way of life not only different but
starkly opposed to that of the classroom. (He enters the house and
hears his parents talking in ways his teachers discourage.)

12   Without extraordinary determination and the great assistance of
others—at home and at school—there is little chance for success. Typically most working-class children are barely changed by the classroom.
The exception succeeds. The relative few become scholarship students.
Of these, Richard Hoggart estimates, most manage a fairly graceful
transition. Somehow they learn to live in the two different worlds of
their day. There are some others, however, those Hoggart pejoratively
terms "scholarship boys," for whom success comes with special anxiety. Scholarship boy: good student, troubled son. The child is "moder-
ately endowed," intellectually mediocre, Hoggart supposes—though
it may be more pertinent to note the special qualities of temperament
in the child. High-strung child. Brooding. Sensitive. Haunted by the
knowledge that one *chooses* to become a student. (Education is not an

inevitable or natural step in growing up.) Here is a child who cannot forget that his academic success distances him from a life he loved; even from his own memory of himself.

13   Initially, he wavers, balances allegiance. ("The boy is himself [until he reaches, say, the upper forms] very much of *both* the worlds of home and school. He is enormously obedient to the dictates of the world or school, but emotionally still strongly wants to continue as part of the family circle.") Gradually, necessarily, the balance is lost. The boy needs to spend more and more time studying, each night enclosing himself in the silence permitted and required by intense concentration. He takes his first step toward academic success, away from his family.

14   From the very first days, through the years following, it will be with his parents—the figures of lost authority, the persons toward whom he feels deepest love—that the change will be most powerfully measured. A separation will unravel between them. Advancing in his studies, the boy notices that his mother and father have not changed as much as he. Rather, when he sees them, they often remind him of the person he once was and the life he earlier shared with them. He realizes what some Romantics also know when they praise the working class for the capacity for human closeness, qualities of passion and spontaneity, that the rest of us experience in like measure only in the earliest part of our youth. For the Romantic, this doesn't make working-class life childish. Working class life challenges precisely because it is an *adult* way of life.

15   The scholarship boy reaches a different conclusion. He cannot afford to admire his parents. (How could he and still pursue such a contrary life?) He permits himself embarrassment at their lack of education. And to evade nostalgia for the life he has lost, he concentrates on the benefits education will bestow upon him. He becomes especially ambitious. Without the support of old certainties and con solations, almost mechanically, he assumes the procedures and doctrines of the classroom. The kind of allegiance the young student might have given his mother and father only days earlier, he transfers to the teacher, the new figure of authority. "[The scholarship boy] tends to make a father-figure of his form-master," Hoggart observes.

16   But Hoggart's calm prose only makes me recall the urgency with which I came to idolize my grammar school teachers. I began by imitating their accents, using their diction, trusting their every direc-

tion. The very first facts they dispensed, I grasped with awe. Any book they told me to read, I read—then waited for them to tell me which books I enjoyed. Their every casual opinion I came to adopt and to trumpet when I returned home. I stayed after school "to help"—to get my teacher's undivided attention. It was the nun's encouragement that mattered most to me. (She understood exactly what—my parents never seemed to appraise so well—all my achievements entailed.) Memory gently caressed each word of praise bestowed in the classroom so that compliments teachers paid me years ago come quickly to mind even today.

17   The enthusiasm I felt in second-grade classes I flaunted before both my parents. The docile, obedient student came home a shrill and precocious son who insisted on correcting and teaching his parents with the remark: "My teacher told us. . . ."

18   I intended to hurt my mother and father. I was still angry at them for having encouraged me toward classroom English. But gradually this anger was exhausted, replaced by guilt as school grew more and more attractive to me. I grew increasingly successful, a talkative student. My hand was raised in the classroom; I yearned to answer any question. At home, life was less noisy than it had been. (I spoke to classmates and teachers more often each day than to family members.) Quiet at home, I sat with my papers for hours each night. I never forgot that schooling had irretrievably changed my family's life. That knowledge, however, did not weaken ambition. Instead, it strengthened resolve. Those times I remembered the loss of my past with regret, I quickly reminded myself of all the things my teachers could give me. (They could make me an educated man.) I tightened my grip on pencil and books. I evaded nostalgia. Tried hard to forget. But one does not forget by trying to forget. One only remembers. I remembered too well that education had changed my family's life. I would not have become a scholarship boy had I not so often remembered.

19   Once she was sure that her children knew English, my mother would tells us, "You should keep up your Spanish." Voices playfully groaned in response. "¡Pochos!" my mother would tease me. I listened silently.

20   After a while, I grew more calm at home. I developed tact. A fourth-grade student, I was no longer the show-off in front of my parents. I became a conventionally dutiful son, politely affectionate,

cheerful enough, even—for reasons beyond choosing—my father's favorite. And much about my family life was easy then, comfortable, happy in the rhythm of our living together: hearing my father getting ready for work; eating the breakfast my mother had made me; looking up from a novel to hear my brother or one of my sisters playing with friends in the backyard; in winter, coming upon the house all lighted up after dark.

21   But withheld from my mother and father was any mention of what most mattered to me: the extraordinary experience of first-learning. Late afternoon: In the midst of preparing dinner, my mother would come up behind me while I was trying to read. Her head just over mine, her breath warmly scented with food. "What are you reading?" Or, "Tell me all about your new courses." I would barely respond, "Just the usual things, nothing special." (A half smile, then silence. Her head moving back in the silence. Silence! Instead of the flood of intimate sounds that had once flowed smoothly between us, there was this silence.) After dinner, I would rush to a bedroom with papers and books. As often as possible, I resisted parental pleas to "save lights" by coming to the kitchen to work. I kept so much, so often, to myself. Sad. Enthusiastic. Troubled by the excitement of coming upon new ideas. Eager. Fascinated by the promising texture of a brand-new book. I hoarded the pleasures of learning. Alone for hours. Enthralled. Nervous. I rarely looked away from my books—or back on my memories. Nights when relatives visited and the front rooms were warmed by Spanish sounds, I slipped quietly out of the house.

22   It mattered that education was changing me. It never ceased to matter. My brother and sisters would giggle at our mother's mispronounced words. They'd correct her gently. My mother laughed girlishly one night, trying to pronounce *sheep* as *ship*. From a distance, I listened sullenly. From that distance, pretending not to notice on another occasion, I say my father looking at the title pages of my library books. That was the scene on my mind when I walked home with a fourth-grade companion and heard him say that his parents read to him every night. (A strange-sounding book—*Winnie the Pooh*.) Immediately, I wanted to know, "What is it like? My companion, however, thought I wanted to know about the plot of the book. Another day, my mother surprised me by asking for a "nice" book to read. "Something not too hard you think I might

like." Carefully I chose one, Willa Cather's *My Ántonia*. But when, several weeks later, I happened to see it next to her bed unread except for the first few pages, I was furious and suddenly wanted to cry. I grabbed up the book and took it back to my room and placed it in its place, alphabetically on my shelf.

Discussion Questions

1. In small groups, discuss whether education was the reason or an excuse for Rodriguez's separating himself culturally from his parents.
2. In paragraph 7, Rodriguez states that it "has taken . . . more than twenty years to admit" what he writes in his essay. Why do you think it took him so long?
3. Throughout his essay, Rodriguez uses parentheses to indicate his unspoken thoughts. Discuss their effectiveness.
4. How well did Rodriguez assimilate into an English-speaking culture? Do you think he was ostracized from his Mexican heritage? Explain your answers.
5. How did schooling change Rodriguez's family life?
6. What made Rodriguez "evade nostalgia" and later regain it?
7. Why does Rodriguez describe the "scholarship boy"?
8. Explain your understanding of the title of this essay.

Writing Assignments

1. In a letter to your parents, discuss how you are different from them and why you do not subscribe to some of their beliefs.
2. In an essay, describe and analyze the ways in which your education has separated you from or drawn you closer to your family and friends.
3. It has long been said that "time is a healer"; it helps to produce distance and objectivity. In an essay, recall an experience in your life when time served such a function, and distinguish between your "before and after" perspectives.

CLASSIC ESSAYS ON

Adolescence

from Incidents in the Life of a Slave Girl

HARRIET JACOBS

Harriet Jacobs (1813–1897) was born in Edenton, North Carolina. After her mother's death in 1819, she was enslaved to Margaret Horniblow, who taught Jacobs how to read and sew. When Horniblow died in 1825, Jacobs became the slave of Horniblow's three-year-old niece, Mary Mathilda Norcom. Mary's father, Dr. James Flint, repeatedly made sexual advances to Jacobs. Jacobs consented to a relationship with Samuel Tredwell Sawyer, a white lawyer, as a way to avoid Norcom's advances; she bore Sawyer's son, Joseph, in 1829 and his daughter, Louisa Mathilda, in 1833. Norcom sent Jacobs to his son's plantation, where she experienced inhumane working conditions. She escaped when she discovered that Norcom planned to sell her children. For almost seven years, Jacobs hid in her grandmother's attic. With the assistance of abolitionists, Jacobs escaped to the North in 1842. Amy Post, a feminist abolitionist, urged Jacobs to write her autobiography. Thus began *Incidents in the Life of a Slave Girl*. Edited by Lydia Maria Child and printed by a Boston publisher, the work appeared in

1862, first under the pseudonym Linda Brent to protect
Jacobs's identity. Among the topics this narrative reveals
are slave women's plights, survival strategies, and the
role of family.

1   During the first years of my service in Dr. Flint's family, I was
accustomed to share some indulgences with the children of my mistress. Though this seemed to me no more than right, I was grateful
for it, and tried to merit the kindness by the faithful discharge of my
duties. But I now entered on my fifteenth year—a sad epoch in the
life of a slave girl. My master began to whisper foul words in my ear.
Young as I was, I could not remain ignorant of their import. I tried
to treat them with indifference or contempt. The master's age, my
extreme youth, and the fear that his conduct would be reported to
my grandmother, made him bear this treatment for many months.
He was a crafty man, and resorted to many means to accomplish his
purposes. Sometimes he had stormy, terrific ways, that made his
victims tremble; sometimes he assumed a gentleness that he thought
must surely subdue. Of the two, I preferred his stormy moods,
although they left me trembling. He tried his utmost to corrupt the
pure principles my grandmother had instilled. He peopled my young
mind with unclean images, such as only a vile monster could think
of. I turned from him with disgust and hatred. But he was my master.
I was compelled to live under the same roof with him—where I
saw a man forty years my senior daily violating the most sacred
commandments of nature. He told me I was his property; that I
must be subject to his will in all things. My soul revolted against the
mean tyranny. But where could I turn for protection? No matter
whether the slave girl be as black as ebony or as fair as her mistress.
In either case, there is no shadow of law to protect her from insult,
from violence, or even from death; all these are inflicted by fiends
who bear the shape of men. The mistress, who ought to protect the
helpless victim, has no other feelings towards her but those of jealousy

and rage. The degradation, the wrongs, the vices, that grow out of slavery, are more than I can describe. They are greater than you would willingly believe. Surely, if you credited one half the truths that are told you concerning the helpless millions suffering in this cruel bondage, you at the north would not help to tighten the yoke. You surely would refuse to do for the master, on your own soil, the mean and cruel work which trained bloodhounds and the lowest class of whites do for him at the south.

2   Every where the years bring to all enough of sin and sorrow; but in slavery the very dawn of life is darkened by these shadows. Even the little child, who is accustomed to wait on her mistress and her children, will learn, before she is twelve years old, why it is that her mistress hates such and such a one among the slaves. Perhaps the child's own mother is among those hated ones. She listens to violent outbreaks of jealous passion, and cannot help understanding what is the cause. She will become prematurely knowing in evil things. Soon she will learn to tremble when she hears her master's footfall. She will be compelled to realize that she is no longer a child. If God has bestowed beauty upon her, it will prove her greatest curse. That which commands admiration in the white woman only hastens the degradation of the female slave. I know that some are too much brutalized by slavery to feel the humiliation of their position; but many slaves feel it most acutely, and shrink from the memory of it. I cannot tell how much I suffered in the presence of these wrongs, nor how I am still pained by the retrospect. My master met me at every turn, reminding me that I belonged to him, and swearing by heaven and earth that he would compel me to submit to him. If I went off for a breath of fresh air, after a day of unwearied toil, his footsteps dogged me. If I knelt by my mother's grave, his dark shadow fell on me even there. The light heart which nature had given me became heavy with sad forebodings. The other slaves in my master's house noticed the change. Many of them pitied me; but none dared to ask the cause. They had no need to inquire. They knew too well the guilty practices under that roof; and they were aware that to speak of them was an offence that never went unpunished.

3   I longed for some one to confide in. I would have given the world to have laid my head on my grandmother's faithful bosom, and told her all my troubles. But Dr. Flint swore he would kill me, if I was

not as silent as the grave. Then, although my grandmother was all in all to me, I feared her as well as loved her. I had been accustomed to look up to her with a respect bordering upon awe. I was very young, and felt shamefaced about telling her such impure things, especially as I knew her to be very strict on such subjects. Moreover, she was a woman of a high spirit. She was usually very quiet in her demeanor; but if her indignation was once roused, it was not very easily quelled. I had been told that she once chased a white gentleman with a loaded pistol, because he insulted one of her daughters. I dreaded the consequences of a violent outbreak; and both pride and fear kept me silent. But though I did not confide in my grandmother, and even evaded her vigilant watchfulness and inquiry, her presence in the neighborhood was some protection to me. Though she had been a slave, Dr. Flint was afraid of her. He dreaded her scorching rebukes. Moreover, she was known and patronized by many people; and he did not wish to have his villainy made public. It was lucky for me that I did not live on a distant plantation, but in a town not so large that the inhabitants were ignorant of each other's affairs. Bad as are the laws and customs in a slaveholding community, the doctor, as a professional man, deemed it prudent to keep up some outward show of decency.

4   O, what days and nights of fear and sorrow that man caused me! Reader, it is not to awaken sympathy for myself that I am telling you truthfully what I suffered in slavery. I do it to kindle a flame of compassion in your hearts for my sisters who are still in bondage, suffering as I once suffered.

5   I once saw two beautiful children playing together. One was a fair white child; the other was her slave, and also her sister. When I saw them embracing each other, and heard their joyous laughter, I turned sadly away from the lovely sight. I foresaw the inevitable blight that would fall on the little slave's heart. I knew how soon her laughter would be changed to sighs. The fair child grew up to be a still fairer woman. From childhood to womanhood her pathway was blooming with flowers, and overarched by a sunny sky. Scarcely one day of her life had been clouded when the sun rose on her happy bridal morning.

6   How had those years dealt with her slave sister, the little playmate of her childhood? She, also, was very beautiful; but the flowers and sunshine of love were not for her. She drank the cup of sin, and

shame, and misery, whereof her persecuted race are compelled to drink.

7   In view of those things, why are ye silent, ye free men and women of the north? Why do your tongues falter in maintenance of the right? Would that I had more ability! But my heart is so full, and my pen is so weak! There are noble men and women who plead for us, striving to help those who cannot help themselves. God bless them! God give them strength and courage to go on! God bless those, every where, who are laboring to advance the cause of humanity!

Discussion Questions

1. Why did Jacobs prefer her master's "stormy moods" over his "gentle" ones?
2. What were the mistress's feelings toward the female slaves? Explain why you think her attitude was justified or unwarranted.
3. How did Jacobs view her grandmother?
4. Why was Dr. Flint afraid of Jacobs's grandmother?
5. In small groups, discuss Jacobs's reasons for having written this essay. Is one reason more convincing than another?
6. Describe the tone of Jacobs's essay. Does it change at any place in the essay? Discuss your answers.
7. Discuss the importance of slave narratives in American literature.

Writing Assignments

1. Write a journal entry that explains how you would have reacted to Dr. Flint had you been in Jacobs's situation.
2. Imagine you are Jacobs and write a letter to Dr. Flint and his wife detailing why their actions were inexcusable and what you learned from your experience.
3. Write an essay in which you draw parallels between Dr. Flint's sexually harassing and stalking Jacobs and sexual harassment and stalking incidents, which are so prevalent today.

4. Read other autobiographies, memoirs, or essays dealing with slav-
    ery. In an essay, compare and contrast the authors' experiences
    with that of Jacobs.
5. Research the history of slave narratives in American literature and
    write an essay that examines why such narratives have an enduring
    importance in literature.

Adolescents

MARGARET
MEAD

Margaret Mead (1901–1978) was born in Philadelphia and grew up in New York. She received a B.A. degree from Barnard College, as well as an M.A. and a Ph.D. from Columbia University. She was a professor at Columbia University for many years and was also a visiting professor or lecturer at such universities as Harvard University, Yale University, Emory University, the University of Colorado, and Stanford University. Mead also worked as a curator at the American Museum of Natural History in New York City. In 1925, Mead made her first of many pilgrimages to the South Pacific Islands to do anthropological research. Her six-month stay on the Samoan island of T'ai resulted in *Coming of Age in Samoa* (1928), a book on the maturation of Samoans from adolescence to adulthood that won Mead great acclaim and established her as one of the United States' most respected anthropologists. A prolific writer, Mead authored more than thirty books, the most famous of which are *Growing Up in New Guinea* (1930), *Sex and Temperament in Three Primitive Societies (1935), And Keep Your Powder Dry* (1942), *Male and Female* (1949), *An Anthropologist at Work* (1959), *Culture and Commitment* (1970), and *Blackberry Winter: A Memoir* (1972). In all of her works, Mead acknowledges the biological factors that affect people but emphasizes the powerful role culture has in shaping human behavior. In the following selection, Mead uses her extensive training in anthropology and rich understanding of human relations to examine the difficulties that face American adolescents.

53

1   At adolescence children begin to move toward an unknown future. The translucent walls of childhood no longer close them in, for suddenly they discover the wide gateways and the gates ready to swing open at a touch of the hand. The way is open for them to move away from the family, away from the familiar gardens and ponds and woods where they came to know the natural world, away from the fireside stories told them by their grandmothers, away from the brothers and sisters who will always be older and younger than they, and away from the playmates who shared their earliest games.

2   Up to adolescence the child lived in a circumscribed world. However individual and gifted, lively and intelligent he seemed to his parents, he was still a child for whom others had to plan, who had to be admonished, hedged about with protective rules, and kept within bounds. But with adolescence the old rules lose their meaning, and children begin to look beyond the old boundaries with new farseeing eyes. The adolescent boy gives up the dream of competition with his father in which he sometimes triumphed and sometimes despaired of ever accomplishing as much as his father had. Instead, he now looks forward to what he actually may become. The adolescent girl who once held her doll as her mother held her baby now looks forward in earnest, picturing the woman she will become and the living child she may rock in her arms. At adolescence, children stand at the gates, vividly seeing—and yet not seeing—the pathways of their own lives. For better or worse, each family has accomplished the task of caring for its sons and daughters, and they have learned, well or badly, the essential lessons their parents could teach them.

3   For the adolescent the paths leading out from the swinging gates are both entrancing and frightening. Even for the youth who has been an intrepid child traveler, the first journeys away from home may seem too difficult to accomplish. Girls who ranged the streams and mountains beside their brothers become shy and timid, their hands hot and cold, their smiles precarious. One day they want to dress as children, the next as women of the world. Each adolescent in his own way hesitates at the threshold. One sallies out and then, frightened by his own temerity, hurries back; but safely inside he looks out longingly, ready to be off again. Another hangs back, willing and unwilling, until at some sign known only to himself he moves ahead boldly, once and for all.

4   Everywhere in the world people mark the moment when a girl passes from childhood to physical maturity and the time when the boy's voice cracks and deepens and his beard, slight as it may be for some racial stocks, begins to grow. For the elders these changes signal the end of one kind of responsibility and the beginning of another more onerous one. Little children must be ceaselessly guarded and cared for, but adolescents, who still are in need of protection, are creatures whom it is almost impossible to protect. Their safety now depends on their earlier learning in childhood and on the way the other adolescents around them are growing toward adulthood.

5   In a society in which boys go out on dangerous raids, a mother may make magic to protect her adolescent son's life, but any attempt to keep him at home when others go out will also endanger him. Where adolescent girls have a special house to which boys come with flutes to court them, a father may tremble for his daughter's safety and fear that the wooing may go wrong, but by interfering he will only create new difficulties. In every society adolescents take over the world's ways and parents must yield their assent.

6   Sometimes parents are permitted to lock up their daughters, and girls can only whisper to their lovers through barred windows. Sometimes boys are shut up in schools where older boys teach and harry them and men wearing the masks of frightening authority give them a last set of admonitions about manliness. Sometimes, at the beginning of adolescence, boys are sent as war scouts on dangerous missions and on long night errands through the enemy-infested bush. And sometimes each boy must go out alone and wait, fasting and vigilant, in the hope of winning the protection of a guardian spirit. Whatever the customary ways are for children to emerge into youth, these indicate the kinds of paths adolescents must take. Individual families can neither shield their children nor safely direct them along different paths. Individual parents who set themselves against custom become involved in a much greater struggle than those who watch with bated breath as their children set out on their first adventures.

7   The world over, adolescence is the period of greatest differentiation between boys and girls, not only in the anxieties felt by their parents but also in the dreams that animate them. Yet the boy and the girl, each in a different way, are equally preoccupied by the task of becoming, physically, a man and a woman—no longer someone's child, but potentially the parent of a child. Within their own bodies

changes are taking place that they cannot ignore, and in the world outside they are confronted by alterations in treatment that match their visible growth and approaching maturity.

8   In some societies adolescents are left to realize change at their own pace. No one records their age. No one complains about the slow pace of this boy or the fast pace of that girl in growing up. Children are safe in their childhood as long as they are unready; and each chooses when to begin courtship and the first tentative search for a mate. One by one, the boys drift away from the boys' gang, take on the stance of young men, and move toward the girls who also, one by one, grow into readiness to receive them. No one will hurry them.

9   But in most societies adults express old fears and new fears, old hopes and new hopes as they urge on and hold back adolescent boys and girls, guard them and leave them to fend for themselves. All the girls may be betrothed early in childhood and sent to their prospective husbands' homes before they reach puberty. In this the girls have no choice. They must accept their new families as unquestioningly as they accepted the families into which they were born. And the boys, given their wives, have as little choice and yet are expected to be grateful to those who have made this provision for their future.

10   At the other extreme are the adolescents who are trapped in the neglect and poverty of great cities. Growing up in families whose kinship ties are disrupted and whose links to a more stable past are broken, they can expect no help from parents who do not understand their new urban life. Unschooled, unprotected, and unguided, each adolescent is left to follow the initiative of other adolescents. In a society that makes no coherent plan for them and coming from families who do not know what plans to make, they turn to radio and television, mass magazines and comic strips in search of guidance. Children of the mass media, they learn from headlines how other adolescents, equally at sea, dress and talk, think and act. In a simpler society, adolescents share the channeled dreams of all young people, and their parents, whose adolescence differed hardly at all from their own, can set up guideposts that will lead a new generation safely into adulthood. In contrast, modern adolescents are exposed to the fads and extreme actions of hundreds of thousands of young people who drift on a chartless course between a narrower, traditional world and a world whose dimensions are still unclear. All they have to

follow are the published statistics of how many of them are now—this year, this month, this week—turning in questing masses first in one direction and then in another. For these adolescents, as in no other generation, the end of the journey in adulthood is unknown.

11   An unbridgeable gulf seems to separate the life of the five boys who are growing up in a shepherd hamlet, each of whom will choose a wife from among the six girls in that hamlet or the twenty girls living in nearby villages, from the life of young people who crowd, ten thousand strong, to welcome a television star at an airport. Yet the tasks confronting the shepherd boy are no different from those facing the teen-age city boy who moves so lightly to the rhythm set last week by a new hit record. For now, at adolescence, both boys must give up the dependence of childhood and move toward the autonomy and interdependence of adulthood.

12   Wherever a boy grows up, he must learn to leave home without fear, leaving behind him the old battles of childhood, and learn to return home from school or work or an assignment in a far city or overseas ready to treat his parents differently. Where he is permitted choice, he must be prepared to make a choice. Where no choice is open to him, the decision to go another way means that he must be prepared to blaze a new and lonely path. If he succeeds, he may open that path to others. If he fails, others coming after him may have a harder time.

13   For the young boy who rebels against the choices that have been made for him—refuses the wife who has been chosen in his name, deserts the craft to which he has been apprenticed, leaves the school or college to which he has been sent—the battle is a lonely one. At the moment of rebellion the battle is joined not with his whole society—for if it is, he becomes a criminal—but with his own parents whose demands he cannot meet. Such a battle generates an almost unbearable tension, as his old childish love and dependence must be opposed both to a desire for independence which his parents approve and to a course which they disapprove. In some societies, it is not only the rebel who suffers, but also the boy struggling to meet the demands made on him—to show bravery in battle, seek a vision on a mountainside, endure a period of poverty and self-discipline in a monastery, work as an ill-fed and much-abused apprentice, last out the hard grind before he can enter a profession, practice every day the difficult skills that will make him an athlete, a mountain guide,

or a pilot. If he fails, or even thinks he has failed, he has been taught
to feel he will betray his parents, and he may be tempted to revenge
himself on them by killing the child they failed to rear in their image
of what their child should be. In still other societies grandfathers
stand behind the springing young boys, guarding their inexperience.
But elsewhere there are no such safeguards. Fathers relinquish their
authority early, and boys of thirteen or fourteen, long before they
can break away in rebellion, are pushed into manhood and have the
cares and responsibilities of manhood thrust on their shoulders.

14   The problems girls face, the world over, are not those that confront
their brothers, but very different ones. For the adolescent girl may
still feel like a child or she may still long to roam the hills with her
brothers as she did when she was a child, but now, unlike a child,
she can conceive. And long before she has the discretion or the
judgment to choose among suitors or to weigh the temptation of
the moment against her hopes for the future, her body, outstripping
her imagination, or her imagination, outstripping her physical readiness, may involve her in an irrevocable act. The boy who breaks his
bow string, turns tail in battle, hesitates before an order, or fails in
school can still retrieve his losses by stringing the bow better,
returning to school, learning to obey and to command. But for the
girl herself and for society, the change is irreversible. It does not
matter whether the child she has conceived is lost immediately after
conception, whether it is born in wedlock or out of wedlock, whether
it lives or dies. The event cannot be set aside. One more child, if it
lives, will have started life in one way and not in another, and the
girl herself can go on, but she cannot begin afresh.

15   Because parenthood for the girl and parenthood for the boy are
fundamentally different, it has taken a very long time to develop
contexts in which girls can be allowed to become persons before
they become mothers. And because, in the end, the education of
boys depends partly on the mothers who rear them, and the sisters
with whom they play and compete or whom they cherish and protect,
it also took a long time before boys were permitted to become full
persons. Throughout human history, most peoples have been intent,
most of the time, on turning most young boys and girls into parents
whose primary task it has been to rear children who, in their turn,
would become parents also. With rare exceptions, girls have always
been reared to become parents, and persons only incidentally, and

boys, too, have been reared to become parents, and persons only if they have belonged to some specially privileged elite.

16 But very slowly the burden has been lifting. Each small savage society had to lay on every able member the responsibility of repro- duction first and then for continual, unremitting daily concern for food and for protection against cold and danger. The burden was lifted first from the sons of those of high rank and, occasionally, the youth of high promise, and later from a few daughters who shared, almost accidentally, in their brothers' privileges. Gradually it has been lifted also from larger and larger numbers of young people in those countries that have conquered the relentless problems of hunger and cold. In the past, most boys, as soon as they left childhood, had no choice but to hunt, herd sheep, fish, toil in the fields, or work at a craft, or, in more recent times, work as unskilled laborers who never earned more than was enough to buy tomorrow's food and pay next week's rent. But in modern societies, it has been possible to keep an ever larger number of adolescents in school and to give them an opportunity to think further than their fathers thought, explore the life of other periods and other cultures, and to become both civilized men, inheritors of the past, and modern men, ready to make a different future. And as our capacity to free more adolescents has increased, our willingness also has grown to permit them to become what they have the potentiality to be as persons.

17 This change has coincided with a tremendous increase in the world's population. In the past, men struggled desperately to preserve the small tribes or nations to which they owed their sense of identity. Today we are engaged in a common enterprise in the attempt to preserve mankind, as all men are endangered by the weapons of destruction they have now—and will always have—the knowledge to build. In the past people counted the children who were born, wept for the many who died, and wondered whether the living were enough to do the work, guard the group from danger, and reproduce the group in the next generation. Now we know we must stem the uncontrolled growth of the earth's population. When almost all children live, fewer children need be born. When almost no mothers die, fewer women need bear children. When as many children grow up in small families as once survived only in very large families, so many of whose children died, men and women need not marry so early or devote so large a part of their lives to parenthood. Now,

when our task is to balance the world's population at a level at which every child who is born anywhere, in the most remote valley and on the highest plateau, will have an opportunity to become a person, we do not need to organize the world in such a way that the relentless, unremitting needs of parenthood and poverty weigh down adolescents as soon as they leave childhood behind, making them old before their time. Our new command of nature, which makes it possible for the first time in human history to organize a world without war, save the children who are born, and feed and clothe every child, also allows us to offer to all adolescents, not only the chosen and privileged few, a chance to grow further.

18   Man's history has been one of longer and longer periods of growth. In the very distant past, before men as we know them had evolved, the period of growth must have been even shorter and boys must have been ready for the tasks of procreation and parenthood very young. Later, when members of our own species were living under extremely primitive conditions, boys had learned all they needed to know in order to survive by the time they were six or seven years of age, but they matured more slowly. At adolescence they were ready to assume the responsibilities of manhood, and so it has remained for primitive men, for peasants, and for the poor in industrial cities. The demands made on them permitted them to grow no more. Even when the years of education lengthened a little in the more fortunate modern countries, the idea survived that growth stopped somewhere in mid-adolescence. There was, as there still is, a general expectation that most young people would give up learning and growing when they left school. Set in a mold, they were ready to work day in and day out, because otherwise they and their children would not eat. They stepped from childhood to adolescence and from early adolescence immediately into maturity, and then aged early.

19   But in the last ten thousand years—and possibly for a longer time—some societies began to benefit from the accumulated knowledge that made it possible for men to plan ahead—to raise more food than they immediately needed, to store food, and to feed a larger number of people—so that some men were freed to study, to think, and to build a larger tradition. In time, in some societies, men watched the stars and measured the phases of the sun and the moon, designed great buildings, carved, painted, created systems of nota-

tion, built cities and organized nations, and dreamed of including all men, not merely the members of their own tribe, their own city, or their own race, within one system of values, cherishing common goals.

20 With leisure and the freedom given to some young men to pursue the new arts and sciences of civilization, a new human capacity was discovered: the idealism of adolescence. Among a primitive people, as each new generation lives much the same life the parent generation also lived, adolescents do not reveal their capacity to dream soaring dreams, make mighty plans, leap in thought to new formulations of the relations of mind and matter, and visualize the place of man on earth, in the solar system, in the galaxy, in an expanding universe. Until men lived in the kinds of societies in which leisure was a possibility, and a few adolescents had time to grow further away from childhood, youth was untouched by idealism. Indeed, in many societies, young people were more cowed, more submissive, and less rebellious than their aging and less responsible elders.

21 With the development of civilization, as knowledge accumulated and systems of writing made it possible to preserve and communicate to others, as yet unborn, what was known, new processes of development were also revealed in adolescents. Moving away from childhood, boys and young men were no longer exposed only to the drudgery and the small excitements of the daily round. Some of them, at least, heard and saw and read about the things earlier great men had dreamed of and sung of, written about, and built. The spacious vision of the exceptional man did not die with him, but became the property of young men who came after him. In each generation there were young men, and occasionally young women, who could match the unsatisfactory present against the prophecies of a better future or the dream of a golden past, and these young people, in their turn, were led to prophesy, strike out in bold adventure, break the bonds of tradition, discover new fields, and plunge forward into some new understanding of the universe and man.

22 In any growing civilization, some young men have been allowed to live out and prolong their adolescence, free from the pressure to marry and from the necessity of working for their bread. This leisure not only has given them time to grow, but also time for friendship before parenthood. It is essentially in the continuation of companionship outside the family, in relationships other than those concerned

with courtship, marriage, and parenthood, that adolescents can seek and find the strength and the vision to carry one step farther the civilization into which they were born and of which they are the heirs. The urgent desire, everywhere in the world, to give children more schooling and more time to learn has at its base a very profound need. The rationale of educational plans in the contemporary world is the necessity of having a more literate population, able to do the work of a more literate and complicated society. But the underlying need goes far beyond this. Giving children time to prolong their growing is intrinsic to the very creation of that literate and complicated society. Without vision the people perish, and the power of seeing visions must be fostered in adolescents if we are to have the visionaries the world needs.

23   For many centuries civilizations have struggled with the problem of how to give men—and sometimes women—the freedom in which inspiration, knowledge, and art can flower. One solution has been to create a dichotomy in which the life of sex and parenthood has been set apart from a life of celibacy, asceticism, and thought or prayer. In a society that accepted this solution, the parent was never so specialized or developed a person as were those who carried on the spiritual, intellectual, and artistic work of the world. Moreover, every child was presented with two conflicting life paths, as he had to choose between the pursuit of knowledge, on the one hand, and the life of the family, on the other. Only in the next generation, if he chose to have children, might a son realize his other dreams and, turning away from parenthood, devote himself entirely to religion, the arts, scholarship, or science. In other societies, all boys have lived for a period apart from the secular world, as a way of giving them access to traditional knowledge and insight into the spiritual resources of a great religion, as one aspect of their on-going lives. In still other societies, childhood and old age were equated in the sense that the intensive learning of childhood, practiced throughout life, came to flower only when men retired from everyday responsibilities and could devote themselves wholly to thought, poetry, painting, and music. But all these have been essentially conservative solutions, the solutions worked out by societies among whom only a few were the chosen carriers of a great tradition, and only a few had the freedom to become creative individuals.

24   In most modern societies this selection and segregation of the few from the many is breaking down. Those who dedicate themselves

wholly to important work now live in the world. Even though they may not marry, they do not live a life apart. However, where once the population was divided into the many who bore and reared children and the few who had time all their lives to think and to grow, there is now developing in many parts of the modern world a new dichotomy based on sex. For increasingly, adolescent boys are being educated, while girls, like the vast majority of men and women in medieval Europe who chose parenthood, are asked to set aside their dreams of what they might become in favor of immediate marriage and parenthood.

25   In creating this new dichotomy we resemble the primitive peoples who did not understand paternity. For we do not take into account fatherhood or realize that in establishing a kind of society in which girls must become mothers as adolescents, before they have had time to become individuals, we also are forcing boys to become fathers before they have become individuals. In our civilization we are the beneficiaries of poor societies in which only a few had leisure, but we are not yet fully conscious of the power our new affluence gives us to make all men the beneficiaries of that past and to open the way for every adolescent to grow slowly through a long youth into mature individuality.

26   All around the world, youth is stirring. Often that stirring is the blind movement of disorganized mobs. There is a restlessness that is widely expressed in demands for privilege, for power, for change, for marriage as a right rather than as a responsibility, and for parenthood as a pleasure rather than as a vocation. That blind movement and those demands express the deep contradictions characteristic of our time—a time of transition.

27   Perhaps even more important than the revolution in the lives of peoples who for centuries have been subjected to tyranny and alien authority is the surging revolution of young people who are seeking a new place in a new kind of world. The more rapidly the world changes, the greater is the contrast between older people, who have had to learn so many new things during their lifetime, and younger people, who take the same things for granted. Young people who all their lives have been familiar with cars and how they are driven, who know how a jet plane is operated and how a computer is built, have an appearance of startling precocity as they move among adults for whom this knowledge and these

skills are still new and strange. How can parents feel that their adolescent children are, in fact, adolescents, when these children know so much that they, the parents, learned only yesterday and with great difficulty? The authority in adult voices flickers, hesitates, grows shrill, and young people, sensing adult uncertainty and weakness, press harder against the barriers that hold them back from full participation in life. From their viewpoint they are asking for full citizenship and the right to be men and women at once, because they are already more skilled and knowledgeable than their parents. But the fulfillment of their demands would have the effect of putting the clock back, rather than moving it forward, and of reinstating a kind of world in which all young people were set to work at sober, confining tasks as soon as they were able to undertake them. At the threshold of a new age, it is as if a generation was turning in blind flight from its vast possibilities.

28   For all over the world a new age is struggling to be born, an age in which all children can grow up in families and all adolescents can have time to become individuals who are able to meet the demands of a fully adult life. In this new age, in which adolescents need not be forced to become mothers and fathers and grow old before their time, we can set a new value on adolescence of the mind and the spirit. In a society in which no one will be forced into premature adulthood, many people will remain adolescents all their lives, following a vision that is not yet clear, puzzling over a theory that is not yet fully formulated, attempting to create in sound or in color, in meditation or in prayer, in the laboratory or in the library, in the halls of government or in the councils of the nations something as yet unknown.

29   For long ages the prospect opening out from childhood closed in almost at once. Only a few were free long enough to glimpse a wider horizon, a visionary gleam. With the knowledge gained through their labor and their imagination, still more could be set free. When childhood stretched only a few years ahead, early man was set free to learn a little; when adolescence was prolonged, the men of earlier civilizations were able to leap ahead. In the future we may hope to meet the magnificent responsibilities of our knowledge through the visions of boys and girls who will remain all their lives, not only as adolescents but as adults, open to the widest prospects, "moving about in worlds not realized."

Discussion Questions

1. In small groups, discuss whether Mead accurately and fairly assesses the problems males and females experience in their adolescence.
2. What in Mead's essay creates the impression that she is sympathetic to what adolescents face?
3. How well do you think Mead describes the role of parents?
4. As someone closer to adolescence than Mead, offer any aspects of adolescence you think she failed to include.
5. What is the significance of Mead's entitling her essay *adolescents* instead of *adolescence*?
6. What does this essay suggest about Mead as an anthropologist and as a human being?

Writing Assignments

1. Write a journal entry that discusses the problems that you have faced as an adolescent.
2. Write a letter to Mead that reports on how effectively she addresses the problems of adolescents in her essay.
3. Are we already living in the "new age" that Mead describes in paragraph 28? Write an essay that examines your answer to this question.
4. Write an essay that either supports or refutes the idea that today's adolescents are faced with a more difficult life than that of previous generations.
5. What benefits do you see emerging from the young people's rebellion that Mead describes in paragraphs 26–27? Write an essay that offers specific examples to support your viewpoint.

The Turning Point of My Life

MARK TWAIN

Mark Twain (1835–1910) was born Samuel Langhorne Clemens in
Florida, Missouri, and grew up in Hannibal, Missouri. As a youth,
Twain was fascinated with the Mississippi River and gathered stories
that he later used in his writing. An aspiring riverboat captain before
riverboat operations ceased about the end of the Civil War, Twain
joined his brother in Nevada and began his career as a humorist.
In 1870, Twain married Olivia Langdon and moved to Hartford,
Connecticut, where he wrote his famous novels, including *The
Adventures of Tom Sawyer* (1876), *The Prince and the Pauper* (1882),
The Adventures of Huckleberry Finn (1884), *A Connecticut Yankee
at King Arthur's Court* (1889), *The American Claimant* (1892),
Tom Sawyer Abroad (1894), *The Tragedy of Pudd'nhead Wilson*
(1894), and *Personal Recollections of Joan of Arc* (1896). Twain
also wrote personal reminiscences and autobiographies: *Roughing
It* (1872), *Life on the Mississippi* (1883), and *Mark Twain's Autobiography* (posthumous, 1924). His travel sketches appear in *The Innocents Abroad* (1869), *A Tramp Abroad* (1880), and *Following the
Equator* (1897). With Charles L. Webster, Twain started a publishing
company that later went bankrupt, forcing him to lecture across the
United States and England to pay his debts. Twain's popularity in
the last thirty years is marked by Hal Holbrook's rendition of *Mark
Twain the Lecturer*, a monologue that Holbrook has performed at
hundreds of theaters and universities across the country. In the

following selection, written one year before his death, Twain describes "Circumstance," a time when outside forces and personal reactions shaped his life.

1   If I understand the idea, the *Bazaar* invites several of us to write upon the above text. It means the change in my life's course which introduced what must be regarded by me as the most *important* condition of my career. But it also implies—without intention, perhaps—that the turning-point *itself* was the creator of the new condition. This gives it too much distinction, too much prominence, too much credit. It is only the *last* link in a very long chain of turning-points commissioned to produce the cardinal result; it is not any more important than the humblest of its ten thousand predecessors. Each of the ten thousand did its appointed share, on its appointed date, in forwarding the scheme, and they were all necessary; to have left out any one of them would have defeated the scheme and brought about *some other* result. I know we have a fashion of saying "such and such an event was the turning-point of my life," but we shouldn't say it. We should merely grant that its place as *last* link in the chain makes it the most *conspicuous* link; in real importance it has no advantage over any one of its predecessors.

2   Perhaps the most celebrated turning-point recorded in history was the crossing of the Rubicon. Suetonius says:

> Coming up with his troops on the banks of the Rubicon, he halted for a while, and, revolving in his mind the importance of the step he was on the point of taking, he turned to those about him and said, "we may still retreat; but if we pass this little bridge, nothing is left for us but to fight it out in arms."

3   This was a stupendously important moment. And all the incidents, big and little, of Caesar's previous life had been leading up to it, stage by stage, link by link. This was the *last* link—merely the last

one, and no bigger than the others; but as we gaze back at it through the inflating mists of our imagination, it looks as big as the orbit of Neptune.

4   You, the reader, have a *personal* interest in that link, and so have I; so has the rest of the human race. It was one of the links in your life chain, and it was one of the links in mine. We may wait, now with bated breath, while Caesar reflects. Your fate and mine are involved in his decision.

5   While he was thus hesitating, the following incident occurred. A person remarked for his noble mien and graceful aspect appeared close at hand, sitting and playing upon a pipe. When not only the shepherds, but a number of soldiers also, flocked to listen to him, and some trumpeters among them, he snatched a trumpet from one of them, ran to the river with it, and, sounding the advance with a piercing blast, crossed to the other side. Upon this, Caesar exclaimed: "Let us go whither the omens of the gods and the iniquity of our enemies call us. *The die is cast.*"

6   So, he crossed—and changed the future of the whole human race, for all time. But that stranger was a link in Caesar's life-chain, too; and a necessary one. We don't know his name, we never hear of him again; he was very casual; he acts like an accident; but he was no accident, he was there by compulsion of *his* life-chain, to blow the electrifying blast that was to make up Caesar's mind for him, and thence go piping down the aisles of history forever.

7   If the stranger hadn't been there! But he *was*. And Caesar crossed. With such results! Such vast events—each a link in the *human* race's life-chain; each event producing the next one, and that one the next one, and so on: the destruction of the republic; the founding of the empire; the breaking up of the empire; the rise of Christianity upon its ruins; the spread of the religion to other lands—and so on; link by link took its appointed place at its appointed time, the discovery of America being one of them; our Revolution another; the inflow of English and other immigrants another; their drift westward (my ancestors among them) another; the settlement of certain of them in Missouri, which resulted in *me*. For I was one of the unavoidable results of the crossing of the Rubicon. If the stranger, with his trumpet blast, had stayed away (which he *couldn't*, for he was an appointed link) Caesar would not have crossed. What would have happened, in that case, we can never guess. We only know that the

things that did happen would not have happened. They might have been replaced by equally prodigious things, of course, but their nature and results are beyond our guessing. But the matter that interests me personally is that I would not be *here* now, but somewhere else; and probably black—there is no telling. Very well, I am glad he crossed. And very really and thankfully glad, too, though I never cared anything about it before.

8   To me, the most important feature of my life is its literary feature. I have been professionally literary something more than forty years. There have been many turning-points in my life, but the one that was the last link in the chain appointed to conduct me to the literary guild is the most *conspicuous* link in that chain. *Because* it was the last one. It was not any more important than its predecessors. All the other links have an inconspicuous look, except the crossing of the Rubicon; but as factors in making me literary they are all of the one size, the crossing of the Rubicon included.

9   I know how I came to be literary, and I will tell the steps that led up to it and brought it about.

10   The crossing of the Rubicon was not the first one, it was hardly even a recent one; I should have to go back ages before Caesar's day to find the first one. To save space I will go back only a couple of generations and start with an incident of my boyhood. When I was twelve and a half years old, my father died. It was in the spring. The summer came, and brought with it an epidemic of measles. For a time, a child died almost every day. The village was paralyzed with fright, distress, despair. Children that were not smitten with the disease were imprisoned in their homes to save them from the infection. In the homes there were no cheerful faces, there was no music, there was no singing but of solemn hymns, no voice but of prayer, no romping was allowed, no noise, no laughter, the family moved spectrally about on tiptoe, in a ghostly hush. I was a prisoner. My soul was steeped in this awful dreariness—and in fear. At some time or other every day and every night a sudden shiver shook me to the marrow, and I said to myself, "There, I've got it! and I shall die." Life on these miserable terms was not worth living, and at last I made up my mind to get the disease and have it over, one way or the other. I escaped from the house and went to the house of a neighbor where a playmate of mine was very ill with the malady. When the chance offered I crept into his room and got into bed

with him. I was discovered by his mother and sent back into captivity. But I had the disease; they could not take that from me. I came near to dying. The whole village was interested, and anxious, and sent for news of me every day; and not only once a day, but several times. Everybody believed I would die; but on the fourteenth day a change came for the worse and they were disappointed.

11   This was a turning-point of my life. (Link number one.) For when I got well my mother closed my school career and apprenticed me to a printer. She was tired of trying to keep me out of mischief, and the adventure of the measles decided her to put me into more masterful hands than hers.

12   I became a printer, and began to add one link after another to the chain which was to lead me into the literary profession. A long road, but I could not know that; and as I did not know what its goal was, even that it had one, I was indifferent. Also contented.

13   A young printer wanders around a good deal, seeking and finding work; and seeking again, when necessity commands. N.B. Necessity is a *Circumstance*; Circumstance is man's master—and when Circumstance commands, he must obey; he may argue the matter—that is his privilege, just as it is the honorable privilege of a falling body to argue with the attraction of gravitation—but it won't do any good, he must *obey*. I wandered for ten years, under the guidance and dictatorship of Circumstance, and finally arrived in a city of Iowa, where I worked several months. Among the books that interested me in those days was one about the Amazon. The traveler told an alluring tale of his long voyage up the great river from Para to the sources of the Madeira, through the heart of an enchanted land, a land wastefully rich in tropical wonders, a romantic land where all the birds and flowers and animals were of the museum varieties, and where the alligator and the crocodile and the monkey seemed as much at home as if they were in the Zoo. Also, he told an astonishing tale about *coca*, a vegetable product of miraculous powers, asserting that it was so nourishing and so strength-giving that the native of the mountains of the Madeira region would tramp up hill and down all day on a pinch of powdered coca and require no other sustenance.

14   I was fired with a longing to ascend the Amazon. Also with a longing to open up a trade in coca with all the world. During months I dreamed that dream, and tried to contrive ways to get to Para and spring that

splendid enterprise upon an unsuspecting planet. But all in vain. A person may *plan* as much as he wants to, but nothing of consequence is likely to come of it until the magician *Circumstance* steps in and takes the matter off his hands. At last Circumstance came to my help. It was in this way. Circumstance, to help or hurt another man, made him lose a fifty-dollar bill in the street; and to help or hurt me, made me find it. I advertised the find, and left for the Amazon the same day. This was another turning-point, another link.

15   Could Circumstance have ordered another dweller in that town to go to the Amazon and open up a world-trade in coca on a fifty-dollar basis and been obeyed? No, I was the only one. There were other fools there—shoals and shoals of them—but they were not of my kind. I was the only one of my kind.

16   Circumstance is powerful, but it cannot work alone; it has to have a partner. Its partner is man's *temperament*—his natural disposition. His temperament is not his invention, it is *born* in him, and he has no authority over it, neither is he responsible for its acts. He cannot change it, nothing can change it, nothing can modify it—except temporarily. But it won't stay modified. It is permanent, like the color of the man's eyes and the shape of his ears. Blue eyes are gray in certain unusual lights; but they resume their natural color when that stress is removed.

17   A Circumstance that will coerce one man will have no effect upon a man of a different temperament. If Circumstance had thrown the bank-note in Caesar's way, his temperament would not have made him start for the Amazon. His temperament would have compelled him to do something with the money, but not that. It might have made him advertise the note—and *wait*. We can't tell. Also, it might have made him go to New York and buy into the Government, with results that would leave Tweed nothing to learn when it came his turn.

18   Very well, Circumstance furnished the capital, and my temperament told me what to do with it. Sometimes a temperament is an ass. When that is the case the owner of it is an ass, too, and is going to remain one. Training, experience, association, can temporarily so polish him, improve him, exalt him that people will think he is a mule, but they will be mistaken. Artificially he is a mule, for the time being, but at bottom he is an ass yet, and will remain one.

19   By temperament I was the kind of person that *does* things. Does them, and reflects afterward. So I started for the Amazon without

reflecting and without asking any questions. That was more than fifty years ago. In all that time my temperament has not changed, by even a shade. I have been punished many and many a time, and bitterly, for doing things and reflecting afterward, but these tortures have been of no value to me: I still do the thing commanded by Circumstance and Temperament, and reflect afterward. Always violently. When I am reflecting, on those occasions, even deaf persons can hear me think.

20   I went by the way of Cincinnati, and down the Ohio and Mississippi. My idea was to take ship, at New Orleans, for Para. In New Orleans I inquired, and found there was no ship leaving for Para. Also, that there never had *been* one leaving for Para. I reflected. A policeman came and asked me what I was doing, and I told him. He made me move on, and said if he caught me reflecting in the public street again he would run me in.

21   After a few days I was out of money. Then Circumstance arrived, with another turning-point of my life—a new link. On my way down, I had made the acquaintance of a pilot. I begged him to teach me the river, and he consented. I became a pilot.

22   By and by Circumstance came again—introducing the Civil War, this time, in order to push me ahead another stage or two toward the literary profession. The boats stopped running, my livelihood was gone.

23   Circumstance came to the rescue with a new turning-point and a fresh link. My brother was appointed secretary to the new Territory of Nevada, and he invited me to go with him and help in his office. I accepted.

24   In Nevada, Circumstance furnished me the silver fever and I went into the mines to make a fortune, as I supposed; but that was not the idea. The idea was to advance me another step toward literature. For amusement I scribbled things for the Virginia City *Enterprise*. One isn't a printer ten years without setting up acres of good and bad literature, and learning—unconsciously at first, consciously later—to discriminate between the two, within his mental limitations; and meantime he is unconsciously acquiring what is called a "style." One of my efforts attracted attention, and the *Enterprise* sent for me and put me on its staff.

25   And so I became a journalist—another link. By and by Circumstance and the Sacramento *Union* sent me to the Sandwich Islands for five or

six months, to write up sugar. I did it; and threw in a good deal of extraneous matter that hadn't anything to do with sugar. But it was this extraneous matter that helped me to another link.

26   It made me notorious, and San Francisco invited me to lecture. Which I did. And profitably. I had long had a desire to travel and see the world, and now Circumstance had most kindly and unexpectedly hurled me upon the platform and furnished me the means. So I joined the "Quaker City Excursion."

27   When I returned to America, Circumstance was waiting on the pier—with the *last* link—the conspicuous, the consummating, the victorious link: I was asked to *write a book*, and I did it, and called it *The Innocents Abroad*. Thus I became at last a member of the literary guild. That was forty-two years ago, and I have been a member ever since. Leaving the Rubicon incident away back where it belongs, I can say with truth that the reason I am in the literary profession is because I had the measles when I was twelve years old.

Discussion Questions

1. In the first paragraph, Twain discusses the implications of "turning points." What does his clarification of *Bazaar*'s writing topic contribute to his essay?
2. In small groups, discuss whether you agree with Twain that "you, the reader, have a *personal* interest in that [*last*] link" (paragraph 4).
3. Explain the connection between Caesar's crossing the Rubicon and Twain's measles when he was twelve years old.
4. Explain Twain's analysis of circumstances that he begins in paragraph 13 and develops throughout the rest of his essay.
5. Why do you think Twain capitalizes the word *circumstance*?
6. What is your overall impression of Twain? Explain.

Writing Assignments

1. Write a journal entry about "the *last* link" in your life that contributed in making you into the person you are today.

2. Write a letter to a stranger describing something about your life that best defines who you are.

3. Write an essay in which you examine the turning points of your life. Carefully analyze the events, people, and personal understanding that have helped to shape you.

4. Twain reports that he was "indifferent" and "contented" when he became a printer. Choose two seemingly incongruous emotions that you once felt and explain how the two were in fact compatible.

5. Examine the relationship between cause and effect; that is, to what extent are the two linked? Do people use the connection more as a reason or as an excuse for events in their life? Support your thinking with specific examples.

An Unfinished Woman

LILLIAN HELLMAN

Lillian Hellman (1905–1984) was born in New Orleans, Louisiana, and lived there for six years before her family moved to New York City. For the next decade, however, Hellman spent half the year in New York and the other half in New Orleans. She studied at New York University from 1922 to 1924 and at Columbia University in 1926. She worked as a manuscript reader, press agent, and book reviewer. In 1930, she met detective-story writer Dashiell Hammett, who remained a central figure in her life. Hellman is the author of *The Children's Hour* (1934), *Days to Come* (1936), *The Little Foxes: A Play in Three Acts* (1939), *Watch on the Rhine: A Play in Three Acts* (1941), *The Autumn Garden: A Play in Three Acts* (1951), *Toys in the Attic* (1960), and *Maybe* (1980). Hellman's plays reveal her interest in social consciousness. Her mastery of dramatic technique—memorable characters, striking dialogue, and explosive confrontation—earned Hellman the reputation as one of the United States' most successful and important playwrights. She received many awards, including the New York Drama Critics Circle Award in 1941 and in 1960. Her life is chronicled in three memoirs: *An Unfinished Woman—A Memoir* (1969), *Pentimento: A Book of Portraits* (1973), and *Scoundrel Time* (1976). She received a National Book Award in

1970 for *An Unfinished Woman,* from which the following selection is taken. In this essay, Hellman recalls some of her experiences
as an adolescent that brought about self-discoveries.

1   I was, they told me, turning into a handful. Mrs. Stillman said I was
wild, Mr. Stillman said that I would, of course, bring pain to my mother
and father, and Fizzy said I was just plain disgusting mean. It had been
a bad month for me. I had, one night, fallen asleep in the fig tree and,
coming down in the morning, refused to tell my mother where I had
been. James Denery the Third had hit me very hard in a tug-of-war
and I had waited until the next day to hit him over the head with a
porcelain coffee pot and then his mother complained to my mother. I
had also refused to go back to dancing class.

2   And I was now spending most of my time with a group from an
orphanage down the block. I guess the orphan group was no more
attractive than any other, but to be an orphan seemed to me desirable
and a self-made piece of independence. In any case, the orphans
were more interesting to me than my schoolmates, and if they played
rougher they complained less. Frances, a dark beauty of my age,
queened it over the others because her father had been killed by the
Mafia. Miriam, small and wiry, regularly stole my allowance from
the red purse my aunt had given me, and the one time I protested
she beat me up. Louis Calda was religious and spoke to me about
it. Pancho was dark, sad, and to me, a poet, because once he said,
"*Yo te amo.*" I could not sleep a full night after this declaration, and
it set up in me forever after both sympathy and irritability with the
first sexual stirrings of little girls, so masked, so complex, so foolish
as compared with the sex of little boys. It was Louis Calda who took
Pancho and me to a Catholic Mass that could have made me a
fourteen-year-old convert. But Louis explained that he did not think
me worthy, and Pancho, to stop my tears, cut off a piece of his hair
with a knife, gave it to me as a gift from royalty, and then shoved
me into the gutter. I don't know why I thought this an act of
affection, but I did, and went home to open the back of a new
wristwatch my father had given me for my birthday and to put the

lock of hair in the back. A day later, when the watched stopped, my father insisted I give it to him immediately, declaring that the jeweler was unreliable.

3   It was that night that I disappeared, and that night that Fizzy said I was disgusting mean, and Mr. Stillman said I would forever pain my mother and father, and my father turned on both of them and said he would handle his family affairs himself without comments from strangers. But he said it too late. He had come home very angry with me: the jeweler, after my father's complaints about his unreliability, had found the lock of hair in the back of the watch. What started out to be a mild reproof on my father's part soon turned angry when I wouldn't explain about the hair. (My father was often angry when I was most like him.) He was so angry that he forgot that he was attacking me in front of the Stillmans, my old rival Fizzy, and the delighted Mrs. Dreyfus, a new, rich boarder who only that afternoon had complained about my bad manners. My mother left the room when my father grew angry with me. Hannah, passing through, put up her hand as if to stop my father and then, frightened of the look he gave her, went out to the porch. I sat on the couch, astonished at the pain in my head. I tried to get up from the couch, but one ankle turned and I sat down again, knowing for the first time the rampage that could be caused in me by anger. The room began to have other forms, the people were no longer men and women, my head was not my own. I told myself that my head had gone somewhere and I have little memory of anything after my Aunt Jenny came into the room and said to my father, "Don't you remember?" I have never known what she meant, but I knew that soon after I was moving up the staircase, that I slipped and fell a few steps, that when I woke up hours later in my bed, I found a piece of angel cake—an old love, an old custom—left by my mother on my pillow. The headache was worse and I vomited out of the window. Then I dressed, took my red purse, and walked a long way down St. Charles Avenue. A St. Charles Avenue mansion had on its back lawn a famous doll's-house, an elaborate copy of the mansion itself, built years before for the small daughter of the house. As I passed this showpiece, I saw a policeman and moved swiftly back to the doll palace and crawled inside. If I had known about the fantasies of the frightened, that ridiculous small house would not have been so terrible for me. I was surrounded by ornate, carved reproductions

of the mansion furniture, scaled for children, bisque figurines in
miniature, a working toilet seat of gold leaf in suitable size, small
draperies of damask with a sign that said "From the damask of Marie
Antoinette," a miniature samovar with small bronze cups, and a tiny
Madame Récamier couch on which I spent the night, my legs on
the floor. I must have slept, because I woke from a nightmare and
knocked over a bisque figurine. The noise frightened me, and since
it was now almost light, in one of those lovely mist mornings of late
spring when every flower in New Orleans seems to melt and mix
with the air, I crawled out. Most of the day I spent walking, although
I had a long session in the ladies' room of the railroad station. I had
four dollars and two bits, but that wasn't much when you meant it
to last forever and when you knew it would not be easy for a fourteen-
year-old girl to find work in a city where too many people knew her.
Three times I stood in line at the railroad ticket windows to ask
where I could go for four dollars, but each time the question seemed
too dangerous and I knew no other way of asking it.

     Toward evening, I moved to the French Quarter, feeling sad and
envious as people went home to dinner. I bought a few Tootsie Rolls
and a half loaf of bread and went to the St. Louis Cathedral in
Jackson Square. (It was that night that I composed the prayer that
was to become, in the next five years, an obsession, mumbled over
and over through the days and nights: "God forgive me, Papa forgive
me, Mama forgive me, Sophronia, Jenny, Hannah, and all others,
through this time and that time, in life and in death." When I was
nineteen, my father, who had made several attempts through the
years to find out what my lip movements meant as I repeated the
prayer, said, "How much would you take to stop that? Name it and
you've got it." I suppose I was sick of the nonsense by that time
because I said, "A leather coat and a feather fan," and the next day
he bought them for me.) After my loaf of bread, I went looking for
a bottle of soda pop and discovered, for the first time, the whorehouse
section around Bourbon Street. The women were ranged in the
doorways of the cribs, making the first early evening offers to sailors,
who were the only men in the streets. I wanted to stick around and
see how things like that worked, but the second or third time I circled
the block, one of the girls called out to me. I couldn't understand the
words, but the voice was angry enough to make me run toward the
French Market.

5   The Market was empty except for two old men. One of them called to me as I went past, and I turned to see that he had opened his pants and was shaking what my circle called "his thing." I flew across the street into the coffee stand, forgetting that the owner had known me since I was a small child when my Aunt Jenny would rest from her marketing tour with a cup of fine strong coffee.

6   He said, in the patois. "*Que faites, ma 'fant? Je suis fermé.*"

7   I said, "*Rien. Ma tante attend*—Could I have a doughnut?

8   He brought me two doughnuts, saying one was *lagniappe*, but I took my doughnuts outside when he said "*Mais où est vo' tante à c'heure?*"

9   I fell asleep with my doughnuts behind a shrub in Jackson Square. The night was damp and hot and through the sleep there were many voices and, much later, there was music from somewhere near the river. When all sounds had ended, I woke, turned my head, and knew I was being watched. Two rats were sitting a few feet from me. I urinated on my dress, crawled backwards to stand up, screamed as I ran up the steps of St. Louis Cathedral and pounded on the doors. I don't know when I stopped screaming or how I got to the railroad station, but I stood against the wall trying to tear off my dress and only knew I was doing it when two women stopped to stare at me. I began to have cramps in my stomach of a kind I had never known before. I went into the ladies' room and sat bent in a chair, whimpering with pain. After a while the cramps stopped, but I had an intimation, when I looked into the mirror, of something happening to me: my face was blotched, and there seemed to be circles and twirls I had never seen before, the straight blonde hair was damp with sweat, and a paste of green from the shrub had made lines on my jaw. I had gotten older.

10   Sometime during that early morning I half washed my dress, threw away my pants, put cold water on my hair. Later in the morning a cleaning woman appeared, and after a while began to ask questions that frightened me. When she put down her mop and went out of the room, I ran out of the station. I walked, I guess, for many hours, but when I saw a man on Canal Street who worked in Hannah's office, I realized that the sections of New Orleans that were known to me were dangerous for me.

11   Years before, when I was a small child, Sophronia and I would go to pick up, or try on, pretty embroidered dresses that were made

for me by a colored dressmaker called Bibettera. A block up from
Bibettera's there had been a large ruin of a house with a sign,
ROOMS—CLEAN—CHEAP, and cheerful people seemed always
to be moving in and out of the house. The door of the house was
painted a bright pink. I liked that and would discuss with Sophronia
why we didn't live in a house with a pink door.

12   Bibettera was long since dead, so I knew I was safe in this Negro
neighborhood. I went up and down the block several times, praying
that things would work and I could take my cramps to bed. I knocked
on the pink door. It was answered immediately by a small young
man.

13   I said, "Hello." He said nothing.

14   I said, "I would like to rent a room, please."

15   He closed the door but I waited, thinking he had gone to get
the lady of the house. After a long time, a middle-aged woman put
her head out of a second-floor window and said, "What you at?"

16   I said, "I would like to rent a room, please. My mama is a widow
and has gone to work across the river. She gave me money and said
to come here until she called for me."

17   "Who your mama?"

18   "Er. My mama."

19   "What you at? Speak out."

20   "I told you. I have money. . . ." But as I tried to open my purse,
the voice grew angry.

21   "This is a nigger house. Get you off. *Vite.*"

22   I said, in a whisper, "I know, I'm part nigger."

23   The small young man opened the front door. He was laughing.
"You part mischief. Get the hell out of here."

24   I said, "Please—and then, "I'm related to Sophronia Mason. She
told me to come. Ask her."

25   Sophronia and her family were respected figures in New Orleans
Negro circles, and because I had some vague memory of her stately
bow to somebody as she passed this house, I believed they knew
her. If they told her about me I would be in trouble; but phones
were not usual then in poor neighborhoods, and I had no other
place to go.

26   The woman opened the door. Slowly I went into the hall.

27   I said, "I won't stay long. I have four dollars and Sophronia will
give more if . . .

28   The woman pointed up the stairs. She opened the door of a small room. "Washbasin place down the hall. Toilet place behind the kitchen. Two-fifty and no fuss, no bother."

29   I said, "Yes ma'am, yes ma'am," but as she started to close the door, the young man appeared.

30   "Where your bag?"

31   "Bag?"

32   "Nobody put up here without no bag."

33   "Oh. You mean the bag with my clothes? It's at the station. I'll go and get it later . . ." I stopped because I knew I was about to say I'm sick, I'm in pain, I'm frightened.

34   He said, "I say you lie. I say you trouble. I say you get out."

35   I said, "And I say you shut up."

36   Years later, I was to understand why the command worked, and to be sorry that it did, but that day I was very happy when he turned and closed the door. I was asleep within minutes.

37   Toward evening, I went down the stairs, saw nobody, walked a few blocks and bought myself an oyster loaf. But the first bite made me feel sick, so I took my loaf back to the house. This time, as I climbed the steps, there were three women in the parlor, and they stopped talking when they saw me. I went back to sleep immediately, dizzy and nauseated.

38   I woke to a high, hot sun and my father standing at the foot of the bed staring at the oyster loaf.

39   He said, "Get up now and get dressed."

40   I was crying as I said, "Thank you, Papa, but I can't."

41   From the hall, Sophronia said, "Get along up now. *Vite.* The morning is late."

42   My father left the room. I dressed and came into the hall carrying my oyster loaf. Sophronia was standing at the head of the stairs. She pointed out, meaning my father was on the street.

43   I said, "He humiliated me. He did. I won't . . ."

44   She said, "Get you going or I will never see you whenever again."

45   I ran past her to the street. I stood with my father until Sophronia joined us, and then we walked slowly, without speaking, to the streetcar line. Sophronia bowed to us, but she refused my father's hand when he attempted to help her into the car. I ran to the car meaning to ask her to take me with her, but the car moved and she raised her hand as if to stop me. My father and I walked again for a long time.

46   He pointed to a trash can sitting in front of a house. "Please put that oyster loaf in the can."

47   At Vanalli's restaurant, he took my arm. "Hungry?"

48   I said, "No, thank you, Papa."

49   But we went through the door. It was, in those days, a New Orleans custom to have an early black coffee, go to the office, and after a few hours have a large breakfast at a restaurant. Vanalli's was crowded, the headwaiter was so sorry, but after my father took him aside, a very small table was put up for us—too small for my large father, who was accommodating himself to it in a manner most unlike him.

50   He said, "Jack, my rumpled daughter would like cold crayfish, a nice piece of pompano, a separate bowl of Béarnaise sauce, don't ask me why, French fried potatoes . . ."

51   I said, "Thank you, Papa, but I am not hungry. I don't want to be here."

52   My father waved the waiter away and we sat in silence until the crayfish came. My hand reached out instinctively and then drew back.

53   My father said, "Your mother and I have had an awful time."

54   I said, "I'm sorry about that. But I don't want to go home, Papa."

55   He said, angrily, "Yes, you do. But you want me to apologize first. I do apologize but you should not have made me say it."

56   After a while I mumbled, "God forgive me, Papa forgive me, Mama forgive me, Sophronia, Jenny, Hannah. . . ."

57   "Eat your crayfish."

58   I ate everything he had ordered and then a small steak. I suppose I had been mumbling through my breakfast.

59   My father said, "You're talking to yourself. I can't hear you. What are you saying?"

60   "God forgive me. Papa forgive me, Mama forgive me, Sophronia, Jenny . . ."

61   My father said, "Where do we start your training as the first Jewish nun on Prytania Street?"

62   When I finished laughing, I liked him again. I said, "Papa, I'll tell you a secret. I've had very bad cramps and I am beginning to bleed. I'm changing life."

63   He started at me for a while. Then he said, "Well, it's not the way it's usually described, but it's accurate, I guess. Let's go home now to your mother."

64   We were never, as long as my mother and father lived, to mention that time again. But it was of great importance to them and I've thought about it all my life. From that day on I knew my power over my parents. That was not to be too important: I was ashamed of it and did not abuse it too much. But I found out something more useful and more dangerous: if you are willing to take the punishment, you are halfway through the battle. That the issue may be trivial, the battle ugly, is another point.

Discussion Questions

1. Cite the reasons why Hellman was called a "handful." Do you think she would be considered as such if she were one of your peers? Why or why not?
2. Describe Hellman's character from what she reports. Would you like her if she were a schoolmate? Why or why not?
3. Explain the symbolism of the angel cake Hellman's mother leaves on Hellman's pillow.
4. Why were Hellman and her father so secretive about the time she ran away?
5. Why did Hellman, as she says in the last paragraph, think about the experience for the rest of her life?
6. Discuss what the title of Hellman's memoir could mean.
7. In small groups, choose which of the two lessons Hellman learned is the more important one. Explain your answer.

Writing Assignments

1. Most children have thought about running away from home, if not having actually done so. In a journal entry, recall a time in your life when you ran away (or thought about it) and describe what precipitated the act and how you felt.
2. Write a letter to a family member in which you discuss an incident you experienced that was so meaningful you have thought about it all of your life.

3. Write an essay about a time when you held power over your parents. Describe the circumstances and the outcome of the experience.

4. Describe a time when you "took the punishment" and found you were "halfway through the battle." What did you learn from the experience and how did it affect your life?

Moment of Wisdom

M. F. K. FISHER

M. F. K. (Mary Frances Kennedy) Fisher (1909–1992) was born in Albion, Michigan. She attended Illinois College, Occidental College, the University of California/Los Angeles, and the University of Dijon in France. Fisher distinguished herself as a prolific writer of books focusing on travel, food, and people. Although her work appeared in such magazines as *Food and Wine, Gourmet,* and *The New Yorker,* she never considered herself a food writer; rather, she used food as a metaphor for inquiry into human emotions. Among her many volumes are *The Gastronomical Me* (1943), *Here Let Us Feast: A Book of Banquets* (1946 and a revised edition, 1986), *An Alphabet for Gourmets* (1949), *With Bold Knife and Fork* (1969), *Among Friends* (1971), *The Art of Eating: Five Gastronomical Works* (1954), *As They Were* (1983), *Sister Age* (1983), *Spirits of the Valley* (1985), *Dubious Honors* (1988), *The Boss Dog* (1991), *Long Ago in France: The Years in Dijon* (1991), *To Begin Again: Stories and Memoirs, 1908–1929* (1992), and *Stay Me, Oh Comfort Me: Journals and Stories, 1933–1945* (1993). Fisher received the California Literature Silver Medal in 1970 and the Robert Kirsch Award in 1984, the latter for a work by a Western author or a work featuring the West. As much as Fisher dealt with people, places, and the art of eating, her writing was a treatise on the art of living. In the following selection, Fisher evokes her family history as a way to examine who she became.

1   Tears do come occasionally into one's eyes, and they are more often than not a good thing. At least they are salty and, no matter what invisible wound they seep from, they purge and seal the tissues. But when they roll out and down the cheeks it is a different thing, and more amazing to one unaccustomed to such an outward and visible sign of an inward cleansing. Quick tears can sting and tease the eyeballs and their lids into suffusion and then a new clarity. The brimming and, perhaps fortunately, rarer kind, however, leaves things pale and thinned out, so that even a gross face takes on a porcelain-like quality, and—in my own case—there is a sensation of great fragility or weariness of the bones and spirit.

2   I have had the experience of such tears very few times. Perhaps it is a good idea to mention one or two of them, if for no other reason than to remind myself that such a pure moment may never come again.

3   When I was twelve years old, my family was slowly installing itself about a mile down Painter Avenue outside Whittier, California, the thriving little Quaker town where I grew up, on an orange ranch with shaggy, neglected gardens and a long row of half-wild roses along the narrow county road. Our house sat far back in the tangle, with perhaps two hundred yards of gravel driveway leading in toward it.

4   There was a wide screened porch across the front of the house, looking into the tangle. It was the heart of the place. We sat there long into the cool evenings of summer, talking softly. Even in winter, we were there for lunch on bright days, and in the afternoon drinking tea or beer. In one corner, there was always a good pile of wood for the hearth fire in the living room, and four wide doors led into that room. They were open most of the time, although the fire burned day and night, brightly or merely a gentle token, all the decades we lived on the Ranch.

5   My grandmother had her own small apartment in the house, as seemed natural and part of the way to coexist, and wandering missionaries and other men of her own cut of cloth often came down the road to see her and discuss convocations and get money and other help. They left books of earnest import and dubious literary worth, like one printed in symbols for the young or illiterate, with Jehovah an eye surrounded by shooting beams of forked fire. Grandmother's friends, of whom I remember not a single one, usually stayed for a meal. Mother was often absent from such unannounced confrontations, prey to almost ritual attacks of what were referred to as "sick headaches," but my father always carved at his seat, head of the table. Grandmother, of course, was there. Father left early, and we children went up to bed, conditioned to complete lack of interest in the murmur of respectful manly voices and our grandmother's clear-cut Victorian guidance of the churchly talk below us. That was the pattern the first months at the Ranch, before the old lady died, and I am sure we ate amply and well, and with good manners, and we accepted sober men in dusty black suits as part of being alive.

6   When we moved down Painter Avenue into what was then real country, I was near intoxication from the flowers growing everywhere—the scraggly roses lining the road, all viciously thorned as they reverted to wildness, and poppies and lupine in the ditches and still between the rows of orange trees (soon to disappear as their seeds got plowed too deeply into the profitable soil), and exotic bulbs springing up hit or miss in our neglected gardens. I rooted around in all of it like a virgin piglet snuffling for truffles. My mother gave me free rein to keep the house filled with my own interpretations of the word "posy." It was a fine season in life.

7   One day, I came inside, very dusty and hot, with a basket of roses and weeds of beauty. The house seemed mine, airy and empty, full of shade. Perhaps everyone was in Whittier, marketing. I leaned my forehead against the screening of the front porch and breathed the wonderful dry air of temporary freedom, and off from the county road and onto our long narrow driveway came a small man, smaller than I, dressed in the crumpled hot black I recognized at once as the Cloth and carrying a small valise.

8   I wiped at my sweaty face and went to the screen door, to be polite to another of my grandmother's visitors. I wished I had stayed

out, anywhere at all, being that age and so on, and aware of rebellion's new pricks.

9   He was indeed tiny and frail in a way I had never noticed before in anyone. (I think this new awareness and what happened later came from the fact that I was alone in the family house and felt for the moment like a stranger made up of Grandmother and my parents and maybe God—that eye, Jehovah, but with no lightning.) He would not come in. I asked him if he would like some cool water, but he said no. His voice was thin. He asked to see Mother Holbrook, and when I told him she had died a few days before he did not seem at all bothered, and neither was I, except that he might be.

10   He asked if I would like to buy a Bible. I said no, we had many of them. His hands were too shaky and weak to open his satchel, but when I asked him again to come in, and started to open the door to go out to help him, he told me in such a firm way to leave him alone that I did. I did not reason about it for it seemed to be an agreement between us.

11   He picked up his dusty satchel, said goodbye in a very gentle voice, and walked back down the long driveway to the county road and then south, thinking God knows what hopeless thoughts. A little past our gate, he stopped to pick one of the dusty roses. I leaned my head against the screening of our porch and was astonished and mystified to feel slow fat quiet tears roll from my unblinking eyes and down my cheeks.

12   I could not believe it was happening. Where did they spring from, so fully formed, so unexpectedly? Where had they been waiting, all my long life as a child? What had just happened to me, to make me cry without volition, without a sound or a sob?

13   In a kind of justification of what I thought was a weakness, for I had been schooled to consider all tears as such, I thought, If I could have given him something of mine . . . If I were rich, I would buy him a new black suit . . . If I had next week's allowance and had not spent this week's on three Cherry Flips. . . If I could have given him some cool water or my love . . .

14   But the tiny old man, dry as a ditch weed, was past all that, as I came to learn long after my first passionate protest—past or beyond.

15   The first of such tears as mine that dusty day, which are perhaps rightly called the tears of new wisdom, are the most startling to one's

supposed equanimity. Later, they have a different taste. Perhaps they seem more bitter because they are recognizable. But they are always as unpredictable. Once, I was lying with my head back, listening to a long program of radio music from New York, with Toscanini drawing the fine blood from his gang. I was hardly conscious of the sound—with my mind, anyway—and when it ended, my two ears, which I had never thought of as cup-like, were so full of silent tears that as I sat up they drenched and darkened my whole front with little gouts of brine. I felt amazed, beyond my embarrassment in a group of near-friends, for the music I had heard was not the kind I thought I liked, and the salty water had rolled down from my half-closed eyes like October rain, with no sting to it but perhaps promising a good winter.

16   Such things are, I repeat to myself, fortunately rare, for they are too mysterious to accept with equanimity. I prefer not to dig too much into their comings, but it is sure that they cannot be evoked or foretold. If anger has a part in them, it is latent, indirect—not an incentive. The helpless weeping and sobbing and retching that sweeps over somebody who inadvertently hears Churchill's voice rallying Englishmen to protect their shores, or Roosevelt telling people not to be afraid of fear, or a civil-rights chieftain saying politely that there is such a thing as democracy—those violent physical reactions are proof of one's being alive and aware. But the slow, large tears that spill from the eye, flowing like unblown rain according to the laws of gravity and desolation—these are the real tears, I think. They are the ones that have been simmered, boiled, sieved, filtered past all anger and into the realm of acceptive serenity.

17   There is a story about a dog and an ape that came to love each other. The dog finally died, trying to keep the ape from returning to the jungle where he should have been all along and where none but another ape could follow. And one becomes the dog, the ape, no matter how clumsily the story is told. One is the hapless lover.

18   I am all of them. I feel again the hot dusty screening on my forehead as I watch the little man walk slowly out to the road and turn down past the ditches and stop for a moment by a scraggly rosebush. If I could only give him something, I think. If I could tell him something true.

19   It was a beginning for me, as the tears popped out so richly and ran down, without a sigh or cry. I could see clearly through them,

with no blurring, and they did not sting. This last is perhaps the most astonishing and fearsome part, past denial of any such encounter with wisdom, or whatever it is.

Discussion Questions

1. In the opening paragraph, what is the purpose of Fisher's distinguishing between the different kinds of tears?
2. What, exactly, was Fisher's "moment of wisdom," and why do you think it qualifies as such?
3. What is the significance of Fisher's tears neither blurring nor stinging?
4. In small groups, discuss what the point is of Fisher's essay.
5. Explain the function of the story about the dog and ape at the end of Fisher's essay.
6. Discuss what Fisher means when she writes in paragraph 18, "I am all of them."
7. Explain your understanding of the three sections of Fisher's essay. What links them?
8. What do you learn about Fisher's character from what she discusses in her essay? Cite specific passages and details that reflect her personality.

Writing Assignments

1. Write a journal entry discussing the importance of crying. Cite specific examples from your own experiences.
2. Write an essay in which you reflect on an event in your life that you could aptly entitle your "moment of wisdom." Describe it so others can experience not only what happened but also your thoughts and feelings at that time.
3. Compare and contrast Fisher's "moment of wisdom" or epiphany with those reached by other authors in this section.
4. Read some Aesop's *Fables* and select one that symbolizes an experience you have had. Write an essay that couples the fable with your experience.

My Horse and I

N. SCOTT MOMADAY

N. Scott Momaday (b. 1934) is a Native American of Kiowa and Cherokee descent and was born in Oklahoma. A poet, novelist, and essayist, Momaday is also an artist, a Kiowa tribal dancer, and a member of the Gourd Dance Society of the Kiowa tribe. Momaday grew up on a reservation in New Mexico and has taught at the University of California at Berkeley. He is currently Regents Professor of English at the University of Arizona. Momaday is the author of *House Made of Dawn* (1969), which won the Pulitzer Prize for fiction; *The Way To Rainy Mountain* (1969), in which the following essay appears; *The Gourd Dancer* (1976); *The Names: A Memoir* (1977); and *In the Presence of the Sun: Stories and Poems, 1961–1991* (1992). Exploring his heritage, customs, and culture, Momaday is one of the most respected contemporary Native American writers. In the following selection, which is representative of his writing style, Momaday examines through his description of his relationship with his horse the process by which he became a man. Momaday uses a relationship with an animal to explore maturation and self-under-standing, a technique other essayists have used.

1   I sometimes think of what it means that in their heyday—in 1830, say—the Kiowas owned more horses *per capita* than any other tribe on the Great Plains, that the Plains Indian culture, the last culture to evolve in North America, is also known as "the horse culture"

and "the centaur culture," that the Kiowas tell the story of a horse
that died of shame after its owner committed an act of cowardice,
that I am a Kiowa, that therefore there is in me, as there is in the
Tartars, an old, sacred notion of the horse. I believe that at some
point in my racial life, this notion must needs be expressed in order
that I may be true to my nature.

2   It happened so: I was thirteen years old, and my parents gave me
a horse. It was a small nine-year-old gelding of that rare, soft color
that is called strawberry roan. This my horse and I came to be, in
the course of our life together, in good understanding, of one mind,
a true story and history of that large landscape in which we made
the one entity of whole motion, one and the same center of an
intricate, pastoral composition, evanescent, ever changing. And to
this my horse I gave the name Pecos.

3   On the back of my horse I had a different view of the world. I
could see more of it, how it reached away beyond all the horizons
I had ever seen; and yet it was more concentrated in its appearance,
too, and more accessible to my mind, my imagination. My mind
loomed upon the farthest edges of the earth, where I could feel the
full force of the planet whirling into space. There was nothing of
the air and light that was not pure exhilaration, and nothing of time
and eternity. Oh, Pecos, *un poquito mas!* Oh, my hunting horse!
Bear me away, bear me away!

4   It was appropriate that I should make a long journey. Accordingly
I set out one early morning, traveling light. Such a journey must
begin in the nick of time, on the spur of the moment, and one must
say to himself at the outset: Let there be wonderful things along the
way; let me hold to the way and be thoughtful in my going; let this
journey be made in beauty and belief.

5   I sang in the sunshine and heard the birds call out on either
side. Bits of down from the cottonwoods drifted across the air, and
butterflies fluttered in the sage. I could feel my horse under me,
rocking at my legs, the bobbing of the reins in my hand; I could
feel the sun on my face and the stirring of a little wind at my hair. And
through the hard hooves, the slender limbs, the supple shoulders, the
fluent back of my horse I felt the earth under me. Everything was

under me, buoying me up; I rode across the top of the world. My mind soared; time and again I saw the fleeting shadow of my mind moving about me as it went winding upon the sun.

6   When the song, which was a song of riding, was finished, I had Pecos pick up the pace. Far down on the road to San Ysidro I overtook my friend Pasqual Fragua. He was riding a rangy, stiff-legged black and white stallion, half wild, which horse he was breaking for the rancher Cass Goodner. The horse skittered and blew as I drew up beside him. Pecos began to prance, as he did always in the company of another horse. "Where are you going?" I asked in the Jemez language. And he replied, "I am going down the road." The stallion was hard to manage, and Pasqual had to keep his mind upon it; I saw that I had taken him by surprise. "You know," he said after a moment, "when you rode up just now I did not know who you were." We rode on for a time in silence, and our horses got used to each other, but still they wanted their heads. The longer I looked at the stallion the more I admired it, and I suppose that Pasqual knew this, for he began to say good things about it: that it was a thing of good blood, that it was very strong and fast, that it felt very good to ride it. The thing was this: that the stallion was half wild, and I came to wonder about the wild half of it; I wanted to know what its wildness was worth in the riding. "Let us trade horses for a while," I said, and, well, all right, he agreed. At first it was exciting to ride the stallion, for every once in a while it pitched and bucked and wanted to run. But it was heavy and raw-boned and full of resistance, and every step was a jolt that I could feel deep down in my bones. I saw soon enough that I had made a bad bargain, and I wanted my horse back, but I was ashamed to admit it. There came a time in the late afternoon, in the vast plain far south of San Ysidro, after thirty miles, perhaps, when I no longer knew whether it was I who was riding the stallion or the stallion who was riding me. "Well, let us go back now," said Pasqual at last. "No, I am going on; and I will have my horse back, please," I said, and he was surprised and sorry to hear it, and we said goodbye. "If you are going south or east," he said, "look out for the sun, and keep your face in the shadow of your hat. *Vaya con Dios.*" and I went on my way alone then, wiser and better mounted, and thereafter I held on to my horse. I saw no one for a long time, but I saw four falling stars and any number of jackrabbits, roadrunners, and coyotes, and

once, across a distance, I saw a bear, small and black, lumbering in a ravine. The mountains drew close and withdrew and drew close again, and after several days I swung east.

7   Now and then I came upon settlements. For the most part they were dry, burnt places with Spanish names: Arroyo Seco, Las Piedras, Tres Casas. In one of these I found myself in a narrow street between high adobe walls. Just ahead, on my left, was a door in the wall. As I approached the door was flung open, and a small boy came running out, rolling a hoop. This happened so suddenly that Pecos shied very sharply, and I fell to the ground, jamming the thumb of my left hand. The little boy looked very worried and said that he was sorry to have caused such an accident. I waved the matter off, as if it were nothing; but as a matter of fact my hand hurt so much that tears welled up in my eyes. And the pain lasted for many days. I have fallen many times from a horse, both before and after that, and a few times I fell from a running horse on dangerous ground, but that was the most painful of them all.

8   In another settlement there were some boys who were interested in racing. They had good horses, some of them, but their horses were not so good as mine, and I won easily. After that, I began to think of ways in which I might even the odds a little, might give some advantage to my competitors. Once or twice I gave them a head start, a reasonable head start of, say, five or ten yards to the hundred, but that was too simple, and I won anyway. Then it came to me that I might try this: we should all line up in the usual way, side by side, but my competitors should be mounted and I should not. When the signal was given I should then have to get up on my horse while the others were breaking away; I should have to mount my horse during the race. This idea appealed to me greatly, for it was both imaginative and difficult, not to mention dangerous; Pecos and I should have to work very closely together. The first few times we tried this I had little success, and over a course of a hundred yards I lost four races out of five. The principal problem was that Pecos simply could not hold still among the other horses. Even before they broke away he was hard to manage, and when they were set running nothing could hold him back, even for an instant. I could not get my foot in the stirrup, but I had to throw myself up across the saddle on my stomach, hold on as best I could, and twist myself into position, and all this while racing at full speed. I could

ride well enough to accomplish this feat, but it was a very awkward and inefficient business. I had to find some way to use the whole energy of my horse, to get it all into the race. Thus far I had managed only to break his motion, to divert him from his purpose and mine. To correct this I took Pecos away and worked with him through the better part of a long afternoon on a broad reach of level ground beside an irrigation ditch. And it was hot, hard work. I began by teaching him to run straight away while I ran beside him a few steps, holding on to the saddle horn, with no pressure on the reins. Then, when we had mastered this trick, we proceeded to the next one, which was this: I placed my weight on my arms, hanging from the saddle horn, threw my feet out in front of me, struck them to the ground, and sprang up against the saddle. This I did again and again, until Pecos came to expect it and did not flinch or lose his stride. I sprang a little higher each time. It was in all a slow process of trial and error, and after two or three hours both Pecos and I were covered with bruises and soaked through with perspiration. But we had much to show for our efforts, and at last the moment came when we must put the whole performance together. I had not yet leaped into the saddle, but I was quite confident that I could now do so; only I must be sure to get high enough. We began this dress rehearsal then from a standing position. At my signal Pecos lurched and was running at once, straight away and smoothly. And at the same time I sprinted forward two steps and gathered myself up, placing my weight precisely at my wrists, throwing my feet out and together, perfectly. I brought my feet down sharply to the ground and sprang up hard, as hard as I could, bringing my legs astraddle of my horse—and everything was just right, except that I sprang too high. I vaulted all the way over my horse, clearing the saddle by a considerable margin, and came down into the irrigation ditch. It was a good trick, but it was not the one I had in mind, and I wonder what Pecos thought of it after all. Anyway, after a while I could mount my horse in this way and so well that there was no challenge in it, and I went on winning race after race.

9   I went on, farther and farther into the wide world. Many things happened. And in all this I knew one thing: I knew where the journey was begun, that it was itself a learning of the beginning, that the beginning was infinitely worth the learning. The journey was well

undertaken, and somewhere in it I sold my horse to an old Spanish man of Vallecitos. I do not know how long Pecos lived. I had used him hard and well, and it may be that in his last days an image of me like thought shimmered in his brain.

Discussion Questions

1. Why does Momaday begin his essay with an explanation of the Kiowa's "horse culture"?
2. What "different view of the world" did Momaday have when he was on his horse?
3. Why do you think Momaday sold Pecos? Are his reasons convincing? Why or why not?
4. In the last paragraph, Momaday states that "the beginning was infinitely worth the learning." In small groups, discuss what he means and what in his essay confirms this observation.
5. What do you know about Momaday's character from what he reveals in the essay?

Writing Assignments

1. Write a journal entry reporting on a time in which you had a "different view of the world."
2. Write an essay examining the circumstances of and your feelings about selling a family pet.
3. In an essay, explore the way(s) in which your behavior or interests are representative of your culture or heritage.
4. Fill in the blank: "My _____ and I" and then write an essay that develops this title.

CLASSIC ESSAYS ON

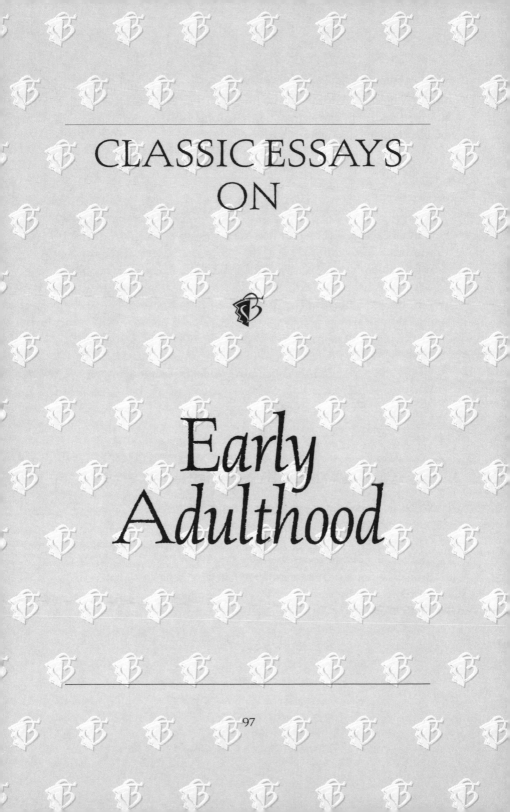

Early Adulthood

University Days

JAMES THURBER

James Thurber (1894–1961) was born in Columbus, Ohio, and attended Ohio State University for three years. From 1918 to 1920, he worked as a clerk in the State Department, stationed in Washington and Paris. He began his career as a journalist in 1920 when he became a writer for the *Columbus Dispatch* in Ohio and later for the *Chicago Tribune* in Paris. In 1925, Thurber returned to the United States to work for the *New York Evening Post*. He began writing articles for *The New Yorker* in 1925. One of America's most famous humorists and cartoonists, Thurber is the author of *Is Sex Necessary?* (1929), cowritten with E. B. White. His many volumes include *The Owl in the Attic* (1931); *The Seal in the Bedroom and Other Predicaments* (1932); *My Life and Hard Times* (1933); *The Middle-Aged Man on the Flying Trapeze* (1935); *Let Your Mind Alone* (1937); *Fables for Our Time* (1940); *My World—and Welcome to It* (1942), in which the following selection appears; *The Thurber Carnival* (1945); *The Beast in Me* (1948); *The Thirteen Clocks* (1950); *The Thurber Album* (1952); *Thurber Country* (1953); *Alarms and Diversions* (1957); *Lanterns and Lances* (1961); and *Credos and Curios*, published posthumously in 1962. Detailing Thurber's experience as a university student, the following essay demonstrates Thurber's lighthearted, whimsical style.

1   I passed all the other courses that I took at my University, but I
could never pass botany. This was because all botany students had
to spend several hours a week in a laboratory looking through a
microscope at plant cells, and I could never see through a microscope.
I never once saw a cell through a microscope. This used to enrage
my instructor. He would wander around the laboratory pleased with
the progress all the students were making in drawing the involved
and, so I am told, interesting structure of flower cells, until he came
to me. I would just be standing there. "I can't see anything," I would
say. He would begin patiently enough, explaining how anybody can
see through a microscope, but he would always end up in a fury;
claiming that I could *too* see through a microscope but just pretended
that I couldn't. "It takes away from the beauty of flowers anyway,"
I used to tell him. "We are not concerned with beauty in this course,"
he would say. "We are concerned solely with what I may call the
mechanics of flars." "Well," I'd say. "I can't see anything." "Try it
just once again," he'd say, and I would put my eye to the microscope
and see nothing at all, except now and again a nebulous milky substance—a phenomenon of maladjustment. You were supposed to see
a vivid, restless clockwork of sharply defined plant cells. "I see what
looks like a lot of milk," I would tell him. This, he claimed, was the
result of my not having adjusted the microscope properly, so he
would readjust it for me, or rather, for himself. And I would look
again and see milk.

2   I finally took a deferred pass, as they called it, and waited a year
and tried again. (You had to pass one of the biological sciences or
you couldn't graduate.) The professor had come back from vacation
brown as a berry, bright-eyed, and eager to explain cell-structure
again to his classes. "Well," he said to me, cheerily, when we met
in the first laboratory hour of the semester, "we're going to see cells
this time, aren't we?" "Yes, sir," I said. Students to the right of me
and left of me and in front of me were seeing cells; what's more,
they were quietly drawing pictures of them in their notebooks. Of
course, I didn't see anything.

3   "We'll try it," the professor said to me, grimly, "with every adjustment of the microscope known to man. As God is my witness, I'll
arrange this glass so that you can see cells through it or I'll give up
teaching. In twenty-two years of botany, I—" He cut off abruptly
for he was beginning to quiver all over, like Lionel Barrymore, and

he genuinely wished to hold onto his temper; his scenes with me had taken a great deal out of him.

4   So we tried it with every adjustment of the microscope known to man. With only one of them did I see anything but blackness or the familiar lacteal opacity, and that time I saw, to my pleasure and amazement, a variegated constellation of flecks, specks, and dots. These I hastily drew. The instructor, noting my activity, came from an adjoining desk, a smile on his lips and his eyebrows high in hope. He looked at my cell drawing. "What's that?" he demanded, with a hint of squeal in his voice. "That's what I saw," I said. "You didn't, you didn't, you *didn't!*" he screamed, losing control of his temper instantly, and he bent over and squinted into the microscope. His head snapped up. "That's your eye!" he shouted. "You've fixed the lens so that it reflects! You've drawn your eye!"

5   Another course that I didn't like, but somehow managed to pass, was economics. I went to that class straight from the botany class, which didn't help me any in understanding either subject. I used to get them mixed up. But not as mixed up as another student in my economics class who came there direct from a physics laboratory. He was a tackle on the football team, named Bolenciecwcz. At that time Ohio State University had one of the best football teams in the country, and Bolenciecwcz was one of its outstanding stars. In order to be eligible to play it was necessary for him to keep up in his studies, a very difficult matter, for while he was not dumber than an ox he was not any smarter. Most of his professors were lenient and helped him along. None gave him more hints, in answering questions, or asked him simpler ones than the economics professor, a thin, timid man named Bassum. One day when we were on the subject of transportation and distribution, it came Bolenciecwcz's turn to answer a question. "Name one means of transportation," the professor said to him. No light came into the big tackle's eyes. "Just any means of transportation," said the professor. Bolenciecwcz sat staring at him. "That is," pursued the professor, "any medium, agency, or method of going from one place to another." Bolenciecwcz had the look of a man who is being led into a trap. "You may choose among steam, horse-drawn, or electrically propelled vehicles," said the instructor. "I might suggest the one which we commonly take in making long journeys across land." There was a profound silence in which everybody stirred uneasily, including Bolenciecwcz and Mr.

Bassum. Mr. Bassum abruptly broke this silence in an amazing manner. "Choo-choo-choo," he said, in a low voice, and turned instantly
scarlet. He glanced appealingly around the room. All of us, of course,
shared Mr. Bassum's desire that Bolenciecwcz should stay abreast of
the class in economics, for the Illinois game, one of the hardest and
most important of the season, was only a week off. "Toot, toot,
tootoooooot!" some student with a deep voice moaned, and we
all looked encouragingly at Bolenciecwcz. Somebody else gave a fine
imitation of a locomotive letting off steam. Mr. Bassum himself
rounded off the little show. "Ding, dong, ding, dong," he said,
hopefully. Bolenciecwcz was staring at the floor now, trying to think,
his great brow furrowed, his huge hands rubbing together, his face
red.

6   "How did you come to college this year, Mr. Bolenciecwcz?"
asked the professor. "*Chu*ffa chuffa, *chu*ffa chuffa."

7   "M'father sent me," said the football player.

8   "What on?" asked Bassum.

9   "I git an 'lowance," said the tackle, in a low, husky voice, obviously
embarrassed.

10   "No, no," said Bassum. "Name a means of transportation. What
did you *ride* here on?"

11   "Train," said Bolenciecwcz.

12   "Quite right," said the professor. "Now, Mr. Nugent, will you
tell us—"

13   If I went through anguish in botany and economics—for different
reasons—gymnasium work was even worse. I don't even like to think
about it. They wouldn't let you play games or join in the exercises
with your glasses on and I couldn't see with mine off. I bumped
into professors, horizontal bars, agricultural students, and swinging
iron rings. Not being able to see, I could take it but I couldn't dish
it out. Also, in order to pass gymnasium (and you had to pass it to
graduate) you had to learn to swim if you didn't know how. I didn't
like the swimming pool, I didn't like swimming, and I didn't like
the swimming instructor, and after all these years I still don't. I never
swam but I passed my gym work anyway, by having another student
give my gymnasium number (978) and swim across the pool in my
place. He was a quiet, amiable blonde youth, number 473, and he
would have seen through a microscope for me if we could have got
away with it, but we couldn't get away with it. Another thing I didn't

like about gymnasium work was that they made you strip the day you registered. It is impossible for me to be happy when I am stripped and being asked a lot of questions. Still, I did better than a lanky agricultural student who was cross-examined just before I was. They asked each student what college he was in—that is, whether Arts, Engineering, Commerce, or Agriculture. "What college are you in?" the instructor snapped at the youth in front of me. "Ohio State University," he said promptly.

14   It wasn't that agricultural student but it was another a whole lot like him who decided to take up journalism, possibly on the ground that when farming went to hell he could fall back on newspaper work. He didn't realize, of course, that that would be very much like falling back full-length on a kit of carpenter's tools. Haskins didn't seem cut out for journalism, being too embarrassed to talk to anybody and unable to use a typewriter, but the editor of the college paper assigned him to the cow barns, the sheep house, the horse pavilion, and the animal husbandry department generally. This was a genuinely big "beat," for it took up five times as much ground and got ten times as great a legislative appropriation as the College of Liberal Arts. The agricultural student knew animals, but nevertheless his stories were dull and colorlessly written. He took all afternoon on each one of them, on account of having to hunt for each letter on the typewriter. Once in a while he had to ask somebody to help him hunt. "C" and "L," in particular, were hard letters for him to find. His editor finally got pretty much annoyed at the farmer-journalist because his pieces were so uninteresting. "See here, Haskins," he snapped at him one day, "why is it we never have anything hot from you on the horse pavilion? Here we have two hundred head of horses on this campus—more than any other university in the Western Conference except Purdue—and yet you never get any real low-down on them. Now shoot over to the horse barns and dig up something lively." Haskins shambled out and came back in about an hour; he said he had something. "Well, start it off snappily," said the editor. "Something people will read." Haskins set to work and in a couple of hours brought a sheet of typewritten paper to the desk; it was a two-hundred word story about some disease that had broken out among the horses. Its opening sentence was simple but arresting. It read: "Who has noticed the sores on the tops of the horses in the animal husbandry building?"

15   Ohio State was a land grant university and therefore two years of
military drill was compulsory. We drilled with old Springfield rifles
and studied the tactics of the Civil War even though the World War
was going on at the time. At 11 o'clock each morning thousands of
freshmen and sophomores used to deploy over the campus, moodily
creeping up on the old chemistry building. It was good training for
the kind of warfare that was waged at Shiloh but it had no connection
with what was going on in Europe. Some people used to think there
was German money behind it, but they didn't dare say so or they
would have been thrown in jail as German spies. It was a period of
muddy thought and marked, I believe, the decline of higher education in the Middle West.

16   As a soldier I was never any good at all. Most of the cadets
were glumly indifferent soldiers, but I was no good at all. Once
General Littlefield, who was commandant of the cadet corps,
popped up in front of me during regimental drill and snapped,
"You are the main trouble with this university!" I think he meant
that my type was the main trouble with the university but he
may have meant me individually. I was mediocre at drill, certainly—
that is, until my senior year. By that time I had drilled longer
than anybody else in the Western Conference, having failed at
military at the end of each preceding year so that I had to do it
all over again. I was the only senior still in uniform. The uniform
which, when new, had made me look like an interurban railway
conductor, now that it had become faded and too tight made
me look like Bert Williams in his bellboy act. This had a definitely
bad effect on my morale. Even so, I had become by sheer practice
little short of wonderful at squad manoeuvres.

17   One day General Littlefield picked our company out of the
whole regiment and tried to get it mixed up by putting it through
one movement after another as fast as we could execute them:
squads right, squads left, squads on right into line, squads right
about, squads left front into line, etc. In about three minutes one
hundred and nine men were marching in one direction and I was
marching away from them at an angle of forty degrees, all alone.
"Company, halt!" shouted General Littlefield, "That man is the
only man who has it right!" I was made a corporal for my
achievement.

18   The next day General Littlefield summoned me to his office.

He was swatting flies when I went in. I was silent and he was silent too, for a long time. I don't think he remembered me or why he had sent for me, but he didn't want to admit it. He swatted some more flies, keeping his eyes on them narrowly before he let go with the swatter. "Button up your coat!" he snapped. Looking back on it now I can see that he meant me although he was looking at a fly, but I just stood there. Another fly came to rest on a paper in front of the general and began rubbing its hind legs together. The general lifted the swatter cautiously. I moved restlessly and the fly flew away. "You startled him!" barked General Littlefield, looking at me severely. I said I was sorry. "That won't help the situation!" snapped the General, with cold military logic. I didn't see what I could do except offer to chase some more flies toward his desk, but I didn't say anything. He stared out the window at the faraway figures of coeds crossing the campus toward the library. Finally, he told me I could go. So I went. He either didn't know which cadet I was or else he forgot what he wanted to see me about. It may have been that he wished to apologize for having called me the main trouble with the university; or maybe he had decided to compliment me on my brilliant drilling of the day before and then at the last minute decided not to. I don't know. I don't think about it much any more.

Discussion Questions

1. What does this essay reveal about Thurber and his classmates?
2. Thurber reports that he "went through anguish" in botany, economics, and gymnasium work. What does he report being good at? Why?
3. Where in the essay is Thurber being serious? Where is he being jocular? Cite examples.
4. Do you find Thurber's use of humor effective? Why or why not?
5. Characterize Thurber from what he reports in this essay, identifying specific passages that lead you to your answer.
6. In small groups, discuss what Thurber seems to be saying about the nature of education.

Writing Assignments

1. Write a caricature of your classmates and/or instructors.
2. Write a letter to an instructor, real or imagined, in which you explain the difficulties you face in learning a particular lesson.
3. Reflect upon the education you have received (or are currently receiving) and critique it in an essay.
4. In an essay, compare and contrast your education with that of Thurber.

Think about It

FRANK
CONROY

Frank Conroy (b. 1936) was born in New York City and graduated from Harvard College in 1958. A fiction writer and jazz pianist, Conroy has taught at Brandeis University, George Mason University, the Massachusetts Institute of Technology, and the University of Iowa, where he has directed the famous Writers' Workshop. Conroy's memoir *Stop-Time* (1967) has won him the acclaim of critics as a classic boy's coming-of-age story. He is also the author of a short-story collection, *Midair* (1985), and a novel, *Body and Soul* (1993). Conroy's writing has appeared in such publications as *The New Yorker, Harper's* magazine, *The New York Times Magazine, GQ,* and the *Chicago Tribune.* In the following essay, Conroy returns to writing about coming of age—again his own experiences in maturing—as he recalls events from his past that helped him to conclude that "Education doesn't end until life ends, because you never know when you're going to understand something you hadn't understood before."

1   When I was sixteen I worked selling hot dogs at a stand in the Fourteenth Street subway station in New York City, one level above the trains and one below the street, where the crowds continually flowed back and forth. I worked with three Puerto Rican men who could not speak English. I had no Spanish, and although we understood each other well with regard to the tasks at hand, sensing and

adjusting to each other's body movements in the extremely confined
space in which we operated, I felt isolated with no one to talk to.
On my break I came out from behind the counter and passed the
time with two old black men who ran a shoeshine stand in a dark
corner of the corridor. It was a poor location, half hidden by columns,
and they didn't have much business. I would sit with my back against
the wall while they stood or moved around their ancient elevated
stand, talking to each other or to me, but always staring into the
distance as they did so.

2   As the weeks went by I realized that they never looked at anything
in their immediate vicinity—not at me or their stand or anybody
who might come within ten or fifteen feet. They did not look at
approaching customers once they were inside the perimeter. Save
for the instant it took to discern the color of the shoes, they did not
even look at what they were doing while they worked, but rubbed
in polish, brushed, and buffed by feel while looking over their shoulders, into the distance, as if awaiting the arrival of an important
person. Of course there wasn't all that much distance in the underground station, but their behavior was so focused and consistent
they seemed somehow to transcend the physical. A powerful mood
was created, and I came almost to believe that these men could see
through walls, through girders, and around corners to whatever
hyperspace it was where whoever it was they were waiting and watching for would finally emerge. Their scattered talk was hip, elliptical,
and hinted at mysteries beyond my white boy's ken, but it was the
staring off, the long, steady staring off, that had me hypnotized. I
left for a better job, with handshakes from both of them, without
understanding what I had seen.

3   Perhaps ten years later, after playing jazz with black musicians in
various Harlem clubs, hanging out uptown with a few young artists
and intellectuals, I began to learn from them something of the
extraordinarily varied and complex riffs and rituals embraced by different people to help themselves get through life in the ghetto.
Fantasy of all kinds—from playful to dangerous—was in the very air
of Harlem. It was the spice of uptown life.

4   Only then did I understand the two shoeshine men. They were
trapped in a demeaning situation in a dark corner in an underground
corridor in a filthy subway system. Their continuous staring off was
a kind of statement, a kind of dance. Our bodies are here, went the

statement, but our souls are receiving nourishment from distant sources only we can see. They were powerful magic dancers, sorcerers almost, and thirty-five years later I can still feel the pressure of their spell.

5 The light bulb may appear over your head, is what I'm saying, but it may be a while before it actually goes on. Early in my attempts to learn jazz piano, I used to listen to recordings of a fine player named Red Garland, whose music I admired. I couldn't quite figure out what he was doing with his left hand, however; the chords eluded me. I went uptown to an obscure club where he was playing with his trio, caught him on his break, and simply asked him. "Sixths," he said cheerfully. And then he went away.

6 I didn't know what to make of it. The basic jazz chord is the seventh, which comes in various configurations, but it is what it is. I was a self-taught pianist, pretty shaky on theory and harmony, and when he said sixths I kept trying to fit the information into what I already knew, and it didn't fit. But it stuck in my mind—a tantalizing mystery.

7 A couple of years later, when I began playing with a bass player, I discovered more or less by accident that if the bass played the root and I played a sixth based on the fifth note of the scale, a very interesting chord involving both instruments emerged. Ordinarily, I suppose I would have skipped over the matter and not paid much attention, but I remembered Garland's remark and so I stopped and spent a week or two working out the voicings, and greatly strengthened my foundations as a player. I had remembered what I hadn't understood, you might say, until my life caught up with the information and the light bulb went on.

8 I remember another, more complicated example from my sophomore year at the small liberal-arts college outside Philadelphia. I seemed never to be able to get up in time for breakfast in the dining hall. I would get coffee and a doughnut in the Coop instead—a basement area with about a dozen small tables where students could get something to eat at odd hours. Several mornings in a row I noticed a strange man sitting by himself with a cup of coffee. He was in his sixties, perhaps, and sat straight in his chair with very little extraneous movement. I guessed he was some sort of distinguished visitor to the college who had decided to put in some time at a

student hangout. But no one ever sat with him. One morning I approached his table and asked if I could join him.

9   "Certainly" he said. "Please do." He had perhaps the clearest eyes I had ever seen, like blue ice, and to be held in their steady gaze was not, at first, an entirely comfortable experience. His eyes gave nothing away about himself while at the same time creating in me the eerie impression that he was looking directly into my soul. He asked a few quick questions, as if to put me at my ease, and we fell into conversation. He was William O. Douglas from the Supreme Court, and when he saw how startled I was he said, "Call me Bill. Now tell me what you're studying and why you get up so late in the morning." Thus began a series of talks that stretched over many weeks. The fact that I was an ignorant sophomore with literary pretensions who knew nothing about the law didn't seem to bother him. We talked about everything from Shakespeare to the possibility of life on other planets. One day I mentioned that I was going to have dinner with Judge Learned Hand. I explained that Hand was my girlfriend's grandfather. Douglas nodded, but I could tell he was surprised at the coincidence of my knowing the chief judge of the most important court in the country save the Supreme Court itself. After fifty years on the bench Judge Hand had become a famous man, both in and out of legal circles—a living legend, to his own dismay. "Tell him hello and give him my best regards," Douglas said.

10   Learned Hand, in his eighties, was a short, barrel-chested man with a large, square head, huge, thick, bristling eyebrows, and soft brown eyes. He radiated energy and would sometimes bark out remarks or questions in the living room as if he were in court. His humor was sharp, but often leavened with a touch of self-mockery. When something caught his funny bone he would burst out with explosive laughter—the laughter of a man who enjoyed laughing. He had a large repertoire of dramatic expressions involving the use of his eyebrows—very useful, he told me conspiratorially, when looking down on things from behind the bench. (The court stenographer could not record the movement of his eyebrows.) When I told him I'd been talking to William O. Douglas, they first shot up in exaggerated surprise, and then lowered and moved forward in a glower.

11   *Justice* William O. Douglas, young man," he admonished. "Justice Douglas, if you please." About the Supreme Court in general, Hand

insisted on a tone of profound respect. Little did I know that in private correspondence he had referred to the Court as "The Blessed Saints Cherubim and Seraphim," "The Jolly Boys," "The Nine Tin Jesuses," "The Nine Blameless Ethiopians," and my particular favorite, "The Nine Blessed Chalices of the Sacred Effluvium."

12   Hand was badly stooped and had a lot of pain in his lower back. Martinis helped, but his strict Yankee wife approved of only one before dinner. It was my job to make the second and somehow slip it to him. If the pain was particularly acute he would get out of his chair and lie flat on the rug, still talking, and finish his point without missing a beat. He flattered me by asking for my impression of Justice Douglas, instructed me to convey his warmest regards, and then began talking about the Dennis case, which he described as a particularly tricky and difficult case involving the prosecution of eleven leaders of the Communist party. He had just started in on the First Amendment and free speech when we were called in to dinner.

13   William O. Douglas loved the outdoors with a passion, and we fell into the habit of having coffee in the Coop and then strolling under the trees down toward the duck pond. About the Dennis case, he said something to this effect: "Eleven Communists arrested by the government. Up to no good, said the government; dangerous people, violent overthrow, etc. First Amendment, said the defense, freedom of speech, etc." Douglas stopped walking. "Clear and present danger."

14   "What?" I asked. He often talked in a telegraphic manner, and one was expected to keep up with him. It was sometimes like listening to a man thinking out loud.

15   "Clear and present danger," he said. "That was the issue. Did they constitute a clear and present danger? I don't think so. I think everybody took the language pretty far in Dennis." He began walking, striding along quickly. Again, one was expected to keep up with him. "The FBI was all over them. Phones tapped, constant surveillance. How could it be clear and present danger with the FBI watching every move they made? That's a ginkgo," he said suddenly, pointing at a tree. "A beauty. You don't see those every day. Ask Hand about clear and present danger."

16   I was in fact reluctant to do so. Douglas's argument seemed to me to be crushing—the last word, really—and I didn't want to

embarrass Judge Hand. But back in the living room, on the second martini, the old man asked about Douglas. I sort of scratched my nose and recapitulated the conversation by the ginkgo tree.

17   "What?" Hand shouted. "Speak up, sir, for heaven's sake."

18   "He said the FBI was watching them all the time so there couldn't be a clear and present danger," I blurted out, blushing as I said it.

19   A terrible silence filled the room. Hand's eyebrows writhed on his face like two huge caterpillars. He leaned forward in the wing chair, his face settling finally, into a grim expression. "I am astonished," he said softly, his eyes holding mine, "at Justice Douglas's newfound faith in the Federal Bureau of Investigation." His big, granite head moved even closer to mine, until I could smell the martini. "I had understood him to consider it a politically corrupt, incompetent organization, directed by a power-crazed lunatic." I realized I had been holding my breath throughout all of this, and as I relaxed, I saw the faintest trace of a smile cross Hand's face. Things are sometimes more complicated than they first appear, his smile seemed to say. The old man leaned back. "The proximity of the danger is something to think about. Ask him about that. See what he says."

20   I chewed the matter over as I returned to campus. Hand had pointed out some of Douglas's language about the FBI from other sources that seemed to bear out his point. I thought about the words "clear and present danger," and the fact that if you looked at them closely they might not be as simple as they had first appeared. What degree of danger? Did the word "present" allude to the proximity of the danger, or just the fact that the danger was there at all—that it wasn't an anticipated danger? Were there other hidden factors these great men were weighing of which I was unaware?

21   But Douglas was gone, back to Washington. (The writer in me is tempted to create a scene here—to invent one for dramatic purposes—but of course I can't do that.) My brief time as a messenger boy was over, and I felt a certain frustration, as if, with a few more exchanges, the matter of *Dennis v. United States* might have been resolved to my satisfaction. They'd left me high and dry. But, of course, it is precisely because the matter did not resolve that has caused me to think about it, off and on, all these years. "The Constitution," Hand used to say to me flatly, "is a piece of paper. The Bill of Rights is a piece of paper." It was many years before I understood

what he meant. Documents alone do not keep democracy alive, nor maintain the state of law. There is no particular safety in them. Living men and women, generation after generation, must continually remake democracy and the law, and that involves an ongoing state of tension between the past and the present which will never completely resolve.

22   Education doesn't end until life ends, because you never know when you're going to understand something you hadn't understood before. For me, the magic dance of the shoeshine men was the kind of experience in which understanding came with a kind of click, a resolving kind of click. The same with the experience at the piano. What happened with Justice Douglas and Judge Hand was different, and makes the point that understanding does not always mean resolution. Indeed, in our intellectual lives, our creative lives, it is perhaps those problems that will never resolve that rightly claim the lion's share of our energies. The physical body exists in a constant state of tension as it maintains homeostasis, and so too does the active mind embrace the tension of never being certain, never being absolutely sure, never being done, as it engages the world. That is our special fate, our inexpressibly valuable condition.

Discussion Questions

1. Are Conroy's experiences typical of that of a young adult?
2. How does Conroy gain and sustain your interest in his experiences?
3. Whom do you think Conroy envisioned as his audience? Explain.
4. To what extent does Conroy preach in the last paragraph? From what Conroy has described up to this point, do you think his preaching is justified?
5. Explain the distinction Conroy makes in the last paragraph between *understanding* and *resolution.*
6. Conroy titled his essay "Think about It." What do you understand "It" to mean, and *did* you think about "it" while reading the essay? Explain.
7. In small groups, discuss what Conroy's main point is in this essay.

Writing Assignments

1. Write an essay in which you describe an event in your life that produced in you a "resolving kind of click."
2. Using personal experiences, observations, and perspectives, write an essay that explores your understanding of the meaning of education.
3. In an essay, compare and contrast Conroy's and Thurber's viewpoints regarding education.
4. Conroy's essay has been termed a classic coming-of-age story. Write an essay outlining the essential ingredients and significance of coming-of-age stories.

Beauty: When the Other Dancer Is the Self

ALICE
WALKER

Alice Walker (b. 1944) was born in Eatonton, Georgia. She attended Spelman College in Atlanta and Sarah Lawrence College in New York. She has been on the faculty at such schools as Brandeis University, Wellesley College, Yale University, and the University of California at Berkeley. Currently living in San Francisco, Walker is the publisher of Wild Trees, a press devoted to publishing works of less well-known writers. Walker is a prolific writer of poetry, novels, short stories, and essays, including *In Love and Trouble: Stories of Black Women* (1973), *Revolutionary Petunias and Other Poems* (1973), *Meridian* (1976), *You Can't Keep a Good Woman Down: Stories* (1981), *Living by the Word: Selected Writings, 1973–1987* (1988), *The Temple of My Familiar* (1989), *Possessing the Secret of Joy* (1992), *Her Blue Body Everything We Know: Earthling Poems* (1991), and *Warrior Marks: Female Genital Mutilation and the Sexual Binding of Women* (1993). Walker is most known for *The Color Purple* (1983), a novel which won a Pulitzer Prize and an American Book Award and was made into a popular film. Walker has also received a Lillian Smith Award, a Rosenthal Award, and a Guggenheim Foundation Award. Although Walker's works distinguish her as one of the most famous African-American writers who addresses feminist issues and race, her writing embraces issues involving women worldwide. In the following essay, which originally appeared in *Ms.* magazine and was later reprinted in *In Search of Our Mothers' Gardens: Womanist Prose* (1983), Walker offers a series of memories that lead to self-discovery. Walker's synthesis of remembrance contributes to this essay's classic theme of reaching a personal understanding of one's self.

1   It is a bright summer day in 1947. My father, a fat, funny man with beautiful eyes and a subversive wit, is trying to decide which of his eight children he will take with him to the county fair. My mother, of course, will not go. She is knocked out from getting most of us ready: I hold my neck stiff against the pressure of her knuckles as she hastily completes the braiding and beribboning of my hair.

2   My father is the driver for the rich old white lady up the road. Her name is Miss Mey. She owns all the land for miles around, as well as the house in which we live. All I remember about her is that she once offered to pay my mother thirty-five cents for cleaning her house, raking up piles of her magnolia leaves, and washing her family's clothes, and that my mother—she of no money, eight children, and a chronic earache—refused it. But I do not think of this in 1947. I am two-and-a-half years old. I want to go everywhere my daddy goes. I am excited at the prospect of riding in a car. Someone has told me fairs are fun. That there is room in the car for only three of us doesn't faze me at all. Whirling happily in my starchy frock, showing off my biscuit-polished patent-leather shoes and lavender socks, tossing my head in a way that makes my ribbons bounce, I stand, hands on hips, before my father. "Take me, Daddy," I say with assurance; "I'm the prettiest!"

3   Later, it does not surprise me to find myself in Miss Mey's shiny black car, sharing the back seat with the other lucky ones. Does not surprise me that I thoroughly enjoy the fair. At home that night I tell the unlucky ones all I can remember about the merry-go-round, the man who eats live chickens, and the teddy bears, until they say: that's enough, baby Alice. Shut up now, and go to sleep.

4   It is Easter Sunday, 1950. I am dressed in a green, flocked, scallop-
ed-hem dress (handmade by my adoring sister, Ruth) that has its
own smooth satin petticoat and tiny hot-pink roses tucked into each
scallop. My shoes, new T-strap patent leather, again highly biscuit-
polished. I am six years old and have learned one of the longest
Easter speeches to be heard that day, totally unlike the speech I said
when I was two: "Easter lilies / pure and white / blossom in / the
morning light." When I rise to give my speech I do so on a great
wave of love and pride and expectation. People in the church stop
rustling their new crinolines. They seem to hold their breath. I can
tell they admire my dress, but it is my spirit, bordering on sassiness
(womanishness), they secretly applaud.

5   "That girl's a little *mess*," they whisper to each other, pleased.

6   Naturally I say my speech without stammer or pause, unlike those
who stutter, stammer, or, worst of all, forget. This is before the word
"beautiful" exists in people's vocabulary, but "Oh, isn't she the
cutest thing!" frequently floats my way. "And got so much sense!"
they gratefully add . . . for which thoughtful addition I thank them
to this day.

7   *It was great fun being cute. But then, one day, it ended.*

8   I am eight years old and a tomboy. I have a cowboy hat, cowboy
boots, checkered shirt and pants, all red. My playmates are my brothers, two and four years older than I. Their colors are black and green,
the only difference in the way we are dressed. On Saturday nights
we all go to the picture show, even my mother; Westerns are her
favorite kind of movie. Back home, "on the ranch," we pretend we
are Tom Mix, Hopalong Cassidy, Lash LaRue (we've even named
one of our dogs Lash LaRue); we chase each other for hours rustling
cattle, being outlaws, delivering damsels from distress. Then my
parents decide to buy my brothers guns. These are not "real" guns.
They shoot BBs, copper pellets my brothers say will kill birds. Because
I am a girl, I do not get a gun. Instantly I am relegated to the
position of Indian. Now there appears a great distance between us.
They shoot and shoot at everything with their new guns. I try to
keep up with my bow and arrows.

9   One day while I am standing on top of our makeshift "garage"—
pieces of tin nailed across some poles—holding my bow and arrow

and looking out toward the fields, I feel an incredible blow in my right eye. I look down just in time to see my brother lower his gun.

10   Both brothers rush to my side. My eye stings, and I cover it with my hand. "If you tell," they say, "we will get a whipping. You don't want that to happen, do you?" I do not. "Here is a piece of wire," says the older brother, picking it up from the roof; "say you stepped on one end of it and the other flew up and hit you." The pain is beginning to start. "Yes," I say. "Yes, I will say that is what happened." If I do not say this is what happened, I know my brothers will find ways to make me wish I had. But now I will say anything that gets me to my mother.

11   Confronted by our parents we stick to the lie agreed upon. They place me on a bench on the porch and I close my left eye while they examine the right. There is a tree growing from underneath the porch that climbs past the railing to the roof. It is the last thing my right eye sees. I watch as its trunk, its branches, and then its leaves are blotted out by the rising blood.

12   I am in shock. First there is intense fever, which my father tries to break using lily leaves bound around my head. Then there are chills: my mother tries to get me to eat soup. Eventually, I do not know how, my parents learn what has happened. A week after the "accident" they take me to see a doctor. "Why did you wait so long to come?" he asks, looking into my eye and shaking his head. "Eyes are sympathetic," he says. "If one is blind, the other will likely become blind too."

13   This comment of the doctor's terrifies me. But it is really how I look that bothers me most. Where the BB pellet struck there is a glob of whitish scar tissue, a hideous cataract, on my eye. Now when I stare at people—a favorite pastime, up to now—they will stare back. Not at the "cute" little girl, but at her scar. For six years I do not stare at anyone, because I do not raise my head.

14   Years later, in the throes of a midlife crisis, I ask my mother and sister whether I changed after the "accident." "No," they say, puzzled. "What do you mean?"

15   *What do I mean?*

16   I am eight, and, for the first time, doing poorly in school, where I have been something of a whiz since I was four. We have just

moved to the place where the "accident" occurred. We do not know any of the people around us because this is a different county. The only time I see the friends I knew is when we go back to our old church. The new school is the former state penitentiary. It is a large stone building, cold and drafty, crammed to overflowing with boisterous, ill-disciplined children. On the third floor there is a huge circular imprint of some partition that has been torn out.

17   "What used to be here?" I ask a sullen girl next to me on our way past it to lunch.

18   "The electric chair," says she.

19   At night I have nightmares about the electric chair, and about all the people reputedly "fried" in it. I am afraid of the school, where all the students seem to be budding criminals.

20   "What's the matter with your eye?" they ask, critically.

21   When I don't answer (I cannot decide whether it was an "accident" or not), they shove me, insist on a fight.

22   My brother, the one who created the story about the wire, comes to my rescue. But then brags so much about "protecting" me, I become sick.

23   After months of torture at the school, my parents decide to send me back to our old community, to my old school. I live with my grandparents and the teacher they board. But there is no room for Phoebe, my cat. By the time my grandparents decide there *is* room, and I ask for my cat, she cannot be found. Miss Yarborough, the boarding teacher, takes me under her wing, and begins to teach me to play the piano. But soon she marries an African—a "prince," she says—and is whisked away to his continent.

24   At my old school there is at least one teacher who loves me. She is the teacher who "knew me before I was born" and bought my first baby clothes. It is she who makes life bearable. It is her presence that finally helps me turn on the one child at the school who continually calls me "one-eyed bitch." One day I simply grab him by his coat and beat him until I am satisfied. It is my teacher who tells me my mother is ill.

25   My mother is lying in bed in the middle of the day, something I have never seen. She is in too much pain to speak. She has an abscess in her ear. I stand looking down on her, knowing that if she dies, I cannot live. She is being treated with warm oils and hot bricks held

against her cheek. Finally a doctor comes. But I must go back to my grandparents' house. The weeks pass but I am hardly aware of it. All I know is that my mother might die, my father is not so jolly, my brothers still have their guns, and I am the one sent away from home.

26   "You did not change," they say.

27   *Did I imagine the anguish of never looking up?*

28   I am twelve. When relatives come to visit, I hide in my room. My cousin Brenda, just my age, whose father works in the post office and whose mother is a nurse, comes to find me. "Hello," she says. And then she asks, looking at my recent school picture, which I did not want taken, and on which the "glob," as I think of it, is clearly visible, "You still can't see out of that eye?"

29   "No," I say, and flop back on the bed over my book.

30   That night, as I do almost every night, I abuse my eye. I rant and rave at it, in front of the mirror. I plead with it to clear up before morning. I tell it I hate and despise it. I do not pray for sight. I pray for beauty.

31   "You did not change," they say.

32   I am fourteen and baby-sitting for my brother Bill, who lives in Boston. He is my favorite brother and there is a strong bond between us. Understanding my feelings of shame and ugliness he and his wife take me to a local hospital, where the "glob" is removed by a doctor named O. Henry. There is still a small bluish crater where the scar tissue was, but the ugly white stuff is gone. Almost immediately I become a different person from the girl who does not raise her head. Or so I think. Now that I've raised my head I win the boyfriend of my dreams. Now that I've raised my head I have plenty of friends. Now that I've raised my head classwork comes from my lips as faultlessly as Easter speeches did, and I leave high school as valedictorian, most popular student, and *queen*, hardly believing my luck. Ironically, the girl who was voted most beautiful in our class (and was) was later shot twice through the chest by a male companion, using a "real" gun, while she was pregnant. But that's another story in itself. Or is it?

33   "You did not change," they say.

34   It is now thirty years since the "accident." A beautiful journalist comes to visit and to interview me. She is going to write a cover story for her magazine that focuses on my latest book. "Decide how you want to look on the cover," she says. "Glamorous, or whatever."

35   Never mind "glamorous," it is the "whatever" that I hear. Suddenly all I can think of is whether I will get enough sleep the night before the photography session: if I don't, my eye will be tired and wander, as blind eyes will.

36   At night in bed with my lover I think up reasons why I should not appear on the cover of a magazine. "My meanest critics will say I've sold out," I say. "My family will now realize I write scandalous books."

37   "But what's the real reason you don't want to do this?" he asks.

38   "Because in all probability," I say in a rush, "my eye won't be straight."

39   "It will be straight enough," he says. Then, "Besides, I thought you'd made your peace with that."

40   And I suddenly remember that I have.

41   *I remember:*

42   I am talking to my brother Jimmy, asking if he remembers anything unusual about the day I was shot. He does not know I consider that day the last time my father, with his sweet home remedy of cool lily leaves, chose me, and that I suffered and raged inside because of this. "Well," he says, "all I remember is standing by the side of the highway with Daddy, trying to flag down a car. A white man stopped, but when Daddy said he needed somebody to take his little girl to the doctor, he drove off."

43   *I remember:*

44   I am in the desert for the first time. I fall totally in love with it. I am so overwhelmed by its beauty, I confront for the first time, consciously, the meaning of the doctor's words years ago: "Eyes are sympathetic. If one is blind, the other will likely become blind too." I realize I have dashed about the world madly, looking at this, looking at that, storing up images against the fading of the light. *But I might have missed seeing the desert!* The shock of that possibility—and gratitude for over twenty-five years of sight—sends me literally to my knees. Poem after poem comes—which is perhaps how poets pray.

ON SIGHT

I am so thankful I have seen
The Desert
And the creatures in the desert
And the desert Itself.

The desert has its own moon
Which I have seen
With my own eye.
There is no flag on it.

Trees of the desert have arms
All of which are always up
That is because the moon is up
The sun is up
Also the sky
The Stars
Clouds
None with flags.

If there were flags, I doubt
the trees would point.
Would you?

45   *But mostly, I remember this:*

46   I am twenty-seven, and my baby daughter is almost three. Since
her birth I have worried about her discovery that her mother's eyes
are different from other people's. Will she be embarrassed? I think.
What will she say? Every day she watches a television program called
Big Blue Marble. It begins with a picture of the earth as it appears
from the moon. It is bluish, a little battered-looking, but full of light,
with whitish clouds swirling around it. Every time I see it I weep
with love, as if it is a picture of Grandma's house. One day when I
am putting Rebecca down for her nap, she suddenly focuses on my
eye. Something inside me cringes, gets ready to try to protect myself.
All children are cruel about physical differences, I know from experience, and that they don't always mean to be is another matter. I
assume Rebecca will be the same.

47   But no-o-o-o. She studies my face intently as we stand, her
inside and me outside her crib. She even holds my face maternally
between her dimpled little hands. Then, looking every bit as

serious and lawyerlike as her father, she says, as if it may just possibly have slipped my attention: "Mommy, there's a *world* in your eye." (As in, "Don't be alarmed, or do anything crazy.") And then, gently, but with great interest: "Mommy, where did you *get* that world in your eye?"

48   For the most part, the pain left then. (So what, if my brothers grew up to buy even more powerful pellet guns for their sons and to carry real guns themselves. So what, if a young "Morehouse man" once nearly fell off the steps of Trevor Arnett Library because he thought my eyes were blue.) Crying and laughing I ran to the bathroom, while Rebecca mumbled and sang herself to sleep. Yes indeed, I realized, looking into the mirror. There *was* a world in my eye. And I saw that it was possible to love it: that in fact, for all it had taught me of shame and anger and inner vision, I *did* love it. Even to see it drifting out of orbit in boredom, or rolling up out of fatigue, not to mention floating back at attention in excitement (bearing witness, a friend has called it), deeply suitable to my personality, and even characteristic of me.

49   That night I dream I am dancing to Stevie Wonder's song "Always" (the name of the song is really "As," but I hear it as "Always"). As I dance, whirling and joyous, happier than I've ever been in my life, another bright-faced dancer joins me. We dance and kiss each other and hold each other through the night. The other dancer has obviously come through all right, as I have done. She is beautiful, whole and free. And she is also me.

Discussion Questions

1. Explain what you think the subtitle of this essay means.
2. Explain the reason for the effect of Walker's using the present tense to describe events that happened in the past.
3. Why does Walker use the one-sentence, italicized paragraphs? What is their impact?
4. What does the poem contribute to Walker's essay? Explain.
5. In small groups, discuss how convincing you find Walker's new-found attitude about beauty. Explain your answer.

6. How representative of most people's thinking is Walker's preoccupation with beauty? Explain your response.
7. Characterize Walker from what she reveals about herself in this essay.

Writing Assignments

1. In an essay, reflect on the ways in which you first recognized what beauty is. How have your viewpoints changed or remained the same?
2. Write an essay in which you define *beauty*. Offer some specific examples to support your thinking.
3. In an essay, analyze the relationship among beauty, femininity, cultural expectations, and the media's role in perpetuating female stereotypes.

Goodbye to All That

JOAN DIDION

Joan Didion (b. 1934) was born in Sacramento, California. She graduated from the University of California at Berkeley. She began her writing career in 1956 at *Vogue* magazine. A prolific writer, Didion is the author of many novels, including *River Run* (1963), *Play It As It Lays* (1970), *A Book of Common Prayer* (1977), *Democracy* (1984), *Sentimental Journeys* (1993), and *Run River* (1994). Her collections of essays, *Slouching towards Bethlehem* (1968) and *The White Album* (1979), examine the deterioration of the American spirit since the 1960s. *Salvador* (1983) and *Miami* (1987) are journalistic accounts of two places that experienced social upheaval in the 1980s. *After Henry* (1992) reports on current events, from the 1988 presidential campaign to the case of a New York investment banker who was raped and beaten nearly to death as she jogged in Central Park. With her spouse, John Gregory Dunne, Didion wrote the screenplay for the popular movie *Up Close and Personal*. Didion's most recent publication is a novel, *The Last Thing He Wanted* (1996). Combining her journalistic skills with her interest in social commentary, Didion has earned the reputation as one of the foremost contemporary American essayists. The following selection, the closing essay in *Slouching towards Bethlehem*, recounts Didion's falling in and out of love with New York City and her maturation while living there.

How many miles to Babylon?
Three score miles and ten—
Can I get there by candlelight?
Yes, and back again—
If your feet are nimble and light
You can get there by candlelight.

1   It is easy to see the beginnings of things, and harder to see the ends. I can remember now, with a clarity that makes the nerves in the back of my neck constrict, when New York began for me, but I cannot lay my finger upon the moment it ended, can never cut through the ambiguities and second starts and broken resolves to the exact place on the page where the heroine is no longer as optimistic as she once was. When I first saw New York I was twenty, and it was summertime, and I got off a DC-7 at the old Idlewild temporary terminal in a new dress which had seemed very smart in Sacramento but seemed less smart already, even in the old Idlewild temporary terminal, and the warm air smelled of mildew, and some instinct, programmed by all the movies I had ever seen and all the songs I had ever heard sung and all the stories I had ever read about New York, informed me that it would never be quite the same again. In fact it never was. Some time later there was a song on all the jukeboxes on the upper East Side that went "but where is the schoolgirl who used to be me," and if it was late enough at night I used to wonder that. I know now that almost everyone wonders something like that, sooner or later and no matter what he or she is doing, but one of the mixed blessings of being twenty and twenty-one and even twenty-three is the conviction that nothing like this, all evidence to the contrary notwithstanding, has ever happened to anyone before.

2   Of course it might have been some other city, had circumstances been different and the time been different and had I been different, might have been Paris or Chicago or even San Francisco, but because I am talking about myself I am talking here about New York. That first night I opened my window on the bus into town and watched for the skyline, but all I could see were the wastes of Queens and the big signs that said MIDTOWN TUNNEL THIS LANE and then a flood of summer rain (even that seemed remarkable and exotic, for I had come out of the West where there was no summer rain), and for the next three days I sat wrapped in blankets in a hotel room air-

conditioned to 35° and tried to get over a bad cold and a high fever. It did not occur to me to call a doctor, because I knew none, and although it did occur to me to call the desk and ask that the air conditioner be turned off, I never called, because I did not know how much to tip whoever might come—was anyone ever so young? I am here to tell you that someone was. All I could do during those three days was talk long-distance to the boy I already knew I would never marry in the spring. I would stay in New York, I told him, just six months, and I could see the Brooklyn Bridge from my window. As it turned out the bridge was the Triborough, and I stayed eight years.

3   In retrospect it seems to me that those days before I knew the names of all the bridges were happier than the ones that came later, but perhaps you will see that as we go along. Part of what I want to tell you is what it is like to be young in New York, how six months can become eight years with the deceptive ease of a film dissolve, for that is how those years appear to me now, in a long sequence of sentimental dissolves and old-fashioned trick shots—the Seagram Building fountains dissolve into snowflakes, I enter a revolving door at twenty and come out a good deal older, and on a different street. But most particularly I want to explain to you, and in the process perhaps to myself, why I no longer live in New York. It is often said that New York is a city for only the very rich and the very poor. It is less often said that New York is also, at least for those of us who came there from somewhere else, a city for only the very young.

4   I remember once, one cold bright December evening in New York, suggesting to a friend who complained of having been around too long that he come with me to a party where there would be, I assured him with the bright resourcefulness of twenty-three, "new faces." He laughed literally until he choked, and I had to roll down the taxi window and hit him on the back. "New faces," he said finally, "don't tell me about *new faces*." It seemed that the last time he had gone to a party where he had been promised "new faces," there had been fifteen people in the room, and he had already slept with five of the women and owed money to all but two of the men. I laughed with him, but the first snow had just begun to fall and the big Christmas trees glittered yellow and white as far as I could see up Park Avenue and I had a new dress and it would be a long

while before I would come to understand the particular moral of the story.

5   It would be a long while because, quite simply, I was in love with New York. I do not mean "love" in any colloquial way, I mean that I was in love with the city, the way you love the first person who ever touches you and never love anyone quite that way again. I remember walking across Sixty-second Street one twilight that first spring, or the second spring, they were all alike for a while. I was late to meet someone but I stopped at Lexington Avenue and bought a peach and stood on the corner eating it and knew that I had come out of the West and reached the mirage. I could taste the peach and feel the soft air blowing from a subway grating on my legs and I could smell lilac and garbage and expensive perfume and I knew that it would cost something sooner or later—because I did not belong there, did not come from there—but when you are twenty-two or twenty-three, you figure that later you will have a high emotional balance, and be able to pay whatever it costs. I still believed in possibilities then, still had the sense, so peculiar to New York, that something extraordinary would happen any minute, any day, any month. I was making only $65 or $70 a week then ("Put yourself in Hattie Carnegie's hands," I was advised without the slightest trace of irony by an editor of the magazine for which I worked), so little money that some weeks I had to charge food at Bloomingdale's gourmet shop in order to eat, a fact which went unmentioned in the letters I wrote to California. I never told my father that I needed money because then he would have sent it, and I would never know if I could do it by myself. At that time making a living seemed a game to me, with arbitrary but quite inflexible rules. And except on a certain kind of winter evening—six-thirty in the Seventies, say, already dark and bitter with a wind off the river, when I would be walking very fast toward a bus and would look in the bright windows of brownstones and see cooks working in clean kitchens and imagine women lighting candles on the floor above and beautiful children being bathed on the floor above that—except on nights like those, I never felt poor; I had the feeling that if I needed money I could always get it. I could write a syndicated column for teenagers under the name "Debbi Lynn" or I could smuggle gold into India or I could become a $100 call girl, and none of it would matter.

6   Nothing was irrevocable; everything was within reach. Just around
every corner lay something curious and interesting, something I had
never before seen or done or known about. I could go to a party
and meet someone who called himself Mr.
Emotional Appeal and
ran The Emotional Appeal Institute or Tina Onassis Blandford or a
Florida cracker who was then a regular on what he called "the Big
C," the Southampton-El Morocco circuit ("I'm well-connected on
the Big C, honey," he would tell me over collard greens on his vast
borrowed terrace), or the widow of the celery king of the Harlem
market or a piano salesman from Bonne Terre, Missouri, or someone
who had already made and lost two fortunes in Midland, Texas. I
could make promises to myself and to other people and there would
be all the time in the world to keep them. I could stay up all night
and make mistakes, and none of it would count.

7   You see I was in a curious position in New York: it never occurred
to me that I was living a real life there. In my imagination I was
always there for just another few months, just until Christmas or
Easter or the first warm day in May. For that reason I was most
comfortable in the company of Southerners. They seemed to be in
New York as I was, on some indefinitely extended leave from wherever they belonged, disinclined to consider the future, temporary
exiles who always knew when the flights left for New Orleans or
Memphis or Richmond or, in my case, California. Someone who
lives always with a plane schedule in the drawer lives on a slightly
different calendar. Christmas, for example, was a difficult season.
Other people could take it in stride, going to Stowe or going abroad
or going for the day to their mothers' places in Connecticut; those
of us who believed that we lived somewhere else would spend it
making and canceling airline reservations, waiting for weatherbound
flights as if for the last plane out of Lisbon in 1940, and finally
comforting one another, those of us who were left, with the oranges
and mementos and smoked-oyster stuffings of childhood, gathering
close, colonials in a far country.

8   Which is precisely what we were. I am not sure that it is possible
for anyone brought up in the East to appreciate entirely what New
York, the idea of New York, means to those of us who came out of
the West and the South. To an Eastern child, particularly a child
who has always had an uncle on Wall Street and who has spent several
hundred Saturdays first at F. A. O. Schwarz and being fitted for

shoes at Best's and then waiting under the Biltmore clock and dancing
to Lester Lanin, New York is just a city, albeit *the* city, a plausible
place for people to live. But to those of us who came from places
where no one had heard of Lester Lanin and Grand Central Station
was a Saturday radio program, where Wall Street and Fifth Avenue
and Madison Avenue were not places at all but abstractions
("Money," and "High Fashion," and "The Hucksters"), New York
was no mere city. It was instead an infinitely romantic notion, the
mysterious nexus of all love and money and power, the shining and
perishable dream itself. To think of "living" there was to reduce the
miraculous to the mundane; one does not "live" at Xanadu.

9   In fact it was difficult in the extreme for me to understand those
young women for whom New York was not simply an ephemeral
Estoril but a real place, girls who bought toasters and installed new
cabinets in their apartments and committed themselves to some reasonable future. I never bought any furniture in New York. For a
year or so I lived in other people's apartments; after that I lived in
the Nineties in an apartment furnished entirely with things taken
from storage by a friend whose wife had moved away. And when I
left the apartment in the Nineties (that was when I was leaving
everything, when it was all breaking up) I left everything in it, even
my winter clothes and the map of Sacramento County I had hung
on the bedroom wall to remind me who I was, and I moved into a
monastic four-room floor-through on Seventy-fifth Street. "Monastic" is perhaps misleading here, implying some chic severity; until
after I was married and my husband moved some furniture in, there
was nothing at all in those four rooms except a cheap double mattress
and box springs, ordered by telephone the day I decided to move,
and two French garden chairs lent me by a friend who imported
them. (It strikes me now that the people I knew in New York all
had curious and self-defeating sidelines. They imported garden chairs
which did not sell very well at Hammacher Schlemmer or they tried
to market hair straighteners in Harlem or they ghosted exposés of
Murder Incorporated for Sunday supplements. I think that perhaps
none of us was very serious, *engagé* only about our most private
lives.)

10   All I ever did to that apartment was hang fifty yards of yellow
theatrical silk across the bedroom windows, because I had some idea
that the gold light would make me feel better, but I did not bother

to weight the curtains correctly and all that summer the long panels of transparent golden silk would blow out the windows and get tangled and drenched in the afternoon thunderstorms. That was the year, my twenty-eighth, when I was discovering that not all of the promises would be kept, that some things are in fact irrevocable and that it had counted after all, every evasion and every procrastination, every mistake, every word, all of it.

11   That is what it was all about, wasn't it? Promises? Now when New York comes back to me it comes in hallucinatory flashes, so clinically detailed that I sometimes wish that memory would effect the distortion with which it is commonly credited. For a lot of the time I was in New York I used a perfume called *Fleurs de Rocaille*, and then *L'Air du Temps*, and now the slightest trace of either can short-circuit my connections for the rest of the day. Nor can I smell Henri Bendel jasmine soap without falling back into the past, or the particular mixture of spices used for boiling crabs. There were barrels of crab boil in a Czech place in the Eighties where I once shopped. Smells, of course, are notorious memory stimuli, but there are other things which affect me the same way. Blue-and-white striped sheets. Vermouth cassis. Some faded nightgowns which were new in 1959 or 1960, and some chiffon scarves I bought about the same time.

12   I suppose that a lot of us who have been young in New York have the same scenes on our home screens. I remember sitting in a lot of apartments with a slight headache about five o'clock in the morning. I had a friend who could not sleep, and he knew a few other people who had the same trouble, and we would watch the sky lighten and have a last drink with no ice and then go home in the early morning light, when the streets were clean and wet (had it rained in the night? we never knew) and the few cruising taxis still had their headlights on and the only color was the red and green of traffic signals. The White Rose bars opened very early in the morning; I recall waiting in one of them to watch an astronaut go into space, waiting so long that at the moment it actually happened I had my eyes not on the television screen but on a cockroach on the tile floor. I liked the bleak branches above Washington Square at dawn, and the monochromatic flatness of Second Avenue, the fire escapes and the grilled storefronts peculiar and empty in their perspective.

13   It is relatively hard to fight at six-thirty or seven in the morning without any sleep, which was perhaps one reason we stayed up all night, and it seemed to me a pleasant time of day. The windows were shuttered in that apartment in the Nineties and I could sleep a few hours and then go to work. I could work then on two or three hours' sleep and a container of coffee from Chock Full O' Nuts. I liked going to work, liked the soothing and satisfactory rhythm of getting out a magazine, liked the orderly progression of four-color closings and two-color closings and black-and-white closings and then The Product, no abstraction but something which looked effortlessly glossy and could be picked up on a newsstand and weighed in the hand. I liked all the minutiae of proofs and layouts, liked working late on the nights the magazine went to press, sitting and reading *Variety* and waiting for the copy desk to call. From my office I could look across town to the weather signal on the Mutual of New York Building and the lights that alternately spelled out TIME and LIFE above Rockefeller Plaza; that pleased me obscurely, and so did walking uptown in the mauve eight o'clocks of early summer evenings and looking at things, Lowestoft tureens in Fifty-seventh Street windows, people in evening clothes trying to get taxis, the trees just coming into full leaf, the lambent air, all the sweet promises of money and summer.

14   Some years passed, but I still did not lose that sense of wonder about New York. I began to cherish the loneliness of it, the sense that at any given time no one need know where I was or what I was doing. I liked walking, from the East River over to the Hudson and back on brisk days, down around the Village on warm days. A friend would leave me the key to her apartment in the West Village when she was out of town, and sometimes I would just move down there, because by that time the telephone was beginning to bother me (the canker, you see, was already in the rose) and not many people had that number. I remember one day when someone who did have the West Village number came to pick me up for lunch there, and we both had hangovers, and I cut my finger opening him a beer and burst into tears, and we walked to a Spanish restaurant and drank Bloody Marys and *gazpacho* until we felt better. I was not then guilt-ridden about spending afternoons that way, because I still had all the afternoons in the world.

15   And even that late in the game I still liked going to parties, all parties, bad parties, Saturday-afternoon parties given by recently

married couples who lived in Stuyvesant Town, West Side parties given by unpublished or failed writers who served cheap red wine and talked about going to Guadalajara, Village parties where all the guests worked for advertising agencies and voted for Reform Democrats, press parties at Sardi's, the worst kinds of parties. You will have perceived by now that I was not one to profit by the experience of others, that it was a very long time indeed before I stopped believing in new faces and began to understand the lesson in that story, which was that it is distinctly possible to stay too long at the Fair.

16   I could not tell you when I began to understand that. All I know is that it was very bad when I was twenty-eight. Everything that was said to me I seemed to have heard before, and I could no longer listen. I could no longer sit in little bars near Grand Central and listen to someone complaining of his wife's inability to cope with the help while he missed another train to Connecticut. I no longer had any interest in hearing about the advances other people had received from their publishers, about plays which were having second-act trouble in Philadelphia, or about people I would like very much if only I would come out and meet them. I had already met them, always. There were certain parts of the city which I had to avoid. I could not bear upper Madison Avenue on weekday mornings (this was a particularly inconvenient aversion, since I then lived just fifty or sixty feet east of Madison), because I would see women walking Yorkshire terriers and shopping at Gristede's, and some Veblenesque gorge would rise in my throat. I could not go to Times Square in the afternoon, or to the New York Public Library for any reason whatsoever. One day I could not go into a Schrafft's; the next day it would be Bonwit Teller.

17   I hurt the people I cared about, and insulted those I did not. I cut myself off from the one person who was closer to me than any other. I cried until I was not even aware when I was crying and when I was not, cried in elevators and in taxis and in Chinese laundries, and when I went to the doctor he said only that I seemed to be depressed, and should see a "specialist." He wrote down a psychiatrist's name and address for me, but I did not go.

18   Instead I got married, which as it turned out was a very good thing to do but badly timed, since I still could not walk on upper

Madison Avenue in the mornings and still could not talk to people and still cried in Chinese laundries. I had never before understood what "despair" meant, and I am not sure that I understand now, but I understood that year. Of course I could not work. I could not even get dinner with any degree of certainty, and I would sit in the apartment on Seventy-fifth Street paralyzed until my husband would call from his office and say gently that I did not have to get dinner, that I could meet him at Michael's Pub or at Toots Shor's or at Sardi's East. And then one morning in April (we had been married in January) he called and told me that he wanted to get out of New York for a while, that he would take a six-month leave of absence, that we would go somewhere.

19   It was three years ago that he told me that, and we have lived in Los Angeles since. Many of the people we knew in New York think this a curious aberration, and in fact tell us so. There is no possible, no adequate answer to that, and so we give certain stock answers, the answers everyone gives. I talk about how difficult it would be for us to "afford" to live in New York right now, about how much "space" we need. All I mean is that I was very young in New York, and that at some point the golden rhythm was broken, and I am not that young any more. The last time I was in New York was in a cold January, and everyone was ill and tired. Many of the people I used to know there had moved to Dallas or had gone on Antabuse or had bought a farm in New Hampshire. We stayed ten days, and then we took an afternoon flight back to Los Angeles, and on the way home from the airport that night I could see the moon on the Pacific and smell jasmine all around and we both knew that there was no longer any point in keeping the apartment we still kept in New York. There were years when I called Los Angeles "the Coast," but they seem a long time ago.

Discussion Questions

1. What do you think the essay's epigraph means?
2. What exemplifies Didion's opening statement, "It is easy to see the beginnings of things, and harder to see the ends"?
3. Describe the effect Didion creates by directly addressing her audience throughout the essay.
4. What is the purpose of Didion's dividing her essay into sections? What are the connections among the sections?
5. Identify what Didion loved about New York and what made her later become disillusioned with it.
6. Describe the tone of Didion's essay. Cite specific examples to support your answer.
7. What is the meaning of the essay's title?
8. In small groups, discuss the purpose of Didion's essay.

Writing Assignments

1. In a journal entry, describe a place with which you fell in love.
2. In an essay, examine a point in your life when it was "easy to see the beginnings of things, and harder to see the ends."
3. Write about a time in your life when you felt that "nothing was irrevocable; everything was within reach."
4. Explain in an essay how the dream of a place is often far better than the reality.

On Being Black and Middle Class

SHELBY
STEELE

Shelby Steele (b. 1946) earned a B.A. from Coe College, an M.A. from Southern Illinois University, and a Ph.D. from the University of Utah. Steele is a professor of English at San Jose State University in California. His numerous articles have appeared in such publications as *The American Scholar*, *Harper's* magazine, and *The New York Times Magazine*. Steele is also the author of *The Content of Our Character: A New Vision of Race in America* (1990), which won the National Book Critics Circle Award in 1990. In the following essay, which originally appeared in *Commentary* and was selected for publication in *The Best American Essays* in 1989, Steele moves between describing personal experiences and discussing the plight of African-Americans as a way to examine what it means to be a black middle-class man. This essay is a forthright, thoughtful, and reflective inquiry into an African-American man's race and social standing.

1   Not long ago a friend of mine, black like myself, said to me that the term "black middle class" was actually a contradiction in terms. Race, he insisted, blurred class distinction among blacks. If you were black, you were just black and that was that. When I argued, he

let his eyes roll at my naiveté. Then he went on. For us, as black professionals, it was an exercise in self-flattery, a pathetic pretension, to give meaning to such a distinction. Worse, the very idea of class threatened the unity that was vital to the black community as a whole. After all, since when had white America taken note of anything but color when it came to blacks? He then reminded me of an old Malcolm X line that had been popular in the sixties. Question: What is a black man with a Ph.D.? Answer: A nigger.

2   For many years I had been on my friend's side of this argument. Much of my conscious thinking on the old conundrum of race and class was shaped during my high school and college years in the race-charged sixties, when the fact of my race took on an almost religious significance. Progressively, from the mid-sixties on, more and more aspects of my life found their explanation, their justification, and their motivation in race. My youthful concerns about career, romance, money, values, and even styles of dress became a subject to consultation with various oracular sources of racial wisdom. And these ranged from a figure as ennobling as Martin Luther King, Jr., to the underworld elegance of dress I found in jazz clubs on the South Side of Chicago. Everywhere there were signals, and in those days I considered myself so blessed with clarity and direction that I pitied my white classmates who found more embarrassment than guidance in the fact of *their* race. In 1968, inflated by my new power, I took a mischievous delight in calling them culturally disadvantaged.

3   But now, hearing my friend's comment was like hearing a priest from a church I'd grown disenchanted with. I understood him, but my faith was weak. What had sustained me in the sixties sounded monotonous and off the mark in the eighties. For me, race had lost much of its juju, its singular capacity to conjure meaning. And today, when I honestly look at my life and the lives of many other middle-class blacks I know, I can see that race never fully explained our situation in American society. Black though I may be, it is impossible for me to sit in my single-family house with two cars in the driveway and a swing set in the back yard and *not* see the role class has played in my life. And how can my friend, similarly raised and similarly situated, not see it?

4   Yet despite my certainty I felt a sharp tug of guilt as I tried to explain myself over my friend's skepticism. He is a man of many comedic facial expressions and, as I spoke, his brow lifted in extreme moral alarm as if I were uttering the unspeakable. His clear implica-

tion was that I was being elitist and possibly (dare he suggest?) anti-
black—crimes for which there might well be no redemption. He
pretended to fear for me. I chuckled along with him, but inwardly
I did wonder at myself. Though I never doubted the validity of what
I was saying, I felt guilty saying it. Why?

5   After he left (to retrieve his daughter from a dance lesson) I realized
that the trap I felt myself in had a tiresome familiarity and, in a sort of
slow-motion epiphany, I began to see its outline. It was like the suddenly sharp vision one has at the end of a burdensome marriage when
all the long-repressed incompatibilities come undeniably to light.

6   What became clear to me is that people like myself, my friend,
and middle-class blacks generally are caught in a very specific double
bind that keeps two equally powerful elements of our identity at
odds with each other. The middle-class values by which we were
raised—the work ethic, the importance of education, the value of
property ownership, of respectability, of "getting ahead," of stable
family life, of initiative, of self-reliance, etc.—are, in themselves, race-
less and even assimilationist. They urge us toward participation in
the American mainstream, toward integration, toward a strong identification with the society—and toward the entire constellation of
qualities that are implied in the word "individualism." These values
are almost rules for how to prosper in a democratic, free-enterprise
society that admires and rewards individual effort. They tell us to
work hard for ourselves and our families and to seek our opportunities
whenever they appear, inside or outside the confines of whatever
ethnic group we may belong to.

7   But the particular pattern of racial identification that emerged in
the sixties and that still prevails today urges middle-class blacks (and
all blacks) in the opposite direction. This pattern asks us to see
ourselves as an embattled minority, and it urges an adversarial stance
toward the mainstream, an emphasis on ethnic consciousness over
individualism. It is organized around an implied separatism.

8   The opposing thrust of these two parts of our identity results in the
double bind of middle-class blacks. There is no forward movement on
either plane that does not constitute backward movement on the
other. This was the familiar trap I felt myself in while talking with
my friend. As I spoke about class, his eyes reminded me that I was
betraying race. Clearly, the two indispensable parts of my identity
were a threat to each other.

9   Of course when you think about it, class and race are both similar in some ways and also naturally opposed. They are two forms of collective identity with boundaries that intersect. But whether they clash or peacefully coexist has much to do with how they are defined. Being both black and middle class becomes a double bind when class and race are defined in sharply antagonistic terms, so that one must be repressed to appease the other.

10   But what is the "substance" of these two identities, and how does each establish itself in an individual's overall identity? It seems to me that when we identify with any collective we are basically identifying with images that tell us what it means to be a member of that collective. Identity is not the same thing as the fact of membership in a collective; it is, rather, a form of self-definition, facilitated by images of what we wish our membership in the collective to mean. In this sense, the images we identify with may reflect the aspirations of the collective more than they reflect reality, and their content can vary with shifts in those aspirations.

11   But the process of identification is usually dialectical. It is just as necessary to say what we are *not* as it is to say what we are—so that finally identification comes about by embracing a polarity of positive and negative images. To identify as middle class, for example, I must have both positive and negative images of what being middle class entails; then I will know what I should and should not be doing in order to be middle class. The same goes for racial identity.

12   In the racially turbulent sixties the polarity of images that came to define racial identification was very antagonistic to the polarity that defined middle-class identification. One might say that the positive images of one lined up with the negative images of the other, so that to identify with both required either a contortionist's flexibility or a dangerous splitting of the self. The double bind of the black middle class was in place.

13   The black middle class has always defined its class identity by means of positive images gleaned from middle- and upper-class white society, and by means of negative images of lower-class blacks. This habit goes back to the institution of slavery itself, when "house" slaves both mimicked the whites they served and held themselves above the "field" slaves. But in the sixties the old bourgeois impulse to dissociate from the lower classes (the "we-they" distinction) back-

fired when racial identity suddenly called for the celebration of this same black lower class. One of the qualities of a double bind is that one feels it more than sees it, and I distinctly remember the tension and strange sense of dishonesty I felt in those days as I moved back and forth like a bigamist between the demands of class and race.

14   Though my father was born poor, he achieved middle-class standing through much hard work and sacrifice (one of his favorite words) and by identifying fully with solid middle-class values—mainly hard work, family life, property ownership, and education for his children (all four of whom have advanced degrees). In his mind these were not so much values as laws of nature. People who embodied them made up the positive images in his class polarity. The negative images came largely from the blacks he had left behind because they were "going nowhere."

15   No one in my family remembers how it happened, but as time went on, the negative images congealed into an imaginary character named Sam, who, from the extensive service we put him to, quickly grew to mythic proportions. In our family lore he was sometimes a trickster, sometimes a boob, but always possessed of a catalogue of sly faults that gave up graphic images of everything we should not be. On sacrifice: "Sam never thinks about tomorrow. He wants it now or he doesn't care about it." On work: "Sam doesn't favor it too much." On children: "Sam likes to have them but not to raise them." On money: "Sam drinks it up and pisses it out." On fidelity: "Sam has to have two or three women." On clothes: "Sam features loud clothes. He likes to see and be seen." And so on. Sam's persona amounted to a negative instruction manual in class identity.

16   I don't think that any of us believed Sam's faults were accurate representations of lower-class black life. He was an instrument of self-definition, not of sociological accuracy. It never occurred to us that he looked very much like the white racist stereotype of blacks, or that he might have been a manifestation of our own racial self-hatred. He simply gave us a counterpoint against which to express our aspirations. If self-hatred was a factor, it was not, for us, a matter of hating lower-class blacks but of hating what we did not want to be.

17   Still, hate or love aside, it is fundamentally true that my middle-class identity involved a dissociation from images of lower-class black life and a corresponding identification with values and patterns of responsibility that are common to the middle class everywhere. These

values sent me a clear message: be both an individual and a responsible citizen; understand that the quality of your life will approximately reflect the quality of effort you put into it; know that individual responsibility is the basis of freedom and that the limitations imposed by fate (whether fair or unfair) are no excuse for passivity.

18 Whether I live up to these values or not, I know that my acceptance of them is the result of lifelong conditioning. I know also that I share this conditioning with middle-class people of all races and that I can no more easily be free of it than I can be free of my race. Whether all this got started because the black middle class modeled itself on the white middle class is no longer relevant. For the middle-class black, conditioned by these values from birth, the sense of meaning they provide is as immutable as the color of his skin.

19 I started the sixties in high school feeling that my class-conditioning was the surest way to overcome racial barriers. My racial identity was pretty much taken for granted. After all, it was obvious to the world that I was black. Yet I ended the sixties in graduate school a little embarrassed by my class background and with an almost desperate need to be "black." The tables had turned. I knew very clearly (though I struggled to repress it) that my aspirations and my sense of how to operate in the world came from my class background, yet "being black" required certain attitudes and stances that made me feel secretly a little duplicitous. The inner compatibility of class and race I had known in 1960 was gone.

20 For blacks, the decade between 1960 and 1969 saw racial identification undergo the same sort of transformation that national identity undergoes in times of war. It became more self-conscious, more narrowly focused, more prescribed, less tolerant of opposition. It spawned an implicit party line, which tended to disallow competing forms of identity. Race-as-identity was lifted from the relative slumber it knew in the fifties and pressed into service in a social and political war against oppression. It was redefined along sharp adversarial lines and directed toward the goal of mobilizing the great mass of black Americans in this warlike effort. It was imbued with a strong moral authority, useful for denouncing those who opposed it and for celebrating those who honored it as a positive achievement rather than as a mere birthright.

21 The form of racial identification that quickly evolved to meet this challenge presented blacks as a racial monolith, a singular people

with a common experience of oppression. Differences within the race, no matter how ineradicable, had to be minimized. Class distinctions were one of the first such differences to be sacrificed, since they not only threatened racial unity but also seemed to stand in contradiction to the principle of equality which was the announced goal of the movement for racial progress. The discomfort I felt in 1969, the vague but relentless sense of duplicity, was the result of a historical necessity that put my race and class at odds, that was asking me to cast aside the distinction of my class and identify with a monolithic view of my race.

22   If the form of this racial identity was the monolith, its substance was victimization. The civil rights movement and the more radical splinter groups of the late sixties were all dedicated to ending racial victimization, and the form of black identity that emerged to facilitate this goal made blackness and victimization virtually synonymous. Since it was our victimization more than any other variable that identified and unified us, moreover, it followed logically that the purest black was the poor black. It was images of him that clustered around the positive pole of the race polarity; all other blacks were, in effect, required to identify with him in order to confirm their own blackness.

23   Certainly there were more dimensions to the black experience than victimization, but no other had the same capacity to fire the indignation needed for war. So, again out of historical necessity, victimization became the overriding focus of racial identity. But this only deepened the double bind for middle-class blacks like me. When it came to class we were accustomed to defining ourselves against lower-class blacks and identifying with at least the values of middle-class whites; when it came to race we were now being asked to identify with images of lower-class blacks and to see whites, middle class or otherwise, as victimizers. Negative lining up with positive, we were called upon to reject what we had previously embraced and to embrace what we had previously rejected. To put it still more personally, the Sam figure I had been raised to define myself against had now become the "real" black I was expected to identify with.

24   The fact that the poor black's new status was only passively earned by the condition of his victimization, not by assertive, positive action, made little difference. Status was status apart from the means by which it was achieved, and along with it came a certain power—the

power to define the terms of access to that status, to say who was black and who was not. If a lower-class black said you were not really "black"—a sellout, an Uncle Tom—the judgment was all the more devastating because it carried the authority of his status. And this judgment soon enough came to be accepted by many whites as well.

25   In graduate school I was once told by a white professor, "Well, but . . . you're not really black. I mean, you're not disadvantaged." In his mind my lack of victim status disqualified me from the race itself. More recently I was complimented by a black student for speaking reasonably correct English, "proper" English as he put it. "But I don't know if I really want to talk like that," he went on. "Why not?" I asked. "Because then I wouldn't be black no more," he replied without a pause.

26   To overcome his marginal status, the middle-class black had to identify with a degree of victimization that was beyond his actual experience. In college (and well beyond) we used to play a game called "nap matching." It was a game of one-upmanship, in which we sat around outdoing each other with stories of racial victimization, symbolically measured by the naps of our hair. Most of us were middle class and so had few personal stories to relate, but if we could not match naps with our own biographies, we would move on to those legendary tales of victimization that came to us from the public domain.

27   The single story that sat atop the pinnacle of racial victimization for us was that of Emmett Till, the Northern black teenager who, on a visit to the South in 1955, was killed and grotesquely mutilated for supposedly looking at or whistling at (we were never sure which, though we argued the point endlessly) a white woman. Oh, how we probed his story, finding in his youth and Northern upbringing the quintessential embodiment of black innocence, brought down by a white evil so portentous and apocalyptic, so gnarled and hideous, that it left us with a feeling not far from awe. By telling his story and others like it, we came to *feel* the immutability of our victimization, its utter indigenousness, as a thing on this earth like dirt or sand or water.

28   Of course, these sessions were a ritual of group identification, a means by which we, as middle-class blacks, could be at one with our race. But why were we, who had only a moderate experience of victimization (and that offset by opportunities our parents never

had), so intent on assimilating or appropriating an identity that in so many ways contradicted our own? Because, I think, the sense of innocence that is always entailed in feeling victimized filled us with a corresponding feeling of entitlement, or even license, that helped us endure our vulnerability on a largely white college campus.

29   In my junior year in college I rode to a debate tournament with three white students and our faculty coach, an elderly English professor. The experience of being the lone black in a group of whites was so familiar to me that I thought nothing of it as our trip began. But then halfway through the trip the professor casually turned to me and, in an isn't-the-world-funny sort of tone, said that he had just refused to rent an apartment in a house he owned to a "very nice" black couple because their color would "offend" the white couple who lived downstairs. His eyebrows lifted helplessly over his hawkish nose, suggesting that he too, like me, was a victim of America's racial farce. His look assumed a kind of comradeship: he and I were above this grimy business of race, though for expediency we had occasionally to concede the world its madness.

30   My vulnerability in this situation came not so much from the professor's blindness to his own racism as from his assumption that I would participate in it, that I would conspire with him against my own race so that he might remain comfortably blind. Why did he think I would be amenable to this? I can only guess that he assumed my middle-class identity was so complete and all-encompassing that I would see his action as nothing more than a trifling concession to the folkways of our land, that I would in fact applaud his decision not to disturb propriety. Blind to both his own racism and to me—one blindness serving the other—he could not recognize that he was asking me to betray my race in the name of my class.

31   His blindness made me feel vulnerable because it threatened to expose my own repressed ambivalence. His comment pressured me to choose between my class identification, which had contributed to my being a college student and a member of the debating team, and my desperate desire to be "black." I could have one but not both; I was double-bound.

32   Because double binds are repressed there is always an element of terror in them: the terror of bringing to the conscious mind the buried duplicity, self-deception, and pretense involved in serving two

masters. This terror is the stuff of vulnerability, and since vulnerability is one of the least tolerable of all human feelings, we usually transform it into an emotion that seems to restore the control of which it has robbed us; most often, that emotion is anger. And so, before the professor had even finished his little story, I had become a furnace of rage. The year was 1967, and I had been primed by endless hours of nap-matching to feel, at least consciously, completely at one with the victim-focused black identity. This identity gave me the license, and the impunity, to unleash upon this professor one of those volcanic eruptions of racial indignation familiar to us from the novels of Richard Wright. Like Cross Damon in *Outsider*, who kills in perfectly righteous anger, I tried to annihilate the man. I punished him not according to the measure of his crime but according to the measure of my vulnerability, a measure set by the cumulative tension of years of repressed terror. Soon I saw that terror in *his* face, as he stared hollow-eyed at the road ahead. My white friends in the back seat, knowing no conflict between their own class and race, were astonished that someone they had taken to be so much like themselves could harbor a rage that for all the world looked murderous.

33   Though my rage was triggered by the professor's comment, it was deepened and sustained by a complex of need, conflict, and repression in myself of which I had been wholly unaware. Out of my racial vulnerability I had developed the strong need of an identity with which to defend myself. The only such identity available was that of me as victim, him as victimizer. Once in the grip of this paradigm, I began to do far more damage to myself than he had done.

34   Seeing myself as a victim meant that I clung all the harder to my racial identity, which, in turn, meant that I suppressed my class identity. This cut me off from all the resources my class values might have offered me. In those values, for instance, I might have found the means to a more dispassionate response, the response less of a victim attacked by a victimizer than of an individual offended by a foolish old man. As an individual I might have reported this professor to the college dean. Or I might have calmly tried to reveal his blindness to him, and possibly won a convert. (The flagrancy of his remark suggested a hidden guilt and even self-recognition on which I might have capitalized. Doesn't confession usually signal a willingness to face oneself?) Or I might have simply chuckled and then let

my silence serve as an answer to his provocation. Would not my composure, in any form it might take, deflect into his own heart the arrow he'd shot at me?

35 Instead, my anger, itself the hair-trigger expression of a long repressed double bind, not only cut me off from the best of my own resources, it also distorted the nature of my true racial problem. The righteousness of this anger and the easy catharsis it brought buoyed the delusion of my victimization and left me as blind as the professor himself.

36 As a middle-class black I have often felt myself *contriving* to be "black." And I have noticed this same contrivance in others—a certain stretching away from the natural flow of one's life to align oneself with a victim-focused black identity. Our particular needs are out of sync with the form of identity available to meet those needs. Middle-class blacks need to identify racially; it is better to think of ourselves as black and victimized than not black at all; so we contrive (more unconsciously than consciously) to fit ourselves into an identity that denies our class and fails to address the true source of our vulnerability.

37 For me this once meant spending inordinate amounts of time at black faculty meetings, though these meetings had little to do with my real racial anxieties or my professional life. I was new to the university, one of two blacks in an English department of over seventy, and I felt a little isolated and vulnerable, though I did not admit it to myself. But at these meetings we discussed the problems of black faculty and students within a framework of victimization. The real vulnerability we felt was covered over by all the adversarial drama the victim/victimized polarity inspired, and hence went unseen and unassuaged. And this, I think, explains our rather chronic ineffectiveness as a group. Since victimization was not our primary problem—the university had long ago opened its doors to us—we had to contrive to make it so, and there is not much energy in contrivance. What I got at these meetings was ultimately an object lesson in how fruitless struggle can be when it is not grounded in actual need.

38 At our black faculty meetings, the old equation of blackness with victimization was ever present—to be black was to be a victim; therefore, not to be a victim was not to be black. As we contrived to meet

the terms of this formula there was an inevitable distortion of both ourselves and the larger university. Through the prism of victimization the university seemed more impenetrable than it actually was, and we more limited in our powers. We fell prey to the victim's myopia, making the university an institution from which we could seek redress but which we could never fully join. And this mind-set often led us to look more for compensations for our supposed victimization than for opportunities we could pursue as individuals.

39 The discomfort and vulnerability felt by middle-class blacks in the sixties, it could be argued, was a worthwhile price to pay considering the progress achieved during that time of racial confrontation. But what may have been tolerable then is intolerable now. Though changes in American society have made it an anachronism, the monolithic form of racial identification that came out of the sixties is still very much with us. It may be more loosely held, and its power to punish heretics has probably diminished, but it continues to catch middle-class blacks in a double bind, thus impeding not only their own advancement but even, I would contend, that of blacks as a group.

40 The victim-focused black identity encourages the individual to feel that his advancement depends almost entirely on that of the group. Thus he loses sight not only of his own possibilities but of the inextricable connection between individual effort and individual advancement. This is a profound encumbrance today, when there is more opportunity for blacks than ever before, for it reimposes limitations that can have the same oppressive effect as those the society has only recently begun to remove.

41 It was the emphasis on mass action in the sixties that made the victim-focused black identity a necessity. But in the eighties and beyond, when racial advancement will come only through a multitude of individual advancements, this form of identity inadvertently adds itself to the forces that hold us back. Hard work, education, individual initiative, stable family life, property ownership—these have always been the means by which ethnic groups have moved ahead in America. Regardless of past or present victimization, these "laws" of advancement apply absolutely to black Americans also. There is no getting around this. What we need is a form of racial identity that energizes the individual by putting him in touch with both his possibilities and his responsibilities.

42   It has always annoyed me to hear from the mouths of certain arbiters of blackness that middle-class blacks should "reach back" and pull up those blacks less fortunate than they—as though middle-class status were an unearned and essentially passive condition in which one needed a large measure of noblesse oblige to occupy one's time. My own image is of reaching back from a moving train to lift on board those who have no tickets. A noble enough sentiment—but might it not be wiser to show them the entire structure of principles, effort, and sacrifice that puts one in a position to buy a ticket any time one likes? This, I think, is something members of the black middle class can realistically offer to other blacks. Their example is not only a testament to possibility but also a lesson in method. But they cannot lead by example until they are released from a black identity that regards that example as suspect, that sees them as "marginally" black, indeed that holds *them* back by catching them in a double bind.

43   To move beyond the victim-focused black identity we must learn to make a difficult but crucial distinction: between actual victimization, which we must resist with every resource, and identification with the victim's status. Until we do this we will continue to wrestle more with ourselves than with the new opportunities which so many paid so dearly to win.

Discussion Questions

1. In small groups, discuss whether you agree with Steele's or his friend's view on the term *black middle class.*
2. What were the benefits and liabilities of Steele's seeing himself as a victim at various times in his life? Explain why you think his reasoning for doing so was sound or faulty.
3. How well does Steele distinguish between reasons and excuses? Cite specific examples from his essay.
4. Steele intersperses personal experiences with analytical discussions of issues. Evaluate the effectiveness of this technique.
5. Whom do you think Steele envisioned as his audience? Explain.
6. Is Steele blaming any particular group in his essay? Explain your answer.

7. In the last paragraph, Steele distinguishes between actual victimization and identification with the victim's status. Explain your understanding of this distinction.

Writing Assignments

1. In a letter to someone who stereotypes people, dispel a seeming contradiction in terms (for example, a National Merit Scholarship football player or a female engineering major). Use as examples people who can be identified with both terms.
2. In a paper, argue whether people will ever be able to "move beyond the victim-focused black identity" that Steele discusses.
3. Discuss the following questions in an essay: Will discrimination end in your own or in the next generation? Why or why not? What are the forces that fuel discrimination? What is needed to end prejudice?
4. Write an essay entitled "On Being _____ and _____."

Conclusion–Baby Doctor

PERRI KLASS

Perri Klass (b. 1958) was born in Tunapuna, Trinidad. She earned her A.B. and M.D. from Harvard University in 1979 and in 1986, respectively. A practicing pediatrician in Boston, Klass is also a writer whose stories and essays have appeared in *The New York Times Magazine*, *Discover Magazine*, *Mademoiselle*, *Esquire*, and *Vogue*. She is the author of two novels, *Recombinations* (1985) and *Other Women's Children* (1990); a collection of short stories, *I Am Having an Adventure* (1986); a collection of autobiographical essays, *A Not Entirely Benign Procedure* (1987); and an autobiography, *Baby Doctor* (1992). Klass chronicled her life as a medical student and a mother while in school through her short and readable essays. Her writing is characterized by introspection and stunning honesty, which culminate in self-revelation. The following essay appears at the end of *Baby Doctor* and reflects the engaging style of writing for which Klass is noted.

1   I am going to be a pediatrician. This is a decision that I started to make even before I had done any pediatrics. During my first three months in the hospital, my general medicine clerkship, I became aware that something was wrong. I was not finding clinical medicine as interesting or as rewarding as I had hoped to. It was more interest-

ing to take care of patients than it had been to memorize diseases for a test, but it wasn't fascinating and all-absorbing—as I had sort of hoped it would be. This, after all, was the big apple, the goal of all those courses, the hospital ward. Why wasn't I more involved, more excited about what I was doing? Some of the answer had to do with my circumstances, the particular hospital I had been assigned to, some of the people with whom I had to work closely, some of those who were supposedly teaching me. But I also began to wonder whether I might prefer working with pediatric patients.

2   And sure enough, when I got to pediatrics I loved it. I was even reasonably happy most of the time—which is not bad for someone who is in the hospital all day every day and all night every fourth night. I felt profoundly involved with my team, with my patients.

3   The kind of adult medicine I was exposed to in a famous teaching hospital does not of course represent all adult medicine. But when I did adult medicine, we seemed to spend a great deal of our time fighting to save people who have very limited prospects. A nursing home would send in an elderly patient who had not walked or talked in two years, who had developed a temperature. A person with a rare and fascinating case of something or other would be referred in for more tests—there would be nothing in particular we could do to help, but everyone would repeat, like a mantra, "Great teaching case." In addition, many of the patients had problems that required other kinds of interventions besides medical treatment   people with chronic lung disease who couldn't stop smoking, for example. As doctors, or medical students, we had to leave these things alone; they were outside our domain, and besides, who had time to talk about smoking or diet or exercise or stress? There are, of course, doctors who address all these subjects, but from my point of view it was just another frustration.

4   But this may all be rationalizing. It's true that in pediatrics you are almost always fighting a battle for a whole lifetime. It's true that you deal much less in what are unfairly stigmatized as "self-induced" problems—the effects of smoking, drinking. (I don't mean to belittle the suffering these substances cause, or imply that sufferers are not entitled to good medical care. I just didn't really get much satisfaction myself from dealing with these problems.) It's also true that in pediatrics you never get to ignore what we rather pompously call the psychosocial aspect of your patients; you always have to deal with

the parents, who provide you with the kind of context which is often missing in adult medicine. But maybe what I really discovered about myself was that I like children, as a group, much better than I like adults. And I also tend to like pediatricians more than I like other doctors. I like them because they are not able to be stiff—the adult doctor can stride grandly into the patient's room and announce, we have decided to do this and that, and command respect from many patients. The pediatrician who says apologetically, to a small patient that such and such a procedure is necessary and will only hurt a tiny bit, is frequently bitten or kicked.

5   Of course, since I had my own child during medical school, and he has grown to the ripe and stubborn age of two and a half while I was a student, I have had a certain amount of contact with pediatrics from the parent's side of the examining table. When I was applying for residency, I tried to pretend that having had a baby naturally gifted me with tremendous expertise, gave me an advantage over other applicants. This, naturally, was nonsense. Of course, there are a few things I know that come in useful in the hospital. I can change diapers in my sleep, for example. And I know all the developmental milestones, when a child can be expected to smile, walk, talk—except I know them only up as far as Benjamin's age. In other words, I could evaluate any child two and a half or under to see if everything was going on schedule, but I would be lost with three-year-olds (can they build tall towers with blocks? catch baseballs? operate heavy machinery? child-raising is full of surprises). By the end of residency, a three-year process, I expect to be fully competent with any child up to five and a half.

6   No, the real advantage of having had a child is that I know a great deal more about parents than I otherwise would have. I have brought my own child to the emergency room where I will begin working in a few months, and I will not forget what it felt like to sit in the waiting room, holding a feverish and alarmingly quiet little boy on my lap, wishing that all the other patients would get out of the way so my child could be seen. I have also in my time called the pediatrician because my tiny baby had a funny-looking poop. One night a year or so ago my son had an ear infection, and his temperature went up over 104, and I began to worry that his brain was melting. Now, I happen to know for a fact that brains do not melt; I even had in my notes a lecture I had attended on the syndrome of so-called fever

phobia—all the myths parents believe about the ill effects of fever, all the damage they can cause their children by overdosing them with antifever drugs. I read over those notes, then I called the pediatrician and told him that I was worried that my baby's brain might be melting. The doctor on call that night was actually someone who knew me; he had taught me during my pediatrics rotation. And he said to me, gently, come on now, Perri, is this kind of fever really unusual in severe otitis media? And of course I blubbered into the phone, don't ask me any questions, dammit, just tell me my baby is going to be okay, his brain isn't cooking. And does he need a spinal tap? Does he need to be admitted to the hospital? And all of this, I suppose, is valuable experience for a pediatrician to have had. Last summer, when I was doing my advanced pediatrics rotation, I admitted a young boy with what we were pretty sure was viral meningitis. We were putting him on antibiotics in case it was bacterial, a much more severe disease, but we weren't really worried. And after I had explained all this to his mother, she suddenly clutched my arm and began to cry. "You can tell me the truth," she sobbed. "He's going to die, he's never going to come out of the hospital alive, is he? My baby's going to die!" It was worth my remembering, right then, despite my impatience that she hadn't heard a word of my brilliant and sensitive explanation, that I am fully capable of the same kind of uncontrollable fears.

7   Like most medical students, and I suspect like many doctors, I tend to deal with my own illness by denying it. Sometimes I indulge myself, especially if I think I can claim a day off, but basically I don't go to doctors and I don't take medicines—or at least not until I absolutely have to. And as an intern, of course, you aren't allowed to be sick. But for my kid, I am a demanding, frightened, overanxious consumer of medical care. For myself, I accept the various unhealthy constraints of residency—no fresh food, no regular hours, no time for exercise, no stress reduction, no doing any of the things we tell patients to do. But for my kid, I want what everyone wants, healthy circumstances and a life tailored to his needs. So having a child has enlarged my perspective on medicine, and on my chosen branch of medicine in particular, in a number of ways. My son has been and will, I expect, continue to be a steady reminder to me of what my patients represent. They are not their diseases, they are—well, I know what they are. I have one of my own.

8   And my own reactions to my child have been and will, I expect, continue to be reminders to me of what parents feel when their children are sick, of the hopes, expectations, and fears with which they bring a child to the doctor.

9   So I am going to be a pediatrician. Two years of preclinical courses, two years of hospital work, and now medical school is ending. I have a great many doubts about the education I have undergone, and most of those doubts are included in these various essays. I do not think my medical education has been extraordinarily well designed, and I think that some of the most effectively conveyed lessons have been the unadvertised teachings about behavior, ethics, style, and power.

10   As I wrote in the introduction, the process of writing about medical school has changed the last four years for me. I think that in many ways it has helped me through; many of the frustrations and furies of medical school have been essentially small and petty (it's amazing how petty you can be when you're really tired and you really want to go home), and trying to put my grievances in writing has sometimes helped me sort that out. In the end, I suppose I understand what has happened to me much better for having written about it; there are people who can keep track of themselves without writing anything down, but I am not like that.

11   I feel obliged to sum it up: am I glad I did it, would I do it again, would I do it differently? I can't answer for myself of four years ago, but I suppose I'm glad, I'd probably do it again. And of course I'd do it differently; I'd do it *right*, whatever that means. I wouldn't let myself be so intimidated, right? I'd defend my dignity, I wouldn't truckle to my superiors, right? I'd really learn everything thoroughly and properly, come out completely *prepared* for internship, right? Well, maybe not.

12   And so, what I am left with is an appreciation that the last four years have certainly accomplished something. Maybe not all they were intended to accomplish, and maybe also some things they were not meant to do, but one way or another, they have served as an initiation. An initiation of blood (not mine) and pain (mine was the least of it), weariness and confusion, of books and cadavers, needles and plastic tubing, patients and doctors. And I, having been initiated, am left saying, well, here I am—a different person. And, as of this writing, almost but not quite a doctor.

Discussion Questions

1. Explain what the title of Klass's essay means.
2. Although Klass restricts her discussion to the field of medicine, her observations could apply to other occupations as well. Explain how this is possible.
3. Whom do you think Klass envisioned as her audience? Explain your answer.
4. Characterize Klass from the perspectives she offers in her essay.
5. State Klass's thesis.

Writing Assignments

1. Write an essay that begins with the statement, "I am going to be a(n) _____."
2. Write about an experience in which "book learning" did not prepare you for the actual experience.
3. Write an essay that argues for a "right" way of doing something as Klass does at the end of her essay.

CLASSIC ESSAYS ON

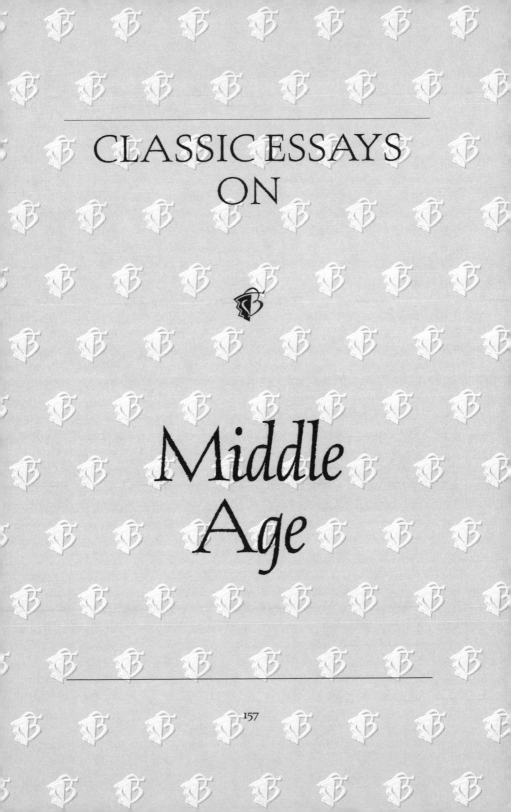

Middle Age

What Life Means to Me

JACK LONDON

Jack London (1876–1916) was born John Griffith London in San Francisco, California. Graduating from grade school at the age of fourteen, London frequented the oceanfront in Oakland, California. With teenage friends, London raided the fisheries and sold what he and his friends stole. In 1893, London became a drifter, traveling to Japan, Canada, and throughout the United States. He studied briefly at the University of California and also joined the gold rush to the Klondike, gathering stories he later used in his writing. London is most famous for two novels, *The Call of the Wild* (1903) and *White Fang* (1906). In the following essay, London addresses a classic theme of essays—the meaning of life—as he muses on the traits of enthusiasm, ambition, and ideals.

1   I was born in the working-class. Early I discovered enthusiasm, ambition, and ideals; and to satisfy these became the problem of my child-life. My environment was crude and rough and raw. I had no outlook, but an uplook rather. My place in society was at the bottom. Here life offered nothing but sordidness and wretchedness, both of the flesh and the spirit; for here flesh and spirit were alike starved and tormented.

2   Above me towered the colossal edifice of society, and to my mind
the only way out was up. Into this edifice I early resolved to climb.
Up above, men wore black clothes and boiled shirts, and women
dressed in beautiful gowns. Also, there were good things to eat, and
there was plenty to eat. This much for the flesh. Then there were
the things of the spirit. Up above me, I knew, were unselfishnesses
of the spirit, clean and noble thinking, keen intellectual living. I
knew all this because I read "Seaside Library" novels, in which, with
the exception of the villains and adventuresses, all men and women
thought beautiful thoughts, spoke a beautiful tongue, and performed
glorious deeds. In short, as I accepted the rising of the sun, I accepted
that up above me was all that was fine and noble and gracious, all
that gave decency and dignity to life, all that made life worth living
and that remunerated one for his travail and misery.

3   But it is not particularly easy for one to climb up out of the working-
class—especially if he is handicapped by the possession of ideals and
illusions. I lived on a ranch in California, and I was hard put to find the
ladder whereby to climb. I early inquired the rate of interest on invested
money, and worried my child's brain into all understanding of the virtues and excellencies of that remarkable invention of man, compound
interest. Further, I ascertained the current rates of wages for workers
of all ages, and the cost of living. From all this data I concluded that if
I began immediately and worked and saved until I was fifty years of
age, I could then stop working and enter into participation in a fair
portion of the delights and goodnesses that would then be open to me
higher up in society. Of course, I resolutely determined not to marry,
while I quite forgot to consider at all that great rock of disaster in the
working-class world—sickness.

4   But the life that was in me demanded more than a meagre existence
of scraping and scrimping. Also, at ten years of age, I became a
newsboy on the streets of a city, and found myself with a changed
uplook. All about me were still the same sordidness and wretchedness,
and up above me was still the same paradise waiting to be gained;
but the ladder whereby to climb was a different one. It was now the
ladder of business. Why save my earnings and invest in government
bonds, when, by buying two newspapers for five cents, with a turn
of the wrist I could sell them for ten cents and double my capital?
The business ladder was the ladder for me, and I had a vision of
myself becoming a hardheaded and successful merchant prince.

5   Alas for visions! When I was sixteen I had already earned the title of "prince." But this title was given me by a gang of cut-throats and thieves, by whom I was called "The Prince of the Oyster Pirates." And at that time I had climbed the first rung of the business ladder. I was a capitalist. I owned a boat and a complete oyster-pirating outfit. I had begun to exploit my fellow-creatures. I had a crew of one man. As captain and owner I took two-thirds of the spoils, and gave the crew one-third, though the crew worked just as hard as I did and risked just as much his life and liberty.

6   This one rung was the height I climbed up the business ladder. One night I went on a raid amongst the Chinese fishermen. Ropes and nets were worth dollars and cents. It was robbery, I grant, but it was precisely the spirit of capitalism. The capitalist takes away the possessions of his fellow-creatures by means of a rebate, or of a betrayal of trust, or by the purchase of senators and supreme court judges. I was merely crude. That was the only difference. I used a gun.

7   But my crew that night was one of those inefficients against whom the capitalist is wont to fulminate, because, forsooth, such inefficients increase expenses and reduce dividends. My crew did both. What of his carelessness: he set fire to the big mainsail and totally destroyed it. There weren't any dividends that night, and the Chinese fishermen were richer by the nets and ropes we did not get. I was bankrupt, unable just then to pay sixty-five dollars for a new mainsail. I left my boat at anchor and went off on a bay-pirate boat on a raid up the Sacramento river. While away on this trip, another gang of bay pirates raided my boat. They stole everything, even the anchors; and later on, when I recovered the drifting hulk, I sold it for twenty dollars. I had slipped back the one rung I had climbed, and never again did I attempt the business ladder.

8   From then on I was mercilessly exploited by other capitalists. I had the muscle, and they made money out of it while I made but a very indifferent living out of it. I was a sailor before the mast, a longshoreman, a roustabout; I worked in canneries, and factories, and laundries; I mowed lawns, and cleaned carpets, and washed windows. And I never got the full product of my toil. I looked at the daughter of the cannery owner, in her carriage, and knew that it was my muscle, in part, that helped drag along that carriage on its rubber tires. I looked at the son of the factory owner, going to

college, and knew that it was my muscle that helped, in part, to pay for the wine and good fellowship he enjoyed.

9 But I did not resent this. It was all in the game. They were the strong. Very well, I was strong. I would carve my way to a place amongst them and make money out of the muscles of other men. I was not afraid of work. I loved hard work. I would pitch in and work harder than ever and eventually become a pillar of society.

10 And just then, as luck would have it, I found an employer that was of the same mind. I was willing to work, and he was more than willing that I should work. I thought I was learning a trade. In reality, I had displaced two men. I thought he was making an electrician out of me; as a matter of fact, he was making fifty dollars per month out of me. The two men I had displaced had received forty dollars each per month; I was doing the work of both for thirty dollars per month.

11 This employer worked me nearly to death. A man may love oysters, but too many oysters will disincline him toward that particular diet. And so with me. Too much work sickened me. I did not wish ever to see work again. I fled from work. I became a tramp, begging my way from door to door, wandering over the United States and sweating bloody sweats in slums and prisons.

12 I had been born in the working-class, and I was now, at the age of eighteen, beneath the point at which I had started. I was down in the cellar of society, down in the subterranean depths of misery about which it is neither nice nor proper to speak. I was in the pit, the abyss, the human cesspool, the shambles and charnel-house of our civilization. This is the part of the edifice of society that society chooses to ignore. Lack of space compels me here to ignore it, and I shall say only that the things I there saw gave me a terrible scare.

13 I was scared into thinking. I saw the naked simplicities of the complicated civilization in which I lived. Life was a matter of food and shelter. In order to get food and shelter men sold things. The merchant sold shoes, the politician sold his manhood, and the representative of the people, with exceptions, of course, sold his trust; while nearly all sold their honor. Women, too, whether on the street or in the holy bond of wedlock, were prone to sell their flesh. All things were commodities, all people bought and sold. The one commodity that labor had to sell was muscle. The honor of labor had no price in the market-place. Labor had muscle, and muscle alone, to sell.

14   But there was a difference, a vital difference. Shoes and trust and honor had a way of renewing themselves. They were imperishable stocks. Muscle, on the other hand, did not renew. As the shoe merchant sold shoes, he continued to replenish his stock. But there was no way of replenishing the laborer's stock of muscle. The more he sold of his muscle, the less of it remained to him. It was his one commodity, and each day his stock of it diminished. In the end, if he did not die before, he sold out and put up his shutters. He was a muscle bankrupt, and nothing remained to him but to go down into the cellar of society and perish miserably.

15   I learned, further, that brain was likewise a commodity. It, too, was different from muscle. A brain seller was only at his prime when he was fifty or sixty years old, and his wares were fetching higher prices than ever. But a laborer was worked out or broken down at forty-five or fifty. I had been in the cellar of society, and I did not like the place as a habitation. The pipes and drains were unsanitary, and the air was bad to breathe. If I could not live on the parlor floor of society, I could, at any rate, have a try at the attic. It was true, the diet there was slim, but the air at least was pure. So I resolved to sell no more muscle, and to become a vender of brains.

16   Then began a frantic pursuit of knowledge. I returned to California and opened the books. While thus equipping myself to become a brain merchant, it was inevitable that I should delve into sociology. There I found, in a certain class of books, scientifically formulated, the simple sociological concepts I had already worked out for myself. Other and greater minds, before I was born, had worked out all that I had thought and a vast deal more. I discovered that I was a socialist.

17   The socialists were revolutionists, inasmuch as they struggled to overthrow the society of the present, and out of the material to build the society of the future. I, too, was a socialist and a revolutionist. I joined the groups of working-class and intellectual revolutionists, and for the first time came into intellectual living. Here I found keen-flashing intellects and brilliant wits; for here I met strong and alert-brained, withal horny-handed, members of the working-class; unfrocked preachers too wide in their Christianity for any congregation of Mammon-worshipers; professors broken on the wheel of university subservience to the ruling class and flung out because they were quick with knowledge which they strove to apply to the affairs of mankind.

18   Here I found, also, warm faith in the human, glowing idealism, sweetnesses of unselfishness, renunciation, and martyrdom—all the splendid, stinging things of the spirit. Here life was clean, noble, and alive. Here life rehabilitated itself, became wonderful and glorious; and I was glad to be alive. I was in touch with great souls who exalted flesh and spirit over dollars and cents, and to whom the thin wail of the starved slum child meant more than all the pomp and circumstance of commercial expansion and world empire. All about me were nobleness of purpose and heroism of effort, and my days and nights were sunshine and starshine, all fire and dew, with before my eyes, ever burning and blazing, the Holy Grail, Christ's own Grail, the warm human, long-suffering and maltreated, but to be rescued and saved at the last.

19   And I, poor foolish I, deemed all this to be a mere foretaste of the delights of living I should find higher above me in society. I had lost many illusions since the day I read "Seaside Library" novels on the California ranch. I was destined to lose many of the illusions I still retained.

20   As a brain merchant I was a success. Society opened its portals to me. I entered right in on the parlor floor, and my disillusionment proceeded rapidly. I sat down to dinner with the masters of society, and with the wives and daughters of the masters of society. The women were gowned beautifully, I admit; but to my naïve surprise I discovered that they were of the same clay as all the rest of the women I had known down below in the cellar. "The colonel's lady and Judy O'Grady were sisters under their skins"—and gowns.

21   It was not this, however, so much as their materialism, that shocked me. It is true, these beautifully gowned, beautiful women prattled sweet little ideals and dear little moralities; but in spite of their prattle the dominant key of the life they lived was materialistic. And they were so sentimentally selfish! They assisted in all kinds of sweet little charities, and informed one of the fact, while all the time the food they ate and the beautiful clothes they wore were bought out of dividends stained with the blood of child labor, and sweated labor, and of prostitution itself. When I mentioned such facts, expecting in my innocence that these sisters of Judy O'Grady would at once strip off their blood-dyed silks and jewels, they became excited and angry, and read me preachments about the lack of thrift, the drink, and the innate depravity that caused all the misery in society's

cellar. When I mentioned that I couldn't quite see that it was the lack of thrift, the intemperance, and the depravity of a half-starved child of six that made it work twelve hours every night in a Southern cotton mill, these sisters of Judy O'Grady attacked my private life and called me an "agitator"—as though that, forsooth, settled the argument.

22   Nor did I fare better with the masters themselves. I had expected to find men who were clean, noble, and alive, whose ideals were clean, noble, and alive. I went about amongst the men who sat in the high places—the preachers, the politicians, the business men, the professors, and the editors. I ate meat with them, drank wine with them, automobiled with them, and studied them. It is true, I found many that were clean and noble; but with rare exceptions, they were not *alive*. I do verily believe I could count the exceptions on the fingers of my two hands. Where they were not alive with rottenness, quick with unclean life, they were merely the unburied dead—clean and noble, like well-preserved mummies, but not alive. In this connection I may especially mention the professors I met, the men who live up to that decadent university ideal, "the passionless pursuit of passionless intelligence."

23   I met men who invoked the name of the Prince of Peace in their diatribes against war, and who put rifles in the hands of Pinkertons with which to shoot down strikers in their own factories. I met men incoherent with indignation at the brutality of prize-fighting, and who, at the same time, were parties to the adulteration of food that killed each year more babies than even red-handed Herod had killed.

24   I talked in hotels and clubs and homes and Pullmans and steamer-chairs with captains of industry, and marveled at how little travelled they were in the realm of intellect. On the other hand, I discovered that their intellect, in the business sense, was abnormally developed. Also, I discovered that their morality, where business was concerned, was nil.

25   This delicate, aristocratic-featured gentleman, was a dummy director and a tool of corporations that secretly robbed widows and orphans. This gentleman, who collected fine editions and was an especial patron of literature, paid blackmail to a heavy-jowled, black-browed boss of a municipal machine. This editor, who published patent medicine advertisements and did not dare print the truth in his paper about said patent medicines for fear of losing the advertising,

called me a scoundrelly demagogue because I told him that his political economy was antiquated and that his biology was contemporaneous with Pliny.

26   This senator was the tool and the slave, the little puppet of a gross, uneducated machine boss; so was this governor and this supreme-court judge; and all three rode on railroad passes. This man, talking soberly and earnestly about the beauties of idealism and the goodness of God, had just betrayed his comrades in a business deal. This man, a pillar of the church and heavy contributor to foreign missions, worked his shop girls ten hours a day on a starvation wage and thereby directly encouraged prostitution. This man, who endowed chairs in universities, perjured himself in courts of law over a matter of dollars and cents. And this railroad magnate broke his word as a gentleman and a Christian when he granted a secret rebate to one of two captains of industry locked together in a struggle to the death.

27   It was the same everywhere, crime and betrayal, betrayal and crime—men who were alive, but who were neither clean nor noble, men who were clean and noble but who were not alive. Then there was a great, hopeless mass, neither noble nor alive, but merely clean. It did not sin positively nor deliberately; but it did sin passively and ignorantly by acquiescing in the current immorality and profiting by it. Had it been noble and alive it would not have been ignorant, and it would have refused to share in the profits of betrayal and crime.

28   I discovered that I did not like to live on the parlor floor of society. Intellectually I was bored. Morally and spiritually I was sickened. I remembered my intellectuals and idealists, my unfrocked preachers, broken professors, and clean-minded, class-conscious workingmen. I remembered my days and nights of sunshine and starshine, where life was all a wild sweet wonder, a spiritual paradise of unselfish adventure and ethical romance. And I saw before me, ever blazing and burning the Holy Grail.

29   So I went back to the working-class, in which I had been born and where I belonged. I care no longer to climb. The imposing edifice of society above my head holds no delights for me. It is the foundation of the edifice that interests me. There I am content to labor, crowbar in hand, shoulder to shoulder with intellectuals, idealists, and class-conscious workingmen, getting a solid pry now

and again and setting the whole edifice rocking. Some day, when we get a few more hands and crowbars to work, we'll topple it over, along with all its rotten life and unburied dead, its monstrous selfishness and sodden materialism. Then we'll cleanse the cellar and build a new habitation for mankind, in which there will be no parlor floor, in which all the rooms will be bright and airy, and where the air that is breathed will be clean, noble, and alive.

30   Such is my outlook. I look forward to a time when man shall progress upon something worthier and higher than his stomach, when there will be a finer incentive to impel men to action than the incentive of today, which is the incentive of the stomach. I retain my belief in the nobility and excellence of the human. I believe that spiritual sweetness and unselfishness will conquer the gross gluttony of today. And last of all, my faith is in the working-class. As some Frenchman has said, "The stairway of time is ever echoing with the wooden shoe going up, the polished boot descending."

Discussion Questions

1. London begins his essay and refers several times to his being born in the working class. Why does he emphasize this fact so strongly?
2. In small groups, discuss whether London really "discovered enthusiasm, ambition, and ideals" as he asserts in the first paragraph.
3. Describe the tone of London's essay. Cite specific passages that inform your response.
4. Do you agree with London when he states in the last paragraph, "I believe that spiritual sweetness and unselfishness will conquer the gross gluttony of today"? Why or why not?
5. Although London wrote his essay almost one hundred years ago, people today still share his view on the meaning of life. To what extent is London's view shared?

Writing Assignments

1. Write a journal entry that examines what life means to you as London did.

2. How pervasive is people's interest in rising above their born socioeconomic status? Write an essay in which you discuss the importance many people place on social class and financial standing.

3. In a paper, compare and contrast London's thinking about class with that of Shelby Steele in "On Being Black and Middle Class."

The Rewards of
Living a Solitary Life

MAY SARTON

May Sarton (1912–1995) was born near Ghent, Belgium. Her family
moved to Cambridge, Massachusetts, where Sarton attended school.
Sarton apprenticed at the Civic Repertory Theater in New York, after
which she founded and directed her own company, the Apprentice
Theater, until it folded in 1936 during the Great Depression. A
prolific writer, Sarton wrote poetry, fiction, memoirs, and journals.
Her most famous poetry collections include *A Grain of Mustard
Seed* (1971), *A Durable Fire* (1972), and *Halfway to Silence* (1980).
Among her most acclaimed novels are *Faithful Are the Wounds*
(1955), *Mrs. Stevens Hears the Mermaids Singing* (1965), *Kinds of
Love* (1970), and *As We Now Are* (1973). Sarton's memoirs and
journals include *I Knew a Phoenix* (1959), *Plant Dreaming Deep*
(1968), *Journals of a Solitude* (1973), *A World of Light* (1976), *The
House by the Sea* (1977), *Recovering: A Journal* (1980), *At Seventy:
A Journal* (1984), *Endgame: A Journal of the Seventy-Ninth Year*
(1992), *Encore: A Journal of the Eightieth Year* (1993), and *At
Eighty-Two: A Journal* (posthumous, 1996). Sarton's published journals and memoirs are strong examples of nonfiction as an important
and powerful genre. In the following selection, Sarton reflects on
living alone, an act that can be seen as not only courageous but
necessary for self-understanding.

1   The other day an acquaintance of mine, a gregarious and charming man, told me he had found himself unexpectedly alone in New York for an hour or two between appointments. He went to the Whitney and spent the "empty" time looking at things in solitary bliss. For him it proved to be a shock nearly as great as falling in love to discover that he could enjoy himself so much alone.

2   What had he been afraid of, I asked myself? That, suddenly alone, he would discover that he bored himself, or that there was, quite simply, no self there to meet? But having taken the plunge, he is now on the brink of adventure; he is about to be launched into his own inner space, space as immense, unexplored, and sometimes frightening as outer space to the astronaut. His every perception will come to him with a new freshness and, for a time, seem startlingly original. For anyone who can see things for himself with a naked eye becomes, for a moment or two, something of a genius. With another human being present vision becomes double vision, inevitably. We are busy wondering, what does my companion see or think of this, and what do I think of it? The original impact gets lost, or diffused.

3   "Music I heard with you was more than music." Exactly. And therefore music *itself* can only be heard alone. Solitude is the salt of personhood. It brings out the authentic flavor of every experience.

4   "Alone one is never lonely: the spirit adventures, walking/In a quiet garden, in a cool house, abiding single there."

5   Loneliness is most acutely felt with other people, for with others, even with a lover sometimes, we suffer from our differences of taste, temperament, mood. Human intercourse often demands that we soften the edge of perception, or withdraw at the very instant of personal truth for fear of hurting, or of being inappropriately present, which is to say naked, in a social situation. Alone we can afford to be wholly whatever we are, and to feel whatever we feel absolutely. That is a great luxury!

6   For me the most interesting thing about a solitary life, and mine has been that for the last twenty years, is that it becomes increasingly rewarding. When I can wake up and watch the sun rise over the ocean, as I do most days, and know that I have an entire day ahead, uninterrupted, in which to write a few pages, take a walk with my dog, lie down in the afternoon for a long think (why does one think better in a horizontal position?), read and listen to music, I am flooded with happiness.

7   I am lonely only when I am overtired, when I have worked too long without a break, when for the time being I feel empty and need filling up. And I am lonely sometimes when I come back home after a lecture trip, when I have seen a lot of people and talked a lot, and am full to the brim with experience that needs to be sorted out.

8   Then for a little while the house feels huge and empty, and I wonder where my self is hiding. It has be recaptured slowly by watering the plants, perhaps, and looking again at each one as though it were a person, by feeding the two cats, by cooking a meal.

9   It takes a while, as I watch the surf blowing up in fountains at the end of the field, but the moment comes when the world falls away, and the self emerges again from the deep unconscious, bringing back all I have recently experienced to be explored and slowly understood, when I can converse again with my hidden powers, and so grow, and so be renewed, till death do us part.

Discussion Questions

1. What was Sarton's purpose in writing this essay: To justify her choice in living alone? To defend her interest in living alone? To persuade others to try the "solitary life"? What in the essay leads you to your answer?
2. What does this essay reveal about Sarton?
3. In small groups, discuss whether most people are afraid of spending time alone. What accounts for their attitude?
4. What does Sarton mean in paragraph 5, when she states, "Loneliness is most acutely felt with other people . . ."?
5. Does Sarton convince you that "living a solitary life" is pleasureful? Why or why not?

Writing Assignments

1. In a journal entry, define with examples the words *alone*, *lonely*, and *solitude*.

2. Spend an entire day (or at least an entire morning or afternoon) alone. In an essay, describe anything you noticed that you had previously been unaware of. Did you feel lonely, or were you pleased with the experience? Recreate the experience of those solitary hours for your readers.

3. Write an essay in which you argue that spending time alone is preferable to spending it with other people (or vice versa).

4. Do you think people's reluctance to spend time alone is peculiar to the latter part of the twentieth century? If so, why might this be the case? In an essay, examine the reasons for people not following Sarton's lead in living a solitary life.

The Discovery of What It Means to Be an American

JAMES
BALDWIN

James Baldwin (1924–1987) was born in the Harlem ghetto of New York City. When he was just eleven years old, Baldwin had already written a history of Harlem, short stories, and editorials for his school newspaper. At the age of fourteen, Baldwin became a preacher at the Fireside Pentecostal Church in Harlem. Family poverty prevented Baldwin from attending college, and his interest in becoming a professional writer further fueled his choice to forgo a formal education in order to devote his energies to writing. A protégé of the novelist Richard Wright, Baldwin worked as a book reviewer and published his famous essay "Harlem Ghetto" in *Commentary* magazine, a publication of the American Jewish Committee. In 1948, he moved to Paris where he did most of his writing. A number of fellowships helped to support Baldwin as he pursued his career: a Sexton in 1945, a Rosenwald in 1948, a Guggenheim in 1954, and a *Partisan Review* in 1956; he also received support from the Ford Foundation in 1959. A prolific writer, Baldwin is the author of the novels *Go Tell It on the Mountain* (1953), *Giovanni's Room* (1956), *Another Country* (1962), and *If Beale Street Could Talk* (1974). His short stories appear in *Going to Meet the Man* (1965). Baldwin is also a playwright whose works include *The Amen Corner* (1955) and *Blues for Mister Charlie* (1964).

His essays are collected in *Notes of a Native Son* (1955), from which
the following essay is taken; *Nobody Knows My Name: More Notes of a
Native Son* (1961); *The Fire Next Time* (1963); *No Name in the Street*
(1972); and *The Price of the Ticket: Collected Nonfiction* (1985). Baldwin is most noted for writing about issues of race, sexual identity, and
social injustice in the United States. In the following essay, Baldwin
describes the social and literary climate in the United States that precipitated his moving to Europe to advance his writing career.

1   "It is a complex fate to be an American," Henry James observed,
and the principal discovery an American writer makes in Europe is
just how complex this fate is. America's history, her aspirations, her
peculiar triumphs, her even more peculiar defeats, and her position
in the world—yesterday and today—are all so profoundly and stub-
bornly unique that the very word "America" remains a new, almost
completely undefined and extremely controversial proper noun. No
one in the world seems to know exactly what it describes, not even
we motley millions who call ourselves Americans.

2   I left America because I doubted my ability to survive the fury of
the color problem here. (Sometimes I still do.) I wanted to prevent
myself from becoming *merely* a Negro; or, even, merely a Negro
writer. I wanted to find out in what way the *specialness* of my experience could be made to connect me with other people instead of
dividing me from them. (I was as isolated from Negroes as I was
from whites, which is what happens when a Negro begins, at bottom,
to believe what white people say about him.)

3   In my necessity to find the terms on which my experience could
be related to that of others, Negroes and whites, writers and non-
writers, I proved, to my astonishment, to be as American as any
Texas G.I. And I found my experience was shared by every American
writer I knew in Paris. Like me, they had been divorced from their
origins, and it turned out to make very little difference that the
origins of white Americans were European and mine were African—
they were no more at home in Europe than I was.

4   The fact that I was the son of a slave and they were the sons of free men meant less, by the time we confronted each other on European soil, than the fact that we were both searching for our separate identities. When we had found these, we seemed to be saying, why, then, we would no longer need to cling to the shame and bitterness which had divided us so long.

5   It became terribly clear in Europe, as it never had been here, that we knew more about each other than any European ever could. And it also became clear that, no matter where our fathers had been born, or what they had endured, the fact of Europe had formed us both, was part of our identity and part of our inheritance.

6   I had been in Paris a couple of years before any of this became clear to me. When it did, I, like many a writer before me upon the discovery that his props have all been knocked out from under him, suffered a species of breakdown and was carried off to the mountains of Switzerland. There, in that absolutely alabaster landscape, armed with two Bessie Smith records and a typewriter, I began to try to re-create the life that I had first known as a child and from which I had spent so many years in flight.

7   It was Bessie Smith, through her tone and her cadence, who helped me to dig back to the way I myself must have spoken when I was a pickaninny, and to remember the things I had heard and seen and felt. I had buried them very deep. I had never listened to Bessie Smith in America (in the same way that, for years, I would not touch watermelon), but in Europe she helped to reconcile me to being a "nigger."

8   I do not think that I could have made this reconciliation here. Once I was able to accept my role—as distinguished, I must say, from my "place"—in the extraordinary drama which is America, I was released from the illusion that I hated America.

9   The story of what can happen to an American Negro writer in Europe simply illustrates, in some relief, what can happen to any American writer there. It is not meant, of course, to imply that it happens to them all, for Europe can be very crippling, too; and, anyway, a writer, when he has made his first breakthrough, has simply won a crucial skirmish in a dangerous, unending and unpredictable battle. Still, the breakthrough is important, and the point is that an American writer, in order to achieve it, very often has to leave this country.

10   The American writer, in Europe, is released, first of all, from
the necessity of apologizing for himself. It is not until he is
released from the habit of flexing his muscles and proving that
he is just a "regular guy" that he realizes how crippling this habit
has been. It is not necessary for him, there, to pretend to be
something he is not, for the artist does not encounter in Europe
the same suspicion he encounters here. Whatever the Europeans
may actually think of artists, they have killed enough of them off
by now to know that they are as real—and as persistent—as rain,
snow, taxes or businessmen.

11   Of course, the reason for Europe's comparative clarity concerning
the different functions of men in society is that European society has
always been divided into classes in a way that American society never
has been. A European writer considers himself to be part of an old
and honorable tradition—of intellectual activity, of letters—and his
choice of a vocation does not cause him any uneasy wonder as to
whether or not it will cost him all his friends. But this tradition does
not exist in America.

12   On the contrary, we have a very deep-seated distrust of real intellectual effort (probably because we suspect that it will destroy, as I
hope it does, that myth of America to which we cling so desperately).
An American writer fights his way to one of the lowest rungs on the
American social ladder by means of pure bullheadedness and an
indescribable series of odd jobs. He probably has been a "regular
fellow" for much of his adult life, and it is not easy for him to step
out of that lukewarm bath.

13   We must, however, consider a rather serious paradox: though
American society is more mobile than Europe's, it is easier to cut
across social and occupational lines there than it is here. This has
something to do, I think, with the problem of status in American
life. Where everyone has status, it is also perfectly possible, after all,
that no one has. It seems inevitable, in any case, that a man may
become uneasy as to just what his status is.

14   But Europeans have lived with the idea of status for a long time.
A man can be as proud of being a good waiter as of being a good
actor, and in neither case feel threatened. And this means that the
actor and the waiter can have a freer and more genuinely friendly
relationship in Europe than they are likely to have here. The waiter
does not feel, with obscure resentment, that the actor has "made

it," and the actor is not tormented by the fear that he may find himself, tomorrow, once again a waiter.

15   This lack of what may roughly be called social paranoia causes the American writer in Europe to feel—almost certainly for the first time in his life—that he can reach out to everyone, that he is accessible to everyone and open to everything. This is an extraordinary feeling. He feels, so to speak, his own weight, his own value.

16   It is as though he suddenly came out of a dark tunnel and found himself beneath the open sky. And, in fact, in Paris, I began to see the sky for what seemed to be the first time. It was borne in on me—and it did not make me feel melancholy—that this sky had been there before I was born and would be there when I was dead. And it was up to me, therefore, to make of my brief opportunity the most that could be made.

17   I was born in New York, but have lived only in pockets of it. In Paris, I lived in all parts of the city—on the Right Bank and the Left, among the bourgeoisie and among *les misérables*, and knew all kinds of people, from pimps and prostitutes in Pigalle to Egyptian bankers in Neuilly. This may sound extremely unprincipled or even obscurely immoral: I found it healthy. I love to talk to people, all kinds of people, and almost everyone, as I hope we still know, loves a man who loves to listen.

18   This perpetual dealing with people very different from myself caused a shattering in me of preconceptions I scarcely knew I held. The writer is meeting in Europe people who are not American, whose sense of reality is entirely different from his own. They may love or hate or admire or fear or envy this country—they see it, in any case, from another point of view, and this forces the writer to reconsider many things he had always taken for granted. This reassessment, which can be very painful, is also very valuable.

19   This freedom, like all freedom, has its dangers and its responsibili ties. One day it begins to be borne in on the writer, and with great force, that he is living in Europe as an American. If he were living there as a European, he would be living on a different and far less attractive continent.

20   This crucial day may be the day on which an Algerian taxi-driver tells him how it feels to be an Algerian in Paris. It may be the day on which he passes a café terrace and catches a glimpse of the tense,

intelligent and troubled face of Albert Camus. Or it may be the day on which someone asks him to explain Little Rock and he begins to feel that it would be simpler—and, corny as the words may sound, more honorable—to go to Little Rock than sit in Europe, on an American passport, trying to explain it.

21   This is a personal day, a terrible day, the day to which his entire sojourn has been tending. It is the day he realizes that there are no untroubled countries in this fearfully troubled world; that if he has been preparing himself for anything in Europe, he has been preparing himself—for America. In short, the freedom that the American writer finds in Europe brings him, full circle, back to himself, with the responsibility for his development where it always was: in his own hands.

22   Even the most incorrigible maverick has to be born somewhere. He may leave the group that produced him—he may be forced to—but nothing will efface his origins, the marks of which he carries with him everywhere. I think it is important to know this and even find it a matter for rejoicing, as the strongest people do, regardless of their station. On this acceptance, literally, the life of a writer depends.

23   The charge has often been made against American writers that they do not describe society, and have no interest in it. They only describe individuals in opposition to it, or isolated from it. Of course, what the American writer is describing is his own situation. But what is Anna Karenina describing if not the tragic fate of the isolated individual, at odds with her time and place?

24   The real difference is that Tolstoy was describing an old and dense society in which everything seemed—to the people in it, though not to Tolstoy—to be fixed forever. And the book is a masterpiece because Tolstoy was able to fathom, and make us see, the hidden laws which really governed this society and made Anna's doom inevitable.

25   American writers do not have a fixed society to describe. The only society they know is one in which nothing is fixed and in which the individual must fight for his identity. This is a rich confusion, indeed, and it creates for the American writer unprecedented opportunities.

26   That the tensions of American life, as well as the possibilities, are tremendous is certainly not even a question. But these are dealt with in contemporary literature mainly compulsively; that is, the book is more likely to be a symptom of our tension than an examination of

it. The time has come, God knows, for us to examine ourselves, but we can only do this if we are willing to free ourselves of the myth of America and try to find out what is really happening here.

27   Every society is really governed by hidden laws, by unspoken but profound assumptions on the part of the people, and ours is no exception. It is up to the American writer to find out what these laws and assumptions are. In a society much given to smashing taboos without thereby managing to be liberated from them, it will be no easy matter.

28   It is no wonder, in the meantime, that the American writer keeps running off to Europe. He needs sustenance for his journey and the best models he can find. Europe has what we do not have yet, a sense of the mysterious and inexorable limits of life, a sense, in a word, of tragedy. And we have what they sorely need: a new sense of life's possibilities.

29   In this endeavor to wed the vision of the Old World with that of the New, it is the writer, not the statesman, who is our strongest arm. Though we do not wholly believe it yet, the interior life is a real life, and the intangible dreams of people have a tangible effect on the world.

Discussion Questions

1. What were Baldwin's reasons for leaving the United States? Which do you find most important and which less so? Explain.
2. Why, according to Baldwin, do American writers benefit from living in Europe?
3. In small groups, discuss Baldwin's analysis of the American versus the European social structure and status and decide whether his analysis is valid.
4. Explain what Baldwin means in paragraph 22 when he states, "Even the most incorrigible maverick has to be born somewhere."
5. Does Baldwin convince you of the reasons for American writers "running off to Europe"? Explain.
6. Although Baldwin focuses on American writers in Europe, his conclusions could apply to other types of artists such as musicians or sculptors. Explain how this is possible.

Writing Assignments

1. In a journal entry, argue whether people, such as Baldwin, who leave their country are courageous or cowardly. Support your stance.
2. Write a letter to Baldwin in which you agree or disagree with his decision to leave the United States.
3. Write an essay in which you explore "What it means to be a(n) _____."
4. Reflect on an event in which dealing with people different from you caused you to confront your own pre- or misconceptions.
5. If you have ever traveled abroad (or to a state far from your home), describe the incident(s) that allowed you to see what it means to be an American (or resident of the state in which you reside).

On Being a Cripple

NANCY MAIRS

Nancy Mairs (b. 1943) was born in Long Beach, California, and grew up in Massachusetts and New Hampshire. She attended Wheaton College and worked as a technical editor at the Smithsonian Astrophysical Observatory, the MIT Press, and the Harvard Law School. In 1972, she moved to Arizona where she earned an M.F.A. and a Ph.D. in English from the University of Arizona where she currently teaches. She was awarded a William P. Sloan Fellowship and a Western States Book Award in 1984 for her poetry collection *All the Rooms in the Yellow House* (1983). Her interest in autobiographical writing led to her experimenting with the genre, and the resulting essays have appeared in numerous publications such as *Triquarterly*, *The New York Times*, *The American Voice*, *Kaleidoscope*, and *Working Mother*. She is the author of six autobiographical essay collections and memoirs: *Plaintext: Deciphering a Woman's Life* (1986), *Remembering the Bone House: An Erotics of Place and Space* (1989), *Carnal Acts* (1990), *Ordinary Time: Cycles in Marriage, Faith, and Renewal* (1993), *Voice Lessons: On Becoming a (Woman) Writer* (1994), and *Waist-High in the World: A Life among the Nondisabled* (1996). These books chronicle Mairs's life as a woman, a mother, a wife, a writer, and a person with multiple sclerosis. In her nonfiction, Mairs concentrates on how living with multiple sclerosis has affected her life since she was diagnosed with the disease in the early 1970s. In the following essay from *Plaintext*, she uses the word *cripple* as a way to explore the physical and emotional ramifications of having multiple sclerosis. The essay is a classic example of how autobiography can be combined with medical information to produce compelling and informative writing.

>To escape is nothing. Not to escape is nothing.
>
>—LOUISE BOGAN

1   The other day I was thinking of writing an essay on being a cripple. I was thinking hard in one of the stalls of the women's room in my office building, as I was shoving my shirt into my jeans and tugging up my zipper. Preoccupied, I flushed, picked up my book bag, took my cane down from the hook, and unlatched the door. So many movements unbalanced me, and as I pulled the door open I fell over backward, landing fully clothed on the toilet seat with my legs splayed in front of me: the old beetle-on-its-back routine. Saturday afternoon, the building deserted, I was free to laugh aloud as I wriggled back to my feet, my voice bouncing off the yellowish tiles from all directions. Had anyone been there with me, I'd have been still and faint and hot with chagrin. I decided that it was high time to write the essay.

2   First, the matter of semantics. I am a cripple. I choose this word to name me. I choose from among several possibilities, the most common of which are "handicapped" and "disabled." I made the choice a number of years ago, without thinking, unaware of my motives for doing so. Even now, I'm not sure what those motives are, but I recognize that they are complex and not entirely flattering. People—crippled or not—wince at the word "cripple," as they do not at "handicapped" or "disabled. " Perhaps I want them to wince. I want them to see me as a tough customer, one to whom the fates/ gods/viruses have not been kind, but who can face the brutal truth of her existence squarely. As a cripple, I swagger.

3   But, to be fair to myself, a certain amount of honesty underlies my choice. "Cripple" seems to me a clean word, straightforward and precise. It has an honorable history, having made its first appear-

ance in the Lindisfarne Gospel in the tenth century. As a lover of
words, I like the accuracy with which it describes my condition: I
have lost the full use of my limbs. "Disabled," by contrast, suggests
any incapacity, physical or mental. And I certainly don't like "handicapped," which implies that I have deliberately been put at a disad-
vantage, by whom I can't imagine (my God is not a Handicapper
General), in order to equalize chances in the great race of life. These
words seem to me to be moving away from my condition, to be
widening the gap between word and reality. Most remote is the
recently coined euphemism "differently abled," which partakes of
the same semantic hopefulness that transformed countries from
"undeveloped" to "underdeveloped," then to "less developed," and
finally to "developing" nations. People have continued to starve in
those countries during the shift. Some realities do not obey the
dictates of language.

4   Mine is one of them. Whatever you call me, I remain crippled.
But I don't care what you call me, so long as it isn't "differently
abled," which strikes me as pure verbal garbage designed, by its
ability to describe anyone, to describe no one. I subscribe to George
Orwell's thesis that "the slovenliness of our language makes it easier
for us to have foolish thoughts." And I refuse to participate in the
degeneration of the language to the extent that I deny that I have
lost anything in the course of this calamitous disease; I refuse to
pretend that the only differences between you and me are the various
ordinary ones that distinguish any one person from another. But call
me "disabled" or "handicapped" if you like. I have long since grown
accustomed to them; and if they are vague, at least they hint at the
truth. Moreover, I use them myself. Society is no readier to accept
crippledness than to accept death, war, sex, sweat, or wrinkles. I
would never refer to another person as a cripple. It is the word I use
to name only myself.

5   I haven't always been crippled, a fact for which I am soundly
grateful. To be whole of limb is, I know from experience, infinitely
more pleasant and useful than to be crippled; and if that knowledge
leaves me open to bitterness at my loss, the physical soundness I
once enjoyed (though I did not enjoy it half enough) is well worth
the occasional stab of regret. Though never any good at sports, I
was a normally active child and young adult. I climbed trees, played
hopscotch, jumped rope, skated, swam, rode my bicycle, sailed. I

despised team sports, spending some of the wretchedest afternoons of my life, sweaty and humiliated, behind a field-hockey stick and under a basketball hoop. I tramped alone for miles along the bridle paths that webbed the woods behind the house I grew up in. I swayed through countless dim hours in the arms of one man or another under the scattered shot of light from mirrored balls, and gyrated through countless more as Tab Hunter and Johnny Mathis gave way to the Rolling Stones, Creedence Clearwater Revival, Cream. I walked down the aisle. I pushed baby carriages, changed tires in the rain, marched for peace.

6   When I was twenty-eight I started to trip and drop things. What at first seemed my natural clumsiness soon became too pronounced to shrug off. I consulted a neurologist, who told me that I had a brain tumor. A battery of tests, increasingly disagreeable, revealed no tumor. About a year and a half later I developed a blurred spot in one eye. I had, at last, the episodes "disseminated in space and time" requisite for a diagnosis: multiple sclerosis. I have never been sorry for the doctor's initial misdiagnosis, however. For almost a week, until the negative results of the tests were in, I thought that I was going to die right away. Every day for the past nearly ten years, then, has been a kind of gift. I accept all gifts.

7   Multiple sclerosis is a chronic degenerative disease of the central nervous system, in which the myelin that sheathes the nerves is somehow eaten away and scar tissue forms in its place, interrupting the nerves' signals. During its course, which is unpredictable and uncontrollable, one may lose vision, hearing, speech, the ability to walk, control of bladder and/or bowels, strength in any or all extremities, sensitivity to touch, vibration, and/or pain, potency, coordination of movements—the list of possibilities is lengthy and, yes, horrifying. One may also lose one's sense of humor. That's the easiest to lose and the hardest to survive without.

8   In the past ten years, I have sustained some of these losses. Characteristic of MS are sudden attacks, called exacerbations, followed by remissions, and these I have not had. Instead, my disease has been slowly progressive. My left leg is now so weak that I walk with the aid of a brace and a cane; and for distances I use an Amigo, a variation on the electric wheelchair that looks rather like an electrified kiddie car. I no longer have much use of my left hand. Now my right side is weakening as well. I still have the blurred spot in my right eye.

Overall, though, I've been lucky so far. My world has, of necessity, been circumscribed by my losses, but the terrain left me has been ample enough for me to continue many of the activities that absorb me: writing, teaching, raising children and cats and plants and snakes, reading, speaking publicly about MS and depression, even playing bridge with people patient and honorable enough to let me scatter cards every which way without sneaking a peek.

9   Lest I begin to sound like Pollyanna, however, let me say that I don't like having MS. I hate it. My life holds realities—harsh ones, some of them—that no right-minded human being ought to accept without grumbling. One of them is fatigue. I know of no one with MS who does not complain of bone-weariness; in a disease that presents an astonishing variety of symptoms, fatigue seems to be a common factor. I wake up in the morning feeling the way most people do at the end of a bad day, and I take it from there. As a result, I spend a lot of time *in extremis* and, impatient with limitation, I tend to ignore my fatigue until my body breaks down in some way and forces rest. Then I miss picnics, dinner parties, poetry readings, the brief visits of old friends from out of town. The offspring of a puritanical tradition of exceptional venerability, I cannot view these lapses without shame. My life often seems a series of small failures to do as I ought.

10   I lead, on the whole, an ordinary life, probably rather like the one I would have led had I not had MS. I am lucky that my predilections were already solitary, sedentary, and bookish—unlike the world-famous French cellist I have read about, or the young woman I talked with one long afternoon who wanted only to be a jockey. I had just begun graduate school when I found out something was wrong with me, and I have remained, interminably, a graduate student. Perhaps I would not have if I'd thought I had the stamina to return to a full-time job as a technical editor; but I've enjoyed my studies.

11   In addition to studying, I teach writing courses. I also teach medical students how to give neurological examinations. I pick up freelance editing jobs here and there. I have raised a foster son and sent him into the world, where he has made me two grandbabies, and I am still escorting my daughter and son through adolescence. I go to Mass every Saturday. I am a superb, if messy, cook. I am also an enthusiastic laundress, capable of sorting a hamper full of

clothes into five subtly differentiated piles, but a terrible housekeeper. I can do italic writing and, in an emergency, bathe an oil-soaked cat. I play a fiendish game of Scrabble. When I have the time and the money, I like to sit on my front steps with my husband, drinking Amaretto and smoking a cigar, as we imagine our counterparts in Leningrad and make sure that the sun gets down once more behind the sharp childish scrawl of the Tucson Mountains.

12   This lively plenty has its bleak complement, of course, in all the things I can no longer do. I will never run again, except in dreams, and one day I may have to write that I will never walk again. I like to go camping, but I can't follow George and the children along the trails that wander out of a campsite through the desert or into the mountains. In fact, even on the level I've learned never to check the weather or try to hold a coherent conversation: I need all my attention for my wayward feet. Of late, I have begun to catch myself wondering how people can propel themselves without canes. With only one usable hand, I have to select my clothing with care not so much for style as for ease of ingress and egress, and even so, dressing can be laborious. I can no longer do fine stitchery, pick up babies, play the piano, braid my hair. I am immobilized by acute attacks of depression, which may or may not be physiologically related to MS but are certainly its logical concomitant.

13   These two elements, the plenty and the privation, are never pure, nor are the delight and wretchedness that accompany them. Almost every pickle that I get into as a result of my weakness and clumsiness— and I get into plenty—is funny as well as maddening and sometimes painful. I recall one May afternoon when a friend and I were going out for a drink after finishing up at school. As we were climbing into opposite sides of my car, chatting, I tripped and fell, flat and hard, onto the asphalt parking lot, my abrupt departure interrupting him in mid-sentence. "Where'd you go?" he called as he came around the back of the car to find me hauling myself up by the door frame. "Are you all right?" Yes, I told him, I was fine, just a bit rattly, and we drove off to find a shady patio and some beer. When I got home an hour or so later, my daughter greeted me with "What have you done to yourself?" I looked down. One elbow of my white turtleneck with the green froggies, one knee of my white trousers, one white kneesock were bloodsoaked. We peeled off the clothes and inspected the damage, which was nasty enough but not alarming. That part

wasn't funny: The abrasions took a long time to heal, and one got a little infected. Even so, when I think of my friend talking earnestly, suddenly, to the hot thin air while I dropped from his view as though through a trap door, I find the image as silly as something from a Marx Brothers movie.

14   I may find it easier than other cripples to amuse myself because I live propped by the acceptance and the assistance and, sometimes, the amusement of those around me. Grocery clerks tear my checks out of my checkbook for me, and sales clerks find chairs to put into dressing rooms when I want to try on clothes. The people I work with make sure I teach at times when I am least likely to be fatigued, in places I can get to, with the materials I need. My students, with one anonymous exception (in an end-of-the-semester evaluation), have been unperturbed by my disability. Some even like it. One was immensely cheered by the information that I paint my own finger-nails; she decided, she told me, that if I could go to such trouble over fine details, she could keep on writing essays. I suppose I became some sort of bright-fingered muse. She wrote good essays, too.

15   The most important struts in the framework of my existence, of course, are my husband and children. Dismayingly few marriages survive the MS test, and why should they? Most twenty-two- and nineteen-year-olds, like George and me, can vow in clear conscience, after a childhood of chicken pox and summer colds, to keep one another in sickness and in health so long as they both shall live. Not many are equipped for catastrophe: the dismay, the depression, the extra work, the boredom that a degenerative disease can insinuate into a relationship. And our society, with its emphasis on fun and its association of fun with physical performance, offers little encour-agement for a whole spouse to stay with a crippled partner. Children experience similar stresses when faced with a crippled parent, and they are more helpless, since parents and children can't usually get divorced. They hate, of course, to be different from their peers, and the child whose mother is tacking down the aisle of a school auditorium packed with proud parents like a Cape Cod dinghy in a stiff breeze jolly well stands out in a crowd. Deprived of legal divorce, the child can at least deny the mother's disability, even her existence, forgetting to tell her about recitals and PTA meetings, refusing to accompany her to stores or church or the movies, never inviting friends to the house. Many do.

16   But I've been limping along for ten years now, and so far George and the children are still at my left elbow, holding tight. Anne and Matthew vacuum floors and dust furniture and haul trash and rake up dog droppings and button my cuffs and bake lasagna and Toll House cookies with just enough grumbling so I know that they don't have brain fever. And far from hiding me, they're forever dragging me by racks of fancy clothes or through teeming school corridors, or welcoming gaggles of friends while I'm wandering through the house in Anne's filmy pink babydoll pajamas. George generally calls before he brings someone home, but he does just as many dumb thankless chores as the children. And they all yell at me, laugh at some of my jokes, write me funny letters when we're apart— in short, treat me as an ordinary human being for whom they have some use. I think they like me. Unless they're faking. . . .

17   Faking. There's the rub. Tugging at the fringes of my consciousness always is the terror that people are kind to me only because I'm a cripple. My mother almost shattered me once, with that instinct mothers have—blind, I think, in this case, but unerring nonetheless— for striking blows along the fault-lines of their children's hearts, by telling me, in an attack on my selfishness, "We all have to make allowances for you, of course, because of the way you are." From the distance of a couple of years, I have to admit that I haven't any idea just what she meant, and I'm not sure that she knew either. She was awfully angry. But at the time, as the words thudded home, I felt my worst fear, suddenly realized. I could bear being called selfish: I am. But I couldn't bear the corroboration that those around me were doing in fact what I'd always suspected them of doing, professing fondness while silently putting up with me because of the way I am. A cripple. I've been a little cracked ever since.

18   Along with this fear that people are secretly accepting shoddy goods comes a relentless pressure to please—to prove myself worth the burdens I impose, I guess, or to build a substantial account of good will against which I may write drafts in times of need. Part of the pressure arises from social expectations. In our society, anyone who deviates from the norm had better find some way to compensate. Like fat people, who are expected to be jolly, cripples must bear their lot meekly and cheerfully. A grumpy cripple isn't playing by the rules. And much of the pressure is self-generated. Early on I vowed that, if I had to have MS, by God I was going to do it well. This is a class

act, ladies and gentlemen. No tears, no recriminations, no faint-heartedness.

19   One way and another, then, I wind up feeling like Tiny Tim, peering over the edge of the table at the Christmas goose, waving my crutch, piping down God's blessing on us all. Only sometimes I don't want to play Tiny Tim. I'd rather be Caliban, a most scurvy monster. Fortunately, at home no one much cares whether I'm a good cripple or a bad cripple as long as I make vichyssoise with fair regularity. One evening several years ago, Anne was reading at the dining-room table while I cooked dinner. As I opened a can of tomatoes, the can slipped in my left hand and juice spattered me and the counter with bloody spots. Fatigued and infuriated, I bellowed, "I'm so sick of being crippled!" Anne glanced at me over the top of her book. "There now," she said, "do you feel better?" "Yes," I said, "yes, I do." She went back to her reading. I felt better. That's about all the attention my scurviness ever gets.

20   Because I hate being crippled, I sometimes hate myself for being a cripple. Over the years I have come to expect—even accept—attacks of violent self-loathing. Luckily, in general our society no longer connects deformity and disease directly with evil (though a charismatic once told me that I have MS because a devil is in me) and so I'm allowed to move largely at will, even among small children. But I'm not sure that this revision of attitude has been particularly helpful. Physical imperfection, even freed of moral disapprobation, still defies and violates the ideal, especially for women, whose confinement in their bodies as objects of desire is far from over. Each age, of course, has its ideal, and I doubt that ours is any better or worse than any other. Today's ideal woman, who lives on the glossy pages of dozens of magazines, seems to be between the age of eighteen and twenty-five: her hair has body, her teach flash white, her breath smells minty, her underarms are dry, she has a career but is still a fabulous cook, especially of meals that take less than twenty minutes to prepare; she does not ordinarily appear to have a husband or children; she is trim and deeply tanned; she jogs, swims, plays tennis, rides a bicycle, sails, but does not bowl; she travels widely, even to out-of-the-way places like Finland and Samoa, always in the company of the ideal man, who possesses a nearly identical set of characteristics. There are a few exceptions. Though usually white and often blond, she may be black, Hispanic, Asian, or Native American, so long as she is unusually

sleek. She may be old, provided she is selling a laxative or is Lauren Bacall. If she is selling a detergent, she may be married and have a flock of strikingly messy children. But she is never a cripple.

21   Like many women I know, I have always had an uneasy relationship with my body. I was not a popular child, largely, I think now, because I was peculiar: intelligent, intense, moody, shy, given to unexpected actions and inexplicable notions and emotions. But as I entered adolescence, I believed myself unpopular because I was homely: my breasts too flat, my mouth too wide, my hips too narrow, my clothing never quite right in fit or style. I was not, in fact, particularly ugly, old photographs inform me, though I was well off the ideal; but I carried this sense of self-alienation with me into adulthood, where it regenerated in response to the depredations of MS. Even with my brace I walk with a limp so pronounced that, seeing myself on the videotape of a television program on the disabled, I couldn't believe that anything but an inchworm could make progress humping along like that. My shoulders droop and my pelvis thrusts forward as I try to balance myself upright, throwing my frame into a bony S. As a result of contractures, one shoulder is higher than the other and I carry one arm bent in front me, the fingers curled into a claw. My left arm and leg have wasted into pipe-stems, and I try always to keep them covered. When I think about how my body must look to others, especially to men, to whom I have been trained to display myself, I feel ludicrous, even loathsome.

22   At my age, however, I don't spend much time thinking about my appearance. The burning egocentricity of adolescence, which assures one that all the world is looking all the time, has passed, thank God, and I'm generally too caught up in what I'm doing to step back, as I used to, and watch myself as though upon a stage. I'm also too old to believe in the accuracy of self-image. I know that I'm not a hideous crone, that in fact, when I'm rested, well dressed, and well made up, I look fine. The self-loathing I feel is neither physically nor intellectually substantial. What I hate is not me but a disease.

23   I am not a disease.

24   And a disease is not—at least not singlehandedly—going to determine who I am, though at first it seemed to be going to. Adjusting to a chronic incurable illness, I have moved through a process similar to that outlined by Elisabeth Kübler-Ross in *On Death and Dying*. The major difference—and it is far more significant than most people recog-

nize—is that I can't be sure of the outcome, as the terminally ill cancer patient can. Research studies indicate that, with proper medical care, I may achieve a "normal" life span. And in our society, with its vision of death as the ultimate evil, worse even than decrepitude, the response to such news is, "Oh well, at least you're not going to *die*." Are there worse things than dying? I think that there may be.

25   I think of two women I know, both with MS, both enough older than I to have served me as models. One took to her bed several years ago and has been there ever since. Although she can sit in a high-backed wheelchair, because she is incontinent she refuses to go out at all, even though incontinence pants, which are readily available at any pharmacy, could protect her from embarrassment. Instead, she stays at home and insists that her husband, a small quiet man, a retired civil servant, stay there with her except for a quick weekly foray to the supermarket. The other woman, whose illness was diagnosed when she was eighteen, a nursing student engaged to a young doctor, finished her training, married her doctor, accompanied him to Germany when he was in the service, bore three sons and a daughter, now grown and gone. When she can, she travels with her husband; she plays bridge, embroiders, swims regularly; she works, like me, as a symptomatic-patient instructor of medical students in neurology. Guess which woman I hope to be.

26   At the beginning, I thought about having MS almost incessantly. And because of the unpredictable course of the disease, my thoughts were always terrified. Each night I'd get into bed wondering whether I'd get out again the next morning, whether I'd be able to see, to speak, to hold a pen between my fingers. Knowing that the day might come when I'd be physically incapable of killing myself, I thought perhaps I ought to do so right away, while I still had the strength. Gradually I came to understand that the Nancy who might one day lie inert under a bedsheet, arms and legs paralyzed, unable to feed or bathe herself, unable to reach out for a gun, a bottle of pills, was not the Nancy I was at present, and that I could not presume to make decisions for that future Nancy, who might well not want in the least to die. Now the only provision I've made for the future Nancy is that when the time comes—and it is likely to come in the form of pneumonia, friend to the weak and the old—I am not to be treated with machines and medications. If she is unable to communicate by then, I hope she will be satisfied with these terms.

27   Thinking all the time about having MS grew tiresome and intru-
sive, especially in the large and tragic mode in which I was accustomed
to considering my plight. Months and even years went by without
catastrophe (at least without one related to MS), and really I was
awfully busy, what with George and children and snakes and students
and poems, and I hadn't the time, let alone the inclination, to devote
myself to being a disease. Too, the richer my life became, the funnier
it seemed, as though there were some connection between largesse
and laughter, and so my tragic stance began to waver until, even
with the aid of a brace and a cane, I couldn't hold it for very long
at a time.

28   After several years I was satisfied with my adjustment. I had suffered my grief and fury and terror, I thought, but now I was at ease
with my lot. Then one summer day I set out with George and the
children across the desert for a vacation in California. Part way to
Yuma I became aware that my right leg felt funny. "I think I've had
an exacerbation," I told George. "What shall we do?" he asked. "I
think we'd better get the hell to California," I said, "because I don't
know whether I'll ever make it again." So we went on to San Diego
and then to Orange, up the Pacific Coast Highway to Santa Cruz,
across to Yosemite, down to Sequoia and Joshua Tree, and so back
over the desert to home. It was a fine two-week trip, filled with
friends and fair weather, and I wouldn't have missed it for the world,
though I did in fact make it back to California two years later. Nor
would there have been any point in missing it, since in MS, once
the symptoms have appeared, the neurological damage has been
done, and there's no way to predict or prevent that damage.

29   The incident spoiled my self-satisfaction, however. It renewed my
grief and fury and terror, and I learned that one never finishes
adjusting to MS. I don't know now why I thought one would. One
does not, after all, finish adjusting to life, and MS is simply a fact of
my life—not my favorite fact, of course—but as ordinary as my nose
and my tropical fish and my yellow Mazda station wagon. It may at
any time get worse, but no amount of worry or anticipation can
prepare me for a new loss. My life is a lesson in losses. I learn one
at a time.

30   And I had best be patient in the learning, since I'll have to do it like
it or not. As any rock fan knows, you can't always get what you want.
Particularly when you have MS. You can't, for example, get cured. In

recent years researchers and the organizations that fund research have started to pay MS some attention even though it isn't fatal; perhaps they have begun to see that life is something other than a quantitative phenomenon, that one may be very much alive for a very long time in a life that isn't worth living. The researchers have made some progress toward understanding the mechanism of the disease: It may well be an auto-immune reaction triggered by a slow-acting virus. But they are nowhere near its prevention, control, or cure. And most of us want to be cured. Some, unable to accept incurability, grasp at one treatment after another, no matter how bizarre: megavitamin therapy, gluten-free diet, injections of cobra venom, hypothermal suits, lymphocyto-pharesis, hyperbaric chambers. Many treatments are probably harmless enough, but none are curative.

31   The absence of a cure often makes MS patients bitter toward their doctors. Doctors are, after all, the priests of modern society, the new shamans, whose business is to heal, and many an MS patient roves from one to another, searching for the "good" doctor who will make him well. Doctors too think of themselves as healers, and for this reason many have trouble dealing with MS patients, whose disease in its intransigence defeats their aims and mocks their skills. Too few doctors, it is true, treat their patients as whole human beings, but the reverse is also true. I have always tried to be gentle with my doctors, who often have more at stake in terms of ego than I do. I may be frustrated, maddened, depressed by the incurability of my disease, but I am not diminished by it, and they are. When I push myself up from my seat in the waiting room and stumble toward them, I incarnate the limitation of their powers. The least I can do is refuse to press on their tenderest spots.

32   This gentleness is part of the reason that I'm not sorry to be a cripple. I didn't have it before. Perhaps I'd have developed it anyway—how could I know such a thing?—and I wish I had more of it, but I'm glad of what I have. It has opened and enriched my life enormously, this sense that my frailty and need must be mirrored in others, that in searching for and shaping a stable core in a life wrenched by change and loss, change and loss, I must recognize the same process, under individual conditions, in the lives around me. I do not deprecate such knowledge, however I've come by it.

33   All the same, if a cure were found, would I take it? In a minute. I may be a cripple, but I'm only occasionally a loony and never a

saint. Anyway, in my brand of theology God doesn't give bonus points for a limp. I'd take a cure; I just don't need one. A friend who also has MS startled me once by asking, "Do you ever say to yourself, 'Why me, Lord?'" "No, Michael, I don't," I told him, "because whenever I try, the only response I can think of is 'Why not?'" If I could make a cosmic deal, who would I put in my place? What in my life would I give up in exchange for sound limbs and a thrilling rush of energy? No one. Nothing. I might as well do the job myself. Now that I'm getting the hang of it.

Discussion Questions

1. Discuss the effectiveness of Mairs's interspersing medical information about multiple sclerosis throughout her essay.
2. What emotions appear in Mairs's essay? Cite specific passages.
3. What does Mairs reveal about her attitude by forthrightly calling herself a cripple?
4. Discuss Mairs's possible reasons for writing this essay.
5. Choose several paragraphs from Mairs's essay and analyze the stylistic devices she uses (for example, imagery, alliteration, one-sentence paragraphs). How do these techniques strengthen the essay?

Writing Assignments

1. Write a journal entry that describes what you envision when you hear or read the word *cripple*.
2. Write a letter to Mairs in which you examine what people who are *not* physically handicapped can learn from her.
3. In recent years, new terminology has replaced words such as *cripple* and *handicap* (for example, *differently abled*). Generate a list of these new terms, and, in an essay, identify which of these should or should not be used. Provide reasons for your suggestions.
4. Most parking lots have places reserved near building entrances for handicapped people, and parking tickets are issued to those

without handicaps who park in these spaces. Are such policies fair? Write an essay supporting your stance.

5. In recent years, the government has passed legislation banning discrimination against handicapped people. Research newspaper and/or magazine articles about such legislation, and write a paper in which you argue for or against the accommodations made for disabled people.

6. Write an essay entitled "On Being a ＿＿＿＿＿＿" as a way to show others what it feels like to be ＿＿＿＿＿＿＿＿＿.

Middle Age: Becoming the Person You Always Were

BARBARA
LAZEAR
ASCHER

Barbara Lazear Ascher (b. 1946) was born in Virginia and attended
Bennington College. She earned her law degree from Cardoza
School of Law in 1979. Ascher was a practicing attorney before
becoming a full-time writer. She has read her essays for National
Public Radio's *Morning Edition*. Her essays have appeared in such
publications as *The New York Times, Saturday Review, The Yale
Review, European Travel and Life*, and *Vogue*. She is the author
of two collections of essays: *The Habit of Loving* (1989) and
Playing after Dark (1986), in which the following essay appears.
She is also the author of *Landscape without Gravity: A Memoir
of Grief* (1993), which relates Ascher's coming to terms with the
death of her brother from AIDS. In the following essay, Ascher
reflects on what it means to be middle-aged.

1   I wish I could remember who said that in middle age we become
the person we always were. I think it might be so. In fact I feel it

happening. Bits and pieces of self, discarded in adolescent frenzy or early adult preoccupation, seem to be floating downstream and fetching up on my shore. I imagine that when I reach middle age I will be a rock covered with moss borne by spores on the wind and lichen brought by who knows what. At any rate, it will all be familiar. We'll all nod to each other—the rock, the moss, the lichen, the visiting toad and the perching dove and say, "Nice to see you again." And then we'll settle in to stay.

2   I've heard others comment on these rumblings, these soft shifts in the soul's crust. Such a stir occurred yesterday before I even knew it. That's how it happens, before you even know it; the way you feel a mild tremor only after the fault has parted and meshed together again.

3   It was a gloomy, damp day. Out of nowhere, or so it seemed, came the idea that I must head directly to the Metropolitan Museum of Art, cross the hall, ascend the staircase, go straight to the Monets, stand and stare. It seems that I thought if I stood long enough, the apple blossoms, gardens, lavender poplars and azure skies would float out of their frames and into me, like ice surrendering to water. Perhaps all that Monet fecundity would crowd out February weariness. Well, of course. Why else do people visit museums?

4   I had avoided them for years, following a girls'-school education that had featured art appreciation—not to be confused with art history—as an intricate step toward becoming a lady. You can't carry your pedigree around with you, our trainers reasoned, but you can acquire certain graces and knowledge that will let the world know. If I remember correctly, these included, in addition to appreciating art, holding a teacup properly and never eating on the street. Somewhere along the line they merged and became confused with the general discomfort of wearing stockings. I rebelled.

5   The fracas of the adolescent heart also dispensed with organized religion. As soon as it was no longer a daily requirement, I refused to go to church. I closed out all memory of comfort or peace found there, the fun of singing hymns louder and higher than the next guy, the soothing familiarity of the *Book of Common Prayer*.

6   Lately I find myself in church and am surprised each time—not knowing why I came, or quite how I got there, but feeling familiar and singing my head off.

7   It's very odd to have parts of the self rubbing up against one like a cat.

8   In her essay "Aces and Eights," Annie Dillard writes, "I am 35; my tolerance for poignancy has diminished to the vanishing point." I would like to ask her, "So how is it at thirty-seven?" If it's not too late, I'd better warn her. I'll tap out the code on a tree trunk or put a note in a bottle and toss it into the East River. In either case the secret will be carried from Manhattan to Tinker Creek. "Pardon the intrusion, Miss Dillard, but I thought you ought to know that in middle age the heart becomes a goldfish."

9   If you have ever had the misfortune of holding a goldfish in your hand, you will know what I mean. There is a wet and desperate thrashing. Unprotected for contact with anything as firm as knuckle and callous, its vulnerability beats against the inside of your fist. You know that your thumb would leave the imprint of its press. if you squeeze too hard the fish will bend and die. If you hold too lightly it will fly away, remembering in midflight that it is wingless. Life! Life! is the code its tail beats out against your hand. Holding it makes you squeamish, letting go is no choice.

10   It's not like catching crickets or flies or lightning bugs. They will protest because, like the rest of us, they don't choose to be contained. But their angry stampings are not the same as a squirm for dear life.

11   If you held a stethoscope to the closed fist grasping the fish, I imagine you would hear a sound similar to a fetal heartbeat. A wet message from another world.

12   It seems that as we become the person we always were, our hearts return to what they once were. Squirming, wet and wingless, sending the message through the wall: Life! Life!

13   I don't think we knew the "person we always were" when we were being it. It's like negative space. When you look at a David Smith sculpture, you don't know which excites you more—where the steel is or where it is not. We don't experience the negative space until time and age have thrown up enough of a structure to give it something to scratch its back against. "Oh, here I am," we say as the familiar floats by and decides to stay.

14   For some, becoming this person is no more, or just as, complicated as becoming one's own mother. I had the fortunate or unfortunate occasion to witness this when I returned for my prep-school reunion. Here is Sarah, who once upon a time had distanced herself from the image of her mother by strict dieting, increasing the space between

them by decreasing her own. Now, eighteen years later, she stands beside me, large and bluff, putting the same strong arm around me that had once made her cringe.

15   And here is Louise with the thin-lipped reserve that had elicited the comment sixteen years ago: "My mother is an iceberg." Now I feel as awkward as Louise herself once felt before this slick of perfection, this perfectly formed icicle.

16   But as I was saying, I had felt the urge to go to the Metropolitan Museum and had raced up the stairs to get to the top before closing time. I would like to tell you, Annie Dillard, that there was a "poignant" moment, a reunion of sorts between the *Path in the Ille St. Martin* and me. But in fact, the guard at the door said, "We're closed, miss."

17   Perhaps the race rather than the getting there was the most important part of this story anyway.

18   So, when it comes, I imagine that middle age will find me as a craggy rock, rough-edged toward the sky and smooth where my base touches water, where rivulets warm in the sun and tadpoles sleep until the next rush of water brought by rain or winds; a sometimes-churchgoing radical who doesn't eat on the street and is mad for Monet.

Discussion Questions

1. How old do you think middle age is? Explain.
2. Explain what the title of Ascher's essay might mean.
3. Describe the tone of Ascher's essay and cite specific lines that contribute to it.
4. Ascher uses imagery to describe her observations and feelings. Evaluate its effectiveness in making her point.
5. What does this essay tell you about Ascher as a woman? Be specific, citing passages that you find most representative.
6. In small groups, discuss whether this essay is optimistic or pessimistic. Identify specific parts of the essay that lead you to your responses.

Writing Assignments

1. Write a journal entry that predicts what you will be like when you reach middle age.
2. In an essay, compare and contrast what you, as a child, thought the teen years would be like and how they actually were.
3. Interview your parents and your peers to find out how they define *middle age*. Write an essay comparing their answers. How do you account for the similarities and differences in their responses?
4. Do you think Americans obsess about age? Write a paper in response to that question.
5. It was once said that the older people get, the more they become who they really are. Using specific examples of people you know, write an essay that supports or refutes this observation.

CLASSIC ESSAYS ON

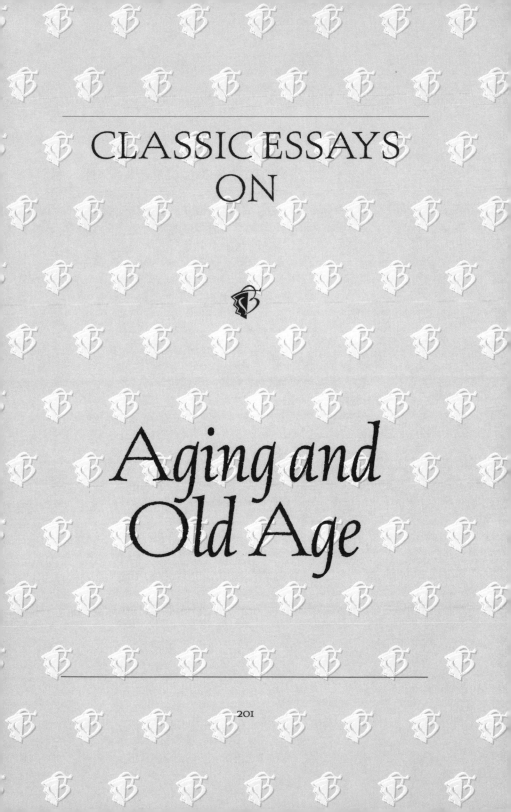

Aging and Old Age

Of Youth
and Age

FRANCIS
BACON

Francis Bacon (1561–1626) was born in London, educated at Trinity College in Cambridge, and trained for the legal profession at Gray's Inn. During his life, he served as solicitor general and lord high chancellor of England. Bacon became Baron Verulam in 1618 and Viscount St. Albans in 1621. While sitting on the judicial bench, he was convicted by Parliament of having accepted bribes. His reputation as an important figure in the emergence of Western thought is the result of his philosophical texts, *The Advancement of Learning* (1605), *Novum Organum* (1620), and *De Augmentis Scientiarum* (1623). These books reflect the change in thinking in the seventeenth century from Aristotelian logic, which favors deductive reasoning, to the inductive approach, which was employed by the physical sciences. Bacon is also the author of *Essayes* (1597), which offers his perspective on a number of topics, from love and marriage to studies and human values. An enlarged edition of the book appeared in 1612, and a final collection was published in 1625, numbering fifty-eight essays. Bacon's short, compact, and rather impersonal essays introduced a distinct version of the genre, one many writers have modeled their work after. In the following selection, taken from *Essayes*, Bacon ponders youth and aging.

1   A man that is young in years may be old in hours, if he have
lost no time. But that happeneth rarely. Generally, youth is like
the first cogitations, not so wise as the second. For there is a
youth in thoughts as well as in ages. And yet the invention of
young men is more lively than that of old, and imaginations
stream into their minds better, and as it were more divinely.
Natures that have much heat, and great and violent desires and
perturbations, are not ripe for action till they have passed the
meridian of their years: as it was with Julius Caesar, and Septimius
Severus. Of the latter of whom it is said, *Juventutem egit erroribus,
imo furoribus, plenam:*[1] and yet he was the ablest emperor, almost,
of all the list. But reposed natures may do well in youth. As it
is seen in Augustus Caesar, Cosmus, Duke of Florence, Gaston
de Foix,[2] and others. On the other side, heat and vivacity in
age is an excellent composition[3] for business. Young men are fitter
to invent than to judge, fitter for execution than for counsel, and
fitter for new projects than for settled business. For the experience
of age, in things that fall within the compass of it, directeth them,
but in new things abuseth[4] them. The errors of young men are
the ruin of business; but the errors of aged men amount but to
this, that more might have been done, or sooner. Young men,
in the conduct and manage of actions, embrace more than they
can hold; stir more than they can quiet; fly to the end, without
consideration of the means and degrees; pursue some few principles
which they have chanced upon absurdly; care not to innovate,
which draws unknown inconveniences; use extreme remedies at
first; and, that which doubleth all errors, will not acknowledge
or retract them; like an unready horse that will neither stop nor
turn. Men of age object too much, consult too long, adventure
too little, repent too soon, and seldom drive business home to
the full period, but content themselves with a mediocrity of success.
Certainly it is good to compound employments of both; for that

1. He passed a youth full of folly, or rather of madness (from Spartianus, *Life of
   Severus*, II).
2. Duke of Nemours, nephew of Louis XII of France.
3. Temperament.
4. Misdirects.

will be good for the present, because the virtues of either age
may correct the defects of both; and good for succession, that
young men may be learners while men in age are actors; and,
lastly, good for extern accidents, because authority followeth old
men, and favour and popularity youth. But for the moral part,
perhaps youth will have the pre-eminence, as age hath for the
politic. A certain rabbin, upon the text, *Your young men shall see
visions, and your old men shall dream dreams*,[5] inferreth that young
men are admitted nearer to God than old, because vision is a
clearer revelation than a dream. And certainly, the more a man
drinketh of the world, the more it intoxicateth; and age doth
profit rather in the powers of understanding than in the virtues
of the will and affections. There be some have an over-early
ripeness in their years, which fadeth betimes. These are, first, such
as have brittle wits, the edge whereof is soon turned; such as was
Hermogenes the rhetorician,[6] whose books are exceeding subtle,
who afterwards waxed stupid. A second sort is of those that have
some natural dispositions which have better grace in youth than
in age, such as is a fluent and luxuriant speech, which becomes
youth well, but not age: so Tully[7] saith of Hortensius,[8] *Idem
manebat, neque idem docebat.*[9] The third is of such as take too
high a strain at the first, and are magnanimous more than tract
of years can uphold. As was Scipio Africanus,[10] of whom Livy
saith in effect, *Ultima primis cedebant.*[11]

5. Joel 2.28. The *rabbin*, or rabbi, is Abravanel.
6. Greek rhetorician of the second century A.D. who is said to have lost his
   memory at the age of twenty-five.
7. Cicero.
8. Roman orator and at one time a rival of Cicero.
9. He remained the same when the same (style) no longer became him (Cicero,
   Brutus, XCV).
10. Roman general. According to Livy, *History* XXXVIII.53, Scipio was more
    suited to war than the peaceful times of his later years.
11. His last actions were not equal to his first (from Ovid, *Heroides*, IX.23).

Discussion Questions

1. Summarize the main points of Bacon's essay.
2. In small groups, discuss whether Bacon is more sympathetic to youth or to older people. Be sure to identify specific passages that lead you to your response.
3. What does Bacon mean when he states, "A man that is young in years may be old in hours, if he have lost no time"?
4. Do you agree with Bacon in what he cites as the errors of youth and those of aged men? Why or why not?
5. Explain the meaning of the quote, "Your young men shall see visions, and your old men shall dream dreams."
6. How valid are Bacon's claims regarding the virtues of young and old men? Explain.

Writing Assignments

1. Write a journal entry examining how Bacon's essay is still relevant.
2. Write a letter to Bacon in which you support or refute his claims regarding youth and old men.
3. Although Bacon writes about the male gender, one could say his observations apply equally to women. In an essay, explain how this is possible.

Of Age

MICHEL DE
MONTAIGNE

Michel de Montaigne (1533–1592) was born in Périgord, France. The son of affluent parents, Montaigne studied law and worked as a civil servant, serving first as counsellor in the Parlement of Bordeaux and then as mayor of Bordeaux in 1551. In 1571, Montaigne returned to his estate in Dordogne to devote the rest of his life to reading and writing. Montaigne is most noted for being the originator of the essay. He is the author of two volumes of *Essais* (1580), which were later revised in 1588 along with a third volume. In 1595, a posthumous version of the three books was published. The essay, as envisioned and written by Montaigne, is an open genre, not restricted by form or content; rather, Montaigne's vision was what the word *essay* actually means: a trying out, an experiment in which the writer discovers meaning through the actual process of writing. An adaptable genre, the essay can be a narrative, a description, an autobiography, an informal argument, or a reflective musing on a topic. The essay, as Montaigne envisioned it, became a popular genre, and writers in the centuries to follow have experimented with and modified the form but never lost sight of Montaigne's original idea. In the following selection from the first book of *Essais*, Montaigne explores his views on aging.

1   I cannot accept the way in which we establish the duration of our life. I see that the sages, as compared with popular opinion, make it a great deal shorter. "What," said the younger Cato to those who wanted to keep him from killing himself, "am I now at an age when I can be reproached for abandoning life too soon?" Yet he was only forty-eight. He regarded that age as quite ripe and quite advanced considering how few men reach it. And those who delude themselves with the idea that some course or other which they call natural promise a few years beyond, might do so properly if they had a privilege to exempt them from the many accidents to which we are all naturally subject, and which can interrupt this course that they promise themselves.

2   What an idle fancy it is to expect to die of a decay of powers brought on by extreme old age, and to set ourselves this term for our duration, since that is the rarest of all deaths and the least customary! We call alone natural, as if it were contrary to nature to see a man break his neck by a fall, be drowned in a shipwreck, or be snatched away by the plague or a pleurisy, and as if our ordinary condition did not expose us to all these mishaps. Let us not flatter ourselves with these fine words: we ought perhaps rather to call natural what is general, common, and universal.

3   Death of old age is a rare, singular, and extraordinary death, and hence less natural than the others; it is the last and ultimate sort of death; the further it is from us, the less it is to be hoped for. It is indeed the bourn beyond which we shall not go, and which the law of nature has prescribed as not to be passed; but it is a very rare privilege of hers to make us last that long. It is an exemption which she grants by special favor to a single person in the space of two or three centuries, relieving him of the misfortunes and difficulties that she has cast in the way of others during this long period.

4   Thus my idea is to consider the age we have reached as one few people reach. Since in the ordinary course of things men do not come thus far, it is a sign that we are well along. And since we have passed the customary limits which are the true measure of our life, we must not hope to go much further. Having escaped so many occasions of dying, at which we see everyone stumble, we must recognize that an extraordinary fortune, and one out of the usual, like the one that is keeping us going, is not due to last much longer.

5   It is a defect in the very laws to hold this false idea: they have it that a man is not capable of the management of his estate until he

is twenty-five, whereas he will hardly keep the management of his life that long. Augustus cut off five years from the ancient Roman ordinances, and declared that it was enough for those assuming the office of judge to be thirty. Servius Tullius released the knights who had passed forty-seven from service in war; Augustus set this back to forty-five. To send men back into retirement before the age of fifty-five or sixty seems not very reasonable to me. I should be of the opinion that our employment and occupation should be extended as far as possible, for the public welfare; I find the fault in the other direction, that of not putting us to work soon enough. Augustus had been universal judge of the world at nineteen, and yet would have a man be thirty in order to pass judgment on the position of a gutter.

6   As for me, I think our souls are as developed at twenty as they are ever to be, and give the promise of all they ever can do. No soul which at that age has not given very evident earnest of its strength has given proof of it later. The natural qualities and virtues give notice within that term, or never, of whatever vigor or beauty they possess:

> If the thorn will not prick at birth,
> It never will prick on earth,

they say in Dauphiné.

7   If I were to enumerate all the beautiful human actions, of whatever kind, that have come to my knowledge, I should think I would find that the greater part were performed, both in ancient times and in our own, before the age of thirty, rather than after. Yes, often even in the lives of the same men.

8   May I not say that with all assurance about those of Hannibal and of Scipio, his great adversary? They lived a good half of their life on the glory acquired in their youth: great men afterward in comparison with all others, but by no means in comparison with themselves.

9   As for me, I hold it as certain that since that age my mind and my body have rather shrunk than grown, and gone backward rather than forward. It is possible that in those who employ their time well, knowledge and experience grow with living; but vivacity, quickness, firmness, and other qualities much more our own, more important and essential, wither and languish.

When age has crushed the body with its might,
The limbs collapse with weakness and decay,
The judgment limps, and mind and speech give
way.

LUCRETIUS

Sometimes it is the body that first surrenders to age, sometimes,
too, it is the mind; and I have seen enough whose brains were
enfeebled before their stomach and legs; and inasmuch as this is
a malady hardly perceptible to the sufferer and obscure in its
symptoms, it is all the more dangerous. For the time, I complain
of the laws, not that they leave us at work too long, but that
they set us to work too late. It seems to me that considering the
frailty of our life and how many ordinary natural reefs it is exposed
to, we should not allot so great a part of it to birth, idleness,
and apprenticeship.

Discussion Questions

1. In small groups, discuss the following statement: Although this
   essay was written in the sixteenth century, its main point is still
   relevant to life in the latter part of the twentieth century.
2. In paragraph 9, Montaigne observes, ". . . I hold it as certain
   that since that age my mind and my body have rather shrunk
   than grown. . . ." Do you think this "process" represents most
   people's experiences? Why or why not?
3. Do you think the body or the mind is the first to "surrender to
   age"? Explain.
4. Why does Montaigne state in the last paragraph that "we should
   not allot so great a part of it [life] to birth, idleness, and apprenticeship"? Do you agree? Why or why not?
5. Is Montaigne more optimistic or pessimistic about old age?
   Explain.

Writing Assignments

1. Write a journal entry in which you examine the benefits of old age.
2. Write a letter to Montaigne describing how old age is viewed in contemporary society.
3. Unlike in the United States, in some cultures old age is honored. What do you think accounts for Americans' attitudes toward the elderly? Explore that question in an essay.

The Shadow of Years

W. E. B. DU BOIS

W. E. B. (William Edward Burghardt) Du Bois (1868–1963) was born in Massachusetts. The descendant of a French Huguenot and an African slave, Du Bois earned his Ph.D. from Harvard University in 1895. A Greek and Latin scholar, he taught history and economics at Atlanta University where he actively sought social justice for African Americans. In 1909, Du Bois helped to found the National Association for the Advancement of Colored People (NAACP). Du Bois was also the publisher and editor of *Moon Illustrated Weekly* and editor-in-chief of *Phylon*. He began his most important work in journalism in 1910 when he began his twenty-four year editorship on *The Crisis*, the journal of the NAACP. His articles, many of which appeared in that journal, reflect his training in history, his interest in social issues, and his literary style of writing. Du Bois often used autobiography as a way to address social and political issues in his writing. A voluminous writer, Du Bois is the author of *The Souls of Black Folk: Essays and Sketches* (1903); *John Brown* (1909); a novel entitled *The Quest of the Fleece* (1911); *The Negro* (1915); *The Gift of Black Folk: The Negroes in the Making of America* (1924); a novel entitled *Dark Princess: A Romance* (1928); *Black Reconstruction in America* (1935); *Black Folk, Then and Now: An Essay in the History and Sociology of the Negro Race* (1939); an autobiography entitled *Dusk at Dawn: An Essay toward an Autobiography of a Race Concept* (1940); *Color and Democracy: Colonies and Peace* (1945); *In Battle for Peace: The Story of My 83rd Birthday* (1952); *The Ordeal of Mansart* (1957); *Worlds of Color* (1961); and *The Autobiography: A Soliloquy on Viewing My Life from the Last Decade of Its First Century* (posthumous, 1968). In 1958, Du Bois, a fervent and well-respected social activist, was awarded the prestigious Lenin International Peace Prize. The following essay is the introduction to *Darkwater: Voices within the Veil* (1920). Its forthright reporting of autobiographical details coupled with sociological, political undertones makes the essay a classic.

1   I was born by a golden river and in the shadow of two great hills, five years after the Emancipation Proclamation. The house was quaint, with clapboards running up and down, neatly trimmed, and there were five rooms, a tiny porch, a rosy front yard, and unbelievably delicious strawberries in the rear. A South Carolinian, lately come to the Berkshire Hills, owned all this—tall, thin, and black, with golden earrings, and given to religious trances. We were his transient tenants for the time.

2   My own people were part of a great clan. Fully two hundred years before, Tom Burghardt had come through the western pass from the Hudson with his Dutch captor, "Coenraet Burghardt," sullen in his slavery and achieving his freedom by volunteering for the Revolution at a time of sudden alarm. His wife was a little, black, Bantu woman, who never became reconciled to this strange land; she clasped her knees and rocked and crooned:

> Do bana coba—gene me, gene me!
> Ben d'nuli, ben d'le—

3   Tom died about 1787, but of him came many sons, and one, Jack, who helped in the War of 1812. Of Jack and his wife, Violet, was born a mighty family, splendidly named: Harlow and Ira, Cloë, Lucinda, Maria, and Othello! I dimly remember my grandfather, Othello—or "Uncle Tallow,"—a brown man, strong-voiced and redolent with tobacco, who sat stiffly in a great high chair because

his hip was broken. He was probably a bit lazy and given to wassail. At any rate, grandmother had a shrewish tongue and often berated him. This grandmother was Sarah—"Aunt Sally"—a stern, tall, Dutch-African woman, beak-nosed, but beautiful-eyed and golden-skinned. Ten or more children were theirs, of whom the youngest was Mary, my mother.

4   Mother was dark shining bronze, with a tiny ripple in her black hair, black-eyed, with a heavy, kind face. She gave one the impression of infinite patience, but a curious determination was concealed in her softness. The family were small farmers on Egremont Plain, between Great Barrington and Sheffield, Massachusetts. The bits of land were too small to support the great families born on them and we were always poor. I never remember being cold or hungry, but I do remember that shoes and coal, and sometimes flour, caused mother moments of anxious thought in winter, and a new suit was an event!

5   At about the time of my birth economic pressure was transmuting the family generally from farmers to "hired" help. Some revolted and migrated westward, others went cityward as cooks and barbers. Mother worked for some years at house service in Great Barrington, and after a disappointed love episode with a cousin, who went to California, she met and married Alfred Du Bois and went to town to live by the golden river where I was born.

6   Alfred, my father, must have seemed a splendid vision in that little valley under the shelter of those mighty hills. He was small and beautiful of face and feature, just tinted with the sun, his curly hair chiefly revealing his kinship to Africa. In nature he was a dreamer,— romantic, indolent, kind, unreliable. He had in him the making of a poet, an adventurer, or a Beloved Vagabond, according to the life that closed round him; and that life gave him all too little. His father, Alexander Du Bois, cloaked under a stern, austere demeanor a passionate revolt against the world. He, too, was small, but squarish. I remember him as I saw him first, in his home in New Bedford,— white hair close-cropped; a seamed, hard face, but high in tone, with a gray eye that could twinkle or glare.

7   Long years before him Louis XIV drove two Huguenots, Jacques and Louis Du Bois, into wild Ulster County, New York. One of them in the third or fourth generation had a descendant, Dr. James Du Bois, a gay, rich bachelor, who made his money in the Bahamas, where he and the Gilberts had plantations. There he took a beautiful little

mulatto slave as his mistress, and two sons were born: Alexander in
1803 and John, later. They were fine, straight, clear-eyed boys, white
enough to "pass." He brought them to America and put Alexander in
the celebrated Cheshire School, in Connecticut. Here he often visited
him, but one last time, fell dead. He left no will, and his relations made
short shrift of these sons. They gathered in the property, apprenticed
grandfather to a shoemaker; then dropped him.

8   Grandfather took his bitter dose like a thoroughbred. Wild as was
his inner revolt against this treatment, he uttered no word against
the thieves and made no plea. He tried his fortunes here and in Haiti,
where, during his short, restless sojourn, my own father was born.
Eventually, grandfather became chief steward on the passenger boat
between New York and New Haven; later he was a small merchant
in Springfield; and finally he retired and ended his days at New
Bedford. Always he held his head high, took no insults, made few
friends. He was not a "Negro"; he was a man! Yet the current was
too strong even for him. Then even more than now a colored man
had colored friends or none at all, lived in a colored world or lived
alone. A few fine, strong, black men gained the heart of this silent,
bitter man in New York and New Haven. If he had scant sympathy
with their social clannishness, he was with them in fighting discrimination. So, when the white Episcopalians of Trinity Parish, New
Haven, showed plainly that they no longer wanted black folk as
fellow Christians, he led the revolt which resulted in St. Luke's Parish,
and was for years its senior warden. He lies dead in the Grove Street
Cemetery, beside Jehudi Ashmun.

9   Beneath his sternness was a very human man. Slyly he wrote
poetry,—stilted, pleading things from a soul astray. He loved women
in his masterful way, marrying three beautiful wives in succession
and clinging to each with a certain desperate, even if unsympathetic,
affection. As a father he was, naturally, a failure,—hard, domineering,
unyielding. His four children reacted characteristically: one was until
past middle life a thin spinster, the mental image of her father; one
died; one passed over into the white world and her children's children
are now white, with no knowledge of their Negro blood; the fourth,
my father, bent before grandfather, but did not break—better if he
had. He yielded and flared back, asked forgiveness and forgot why,
became the harshly-held favorite, who ran away and rioted and
roamed and loved and married my brown mother.

10   So with some circumstance having finally gotten myself born, with
a flood of Negro blood, a strain of French, a bit of Dutch, but, thank
God! no "Anglo-Saxon," I come to the days of my childhood.

11   They were very happy. Early we moved back to Grandfather Burghardt's home,—I barely remember its stone fireplace, big kitchen,
and delightful woodshed. Then this house passed to other branches
of the clan and we moved to rented quarters in town,—to one
delectable place "upstairs," with a wide yard full of shrubbery, and
a brook; to another house abutting a railroad, with infinite interests
and astonishing playmates; and finally back to the quiet street on
which I was born,—down a long lane and in a homely, cozy cottage,
with a living-room, a tiny sitting-room, a pantry, and two attic bedrooms. Here mother and I lived until she died, in 1884, for father
early began his restless wanderings. I last remember urgent letters
for us to come to New Milford, where he had started a barber shop.
Later he became a preacher. But mother no longer trusted his dreams,
and he soon faded out of our lives into silence.

12   From the age of five until I was sixteen I went to school on the
same grounds,—down a lane, into a widened yard, with a big choke-
cherry tree and two buildings, wood and brick. Here I got acquainted
with my world, and soon had my criterions of judgment.

13   Wealth had no particular lure. On the other hand, the shadow of
wealth was about us. That river of my birth was golden because of
the woolen and paper waste that soiled it. The gold was theirs, not
ours; but the gleam and glint was for all. To me it was all in order
and I took it philosophically. I cordially despised the poor Irish and
South Germans, who slaved in the mills, and annexed the rich and
well-to-do as my natural companions. Of such is the kingdom of
snobs!

14   Most of our townfolk were, naturally, the well-to-do, shading
downward, but seldom reaching poverty. As playmate of the children
I saw the homes of nearly every one, except a few immigrant New
Yorkers, of whom none of us approved. The homes I saw impressed
me, but did not overwhelm me. Many were bigger than mine, with
newer and shinier things, but they did not seem to differ in kind. I
think I probably surprised my hosts more than they me, for I was
easily at home and perfectly happy and they looked to me just like
ordinary people, while my brown face and frizzled hair must have
seemed strange to them.

15   Yet I was very much one of them. I was a center and sometimes the leader of the town gang of boys. We were noisy, but never very bad,—and, indeed, my mother's quiet influence came in here, as I realize now. She did not try to make me perfect. To her I was already perfect. She simply warned me of a few things, especially saloons. In my town the saloon was the open door to hell. The best families had their drunkards and the worst had little else.

16   Very gradually,—I cannot now distinguish the steps, though here and there I remember a jump or a jolt—but very gradually I found myself assuming quite placidly that I was different from other children. At first I think I connected the difference with a manifest ability to get my lessons rather better than most and to recite with a certain happy, almost taunting, glibness, which brought frowns here and there. Then, slowly, I realized that some folks, a few, even several, actually considered my brown skin a misfortune; once or twice I became painfully aware that some human beings even thought it a crime. I was not for a moment daunted,—although, of course, there were some days of secret tears—rather I was spurred to tireless effort. If they beat me at anything, I was grimly determined to make them sweat for it! Once I remember challenging a great, hard farmer-boy to battle, when I knew he could whip me; and he did. But ever after, he was polite.

17   As time flew I felt not so much disowned and rejected as rather drawn up into higher spaces and made part of a mightier mission. At times I almost pitied my pale companions, who were not of the Lord's anointed and who saw in their dreams no splendid quests of golden fleeces.

18   Even in the matter of girls my peculiar phantasy asserted itself. Naturally, it was in our town voted bad form for boys of twelve and fourteen to show any evident weakness for girls. We tolerated them loftily, and now and then they played in our games, when I joined in quite as naturally as the rest. It was when strangers came, or summer boarders, or when the oldest girls grew up that my sharp senses noted little hesitancies in public and searchings for possible public opinion. Then I flamed! I lifted my chin and strode off to the mountains, where I viewed the world at my feet and strained my eyes across the shadow of the hills.

19   I was graduated from high school at sixteen, and I talked of "Wendell Phillips." This was my first sweet taste of the world's applause. There were flowers and upturned faces, music and

marching, and there was my mother's smile. She was lame, then, and a bit drawn, but very happy. It was her great day and that very year she lay down with a sigh of content and has not yet awakened. I felt a certain gladness to see her, at last, at peace, for she had worried all her life. Of my own loss I had then little realization. That came only with the after-years. Now it was the choking gladness and solemn feel of wings! At last, I was going beyond the hills and into the world that beckoned steadily.

20   There came a little pause,—a singular pause. I was given to understand that I was almost too young for the world. Harvard was the goal of my dreams, but my white friends hesitated and my colored friends were silent. Harvard was a mighty conjure-word in that hill town, and even the mill owners' sons had aimed lower. Finally it was tactfully explained that the place for me was in the South among my people. A scholarship had been already arranged at Fisk, and my summer earnings would pay the fare. My relatives grumbled, but after a twinge I felt a strange delight! I forgot, or did not thoroughly realize, the curious irony by which I was not looked upon as a real citizen of my birth-town, with a future and a career, and instead was being sent to a far land among strangers who were regarded as (and in truth were) "mine own people."

21   Ah! the wonder of that journey, with its faint spice of adventure, as I entered the land of slaves; the never-to-be-forgotten marvel of that first supper at Fisk with the world "colored" and opposite two of the most beautiful beings God ever revealed to the eyes of seventeen. I promptly lost my appetite, but I was deliriously happy!

22   As I peer back through the shadow of my years, seeing not too clearly, but through the thickening veil of wish and after-thought, I seem to view my life divided into four distinct parts: the Age of Miracles, the Days of Disillusion, the Discipline of Work and Play, and the Second Miracle Age.

23   The Age of Miracles began with Fisk and ended with Germany. I was bursting with the joy of living. I seemed to ride in conquering might. I was captain of my soul and master of fate! I *willed* to do! It was done. I *wished!* The wish came true.

24   Now and then out of the void flashed the great sword of hate to remind me of the battle. I remember once, in Nashville, brushing by accident against a white woman on the street. Politely and eagerly I raised my hat to apologize. That was thirty-five years ago. From

that day to this I have never knowingly raised my hat to a Southern white woman.

25   I suspect that beneath all of my seeming triumphs there were many failures and disappointments, but the realities loomed so large that they swept away even the memory of other dreams and wishes. Consider, for a moment, how miraculous it all was to a boy of seventeen, just escaped from a narrow valley: I willed and lo! my people came dancing about me,—riotous in color, gay in laughter, full of sympathy, need, and pleading; darkly delicious girls—"colored" girls—sat beside me and actually talked to me while I gazed in tongue-tied silence or babbled in boastful dreams. Boys with my own experiences and out of my own world, who knew and understood, wrought out with me great remedies. I studied eagerly under teachers who bent in subtle sympathy, feeling themselves some shadow of the Veil and lifting it gently that we darker souls might peer through to other worlds.

26   I willed and lo! I was walking beneath the elms of Harvard,—the name of allurement, the college of my youngest, wildest visions! I needed money; scholarships and prizes fell into my lap,—not all I wanted or strove for, but all I needed to keep in school. Commencement came and standing before governor, president, and grave, gowned men, I told them certain astonishing truths, waving my arms and breathing fast! They applauded with what now seems to me uncalled-for fervor, but then! I walked home on pink clouds of glory! I asked for a fellowship and got it. I announced my plan of studying in Germany, but Harvard had no more fellowships for me. A friend, however, told me of the Slater Fund and how the Board was looking for colored men worth educating. No thought of modest hesitation occurred to me. I rushed at the chance.

27   The trustees of the Slater Fund excused themselves politely. They acknowledged that they had in the past looked for colored boys of ability to educate, but, being unsuccessful, they had stopped searching. I went at them hammer and tongs! I plied them with testimonials and mid-year and final marks. I intimated plainly, impudently, that they were "stalling"! In vain did the chairman, Ex-President Hayes, explain and excuse. I took no excuses and brushed explanations aside. I wonder now that he did not brush me aside, too, as a conceited meddler, but instead he smiled and surrendered.

28   I crossed the ocean in a trance. Always I seemed to be saying, "It is not real; I must be dreaming!" I can live it again—the little, Dutch

ship—the blue waters—the smell of new-mown hay—Holland and
the Rhine. I saw the Wartburg and Berlin; I made the Harzreise and
climbed the Brocken; I saw the Hansa towns and the cities and dorfs
of South Germany; I saw the Alps at Berne, the Cathedral at Milan,
Florence, Rome, Venice, Vienna, and Pesth; I looked on the boundaries of Russia; and I sat in Paris and London.

29   On mountain and valley, in home and school, I met men and
women as I had never met them before. Slowly they became, not
white folks, but folks. The unity beneath all life clutched me. I
was not less fanatically a Negro, but "Negro" meant a greater,
broader sense of humanity and world-fellowship. I felt myself
standing, not against the world, but simply against American
narrowness and color prejudice, with the greater, finer world at
my back urging me on.

30   I builded great castles in Spain and lived therein. I dreamed and
loved and wandered and sang; then, after two long years, I dropped
suddenly back into "nigger"-hating America!

31   My Days of Disillusion were not disappointing enough to discourage me. I was still upheld by that fund of infinite faith, although
dimly about me I saw the shadow of disaster. I began to realize how
much of what I had called Will and Ability was sheer Luck! *Suppose*
my good mother had preferred a steady income from my child labor
rather than bank on the precarious dividend of my higher training?
Suppose that pompous old village judge, whose dignity we often
ruffled and whose apples we stole, had had his way and sent me
while a child to a "reform" school to learn a "trade"? *Suppose* Principal Hosmer had been born with no faith in "darkies," and instead
of giving me Greek and Latin had taught me carpentry and the
making of tin pans? *Suppose* I had missed a Harvard scholarship?
Suppose the Slater Board had then, as now, distinct ideas as to where
the education of Negroes should stop? Suppose *and* suppose! As I
sat down calmly on flat earth and looked at my life a certain great
fear seized me. Was I the masterful captain or the pawn of laughing
sprites? Who was I to fight a world of color prejudice? I raise my
hat to myself when I remember that, even with these thoughts, I
did not hesitate or waver; but just went doggedly to work, and
therein lay whatever salvation I have achieved.

32   First came the task of earning a living. I was not nice or hard to
please. I just got down on my knees and begged for work, anything

and anywhere. I wrote to Hampton, Tuskegee, and a dozen other places. They politely declined, with many regrets. The trustees of a backwoods Tennessee town considered me, but were eventually afraid. Then, suddenly, Wilberforce offered to let me teach Latin and Greek at $750 a year. I was overjoyed!

33   I did not know anything about Latin and Greek, but I did know of Wilberforce. The breath of that great name had swept the water and dropped into southern Ohio, where Southerners had taken their cure at Tawawa Springs and where white Methodists had planted a school; then came the little bishop, Daniel Payne, who made it a school of the African Methodists. This was the school that called me, and when re-considered offers from Tuskegee and Jefferson City followed, I refused; I was so thankful for that first offer.

34   I went to Wilberforce with high ideals. I wanted to help to build a great university. I was willing to work night as well as day. I taught Latin, Greek, English, and German. I helped in the discipline, took part in the social life, begged to be allowed to lecture on sociology, and began to write books. But I found myself against a stone wall. Nothing stirred before my impatient pounding! Or if it stirred, it soon slept again.

35   Of course, I was too impatient! The snarl of years was not to be undone in days. I set at solving the problem before I knew it. Wilberforce was a colored church-school. In it were mingled the problems of poorly-prepared pupils, an inadequately-equipped plant, the natural politics of bishoprics, and the provincial reactions of a country town loaded with traditions. It was my first introduction to a Negro world, and I was at once marvelously inspired and deeply depressed. I was inspired with the children,—had I not rubbed against the children of the world and did I not find here the same eagerness, the same joy of life, the same brains as in New England, France, and Germany? But, on the other hand, the ropes and myths and knots and hindrances; the thundering waves of the white world beyond beating us back; the scalding breakers of this inner world,—its currents and back eddies—its meanness and smallness—its sorrow and tragedy—its screaming farce!

36   In all this I was as one bound hand and foot. Struggle, work, fight as I would, I seemed to get nowhere and accomplish nothing. I had all the wild intolerance of youth, and no experience in human tangles. For the first time in my life I realized that there were limits

to my will to do. The Day of Miracles was past, and a long, gray road of dogged work lay ahead.

37   I had, naturally, my triumphs here and there. I defied the bishops in the matter of public extemporaneous prayer and they yielded. I bearded the poor, hunted president in his den, and yet was re-elected to my position. I was slowly winning a way, but quickly losing faith in the value of the way won. Was this the place to begin my life work? Was this the work which I was best fitted to do? What business had I, anyhow, to teach Greek when I had studied men? I grew sure that I had made a mistake. So I determined to leave Wilberforce and try elsewhere. Thus, the third period of my life began.

38   First, in 1896, I married—a slip of a girl, beautifully dark-eyed and thorough and good as a German housewife. Then I accepted a job to make a study of Negroes in Philadelphia for the University of Pennsylvania,—one year at six hundred dollars. How did I dare these two things? I do not know. Yet they spelled salvation. To remain at Wilberforce without doing my ideals meant spiritual death. Both my wife and I were homeless. I dared a home and a temporary job. But it was a different daring from the days of my first youth. I was ready to admit that the best of men might fail. I meant still to be captain of my soul, but I realized that even captains are not omnipotent in uncharted and angry seas.

39   I essayed a thorough piece of work in Philadelphia. I labored morning, noon, and night. Nobody ever reads that fat volume on "The Philadelphia Negro," but they treat it with respect, and that consoles me. The colored people of Philadelphia received me with no open arms. They had a natural dislike to being studied like a strange species. I met again and in different guise those curious cross-currents and inner social whirlings of my own people. They set me to groping. I concluded that I did not know so much as I might about my own people, and when President Bumstead invited me to Atlanta University the next year to teach sociology and study the American Negro, I accepted gladly, at a salary of twelve hundred dollars.

40   My real life work was done at Atlanta for thirteen years, from my twenty-ninth to my forty-second birthday. They were years of great spiritual upturning, of the making and unmaking of ideals, of hard work and hard play. Here I found myself. I lost most of my mannerisms. I grew more broadly human, made my closest and most holy

friendships, and studied human beings. I became widely-acquainted with the real condition of my people. I realized the terrific odds which faced them. At Wilberforce I was their captious critic. In Philadelphia I was their cold and scientific investigator, with microscope and probe. It took but a few years of Atlanta to bring me to hot and indignant defense. I saw the race-hatred of the whites as I had never dreamed of it before,—naked and unashamed! The faint discrimination of my hopes and intangible dislikes paled into nothing before this great, red monster of cruel oppression. I held back with more difficulty each day my mounting indignation against injustice and misrepresentation.

41   With all this came the strengthening and hardening of my own character. The billows of birth, love, and death swept over me. I saw life through all its paradox and contradiction of streaming eyes and mad merriment. I emerged into full manhood, with the ruins of some ideals about me, but with others planted above the stars; scarred and a bit grim, but hugging to my soul the divine gift of laughter and withal determined, even unto stubbornness, to fight the good fight.

42   At last, forbear and waver as I would, I faced the great Decision. My life's last and greatest door stood ajar. What with all my dreaming, studying, and teaching was I going to *do* in this fierce fight? Despite all my youthful conceit and bumptiousness, I found developed beneath it all a reticence and new fear of forwardness, which sprang from searching criticisms of motive and high ideals of efficiency; but contrary to my dream of racial solidarity and notwithstanding my deep desire to serve and follow and think, rather than to lead and inspire and decide, I found myself suddenly the leader of a great wing of people fighting against another and greater wing.

43   Nor could any effort of mine keep this fight from sinking to the personal plane. Heaven knows I tried. That first meeting of a knot of enthusiasts, at Niagara Falls, had all the earnestness of self-devotion. At the second meeting, at Harper's Ferry, it arose to the solemnity of a holy crusade and yet without and to the cold, hard stare of the world it seemed merely the envy of fools against a great man, Booker Washington.

44   Of the movement I was willy-nilly leader. I hated the role. For the first time I faced criticism and *cared*. Every ideal and habit of my life was cruelly misjudged. I who had always overstriven to give credit for good work, who had never consciously stooped to envy

was accused by honest colored people of every sort of small and petty jealousy, while white people said I was ashamed of my race and wanted to be white! And this of me, whose one life fanaticism had been belief in my Negro blood!

45   Away back in the little years of my boyhood I had sold the Springfield *Republican* and written for Mr. Fortune's *Globe*. I dreamed of being an editor myself some day. I am an editor. In the great, slashing days of college life I dreamed of a strong organization to fight the battles of the Negro race. The National Association for the Advancement of Colored People is such a body, and it grows daily. In the dark days at Wilberforce I planned a time when I could speak freely to my people and of them, interpreting between two worlds. I am speaking now. In the study at Atlanta I grew to fear lest my radical beliefs should so hurt the college that either my silence or the institution's ruin would result. Powers and principalities have not yet curbed my tongue and Atlanta still lives.

46   It all came—this new Age of Miracles—because a few persons in 1909 determined to celebrate Lincoln's Birthday properly by calling for the final emancipation of the American Negro. I came at their call. My salary even for a year was not assured, but it was the "Voice without reply." The result has been the National Association for the Advancement of Colored People and *The Crisis* and this book, which I am finishing on my Fiftieth Birthday.

47   Last year I looked death in the face and found its lineaments not unkind. But it was not my time. Yet in nature some time soon and in the fullness of days I shall die, quietly, I trust, with my face turned South and eastward; and, dreaming or dreamless, I shall, I am sure, enjoy death as I have enjoyed life.

Discussion Questions

1. In small groups, discuss what the title of this essay means.
2. Why does Du Bois present his rather lengthy family history? How does Du Bois sustain your interest in it?
3. How would you characterize Du Bois from what he writes in his essay?

4. What qualities do you think Du Bois inherited from his ancestors? What leads you to your answer?
5. Why, when facing death, do you think Du Bois "found its lineaments not unkind"?
6. What in his essay makes you believe (or disbelieve) Du Bois when he states in the last paragraph that "I shall, I am sure, enjoy death as I have enjoyed life"? Are you able to say the same thing? Why or why not?

Writing Assignments

1. If you could divide your life into distinct parts, as Du Bois did, what would they be? In a journal entry, name each part and explain its significance.
2. Imagine that you are a parent and write a letter to your child explaining how your ancestry has had an effect on the person you are today.
3. Write an essay in which you examine how an event in your life gave you a newfound perspective. Describe the event clearly so others can see what you experienced. Analyze any new understandings you reached.

The Ring of Time

E. B. WHITE

E. B. (Elwyn Brooks) White (1899–1985) grew up in New York City and graduated from Cornell University in 1921. He worked as a reporter for several New York news services and as a newspaper writer and a copywriter. White's writing was published by *The New Yorker* when the magazine was in its infancy. His work was so well received, he became the author of the highly sought after "Talk of the Town" section of the magazine. In 1937, he started "One Man's Meat," a monthly column for *Harper's* magazine. A prolific writer, White is most famous for his books of children's literature, which include *Stuart Little* (1945), *Charlotte's Web* (1952), and *The Trumpet of the Swan* (1970). Among his essay collections are *One Man's Meat* (1942), *Every Day is Saturday* (1934), *The Second Tree from the Corner* (1954), and *The Points of My Compass* (1962). Many students and teachers are familiar with *The Elements of Style* (1959), a small book on writing, which he edited for his professor from Cornell, William Strunk, Jr. White's many honors include the Gold Medal of the American Academy of Arts and Letters, a Presidential Medal of Freedom, and a National Medal for Literature. White's essays are noted for their perceptive insights, graceful style, and enduring ideas. In the following selection, White ruminates on the passage of time.

I

Fiddler Bayou, March 22, 1956

1   After the lions had returned to their cages, creeping angrily through the chutes, a little bunch of us drifted away and into an open doorway nearby, where we stood for a while in semidarkness, watching a big brown circus horse go harumphing around the practice ring. His trainer was a woman of about forty, and the two of them, horse and woman, seemed caught up in one of those desultory treadmills of afternoon from which there is no apparent escape. The day was hot, and we kibitzers were grateful to be briefly out of the sun's glare. The long rein, or tape by which the woman guided her charge counterclockwise in his dull career formed the radius of their private circle of which she was the revolving center; and she, too, stepped a tiny circumference of her own, in order to accommodate the horse and allow him his maximum scope. She had on a short-skirted costume and a conical straw hat. Her legs were bare and she wore high heels, which probed deep into the loose tanbark and kept her ankles in a state of constant turmoil. The great size and meekness of the horse, the repetitious exercise, the heat of the afternoon, all exerted a hypnotic charm that invited boredom; we spectators were experiencing a languor—we neither expected relief nor felt entitled to any. We had paid a dollar to get into the grounds, to be sure, but we had got our dollar's worth a few minutes before, when the lion trainer's whiplash had got caught around a toe of one of the lions. What more did we want for a dollar?

2   Behind me I heard someone say, "Excuse me, please," in a low voice. She was halfway into the building when I turned and saw her—a girl of sixteen or seventeen, politely threading her way through us onlookers who blocked the entrance. As she emerged in front of us, I saw that she was barefoot, her dirty little feet fighting the uneven ground. In most respects she was like any of two or three dozen showgirls you encounter if you wander about the winter quarters of Mr. John Ringling North's circus, in Sarasota—cleverly proportioned, deeply browned by the sun, dusty, eager, and almost naked. But her grave face and the naturalness of her manner gave her a sort of quick distinction and brought a new note into the gloomy

octagonal building where we had all cast our lot for a few moments. As soon as she had squeezed through the crowd, she spoke a word or two to the older woman, whom I took to be her mother, stepped to the ring, and waited while the horse coasted to a stop in front of her. She give the animal a couple of affectionate swipes on his enormous neck and then swung herself aboard. The horse immediately resumed his rocking canter, the woman gliding him on, chanting something that sounded like "Hop! Hop!"

3   In attempting to recapture this mild spectacle, I am merely acting as recording secretary for one of the oldest of societies—the society of those who, at one time or another, have surrendered, without even a show of resistance, to the bedazzlement of a circus rider. As a writing man, or secretary, I have always felt charged with the safekeeping of all unexpected items of worldly or unworldly enchantment, as though I might be held personally responsible if even a small one were to be lost. But it is not easy to communicate anything of this nature. The circus comes as close to being the world in microcosm as anything I know; in a way, it puts all the rest of show business in the shade. Its magic is universal and complex. Out of its wild disorder comes order; from its rank smell rises the good aroma of courage and daring; out of its preliminary shabbiness comes the final splendor. And buried in the familiar boasts of its advance agents lies the modesty of most of its people. For me the circus is at its best before it has been put together. It is at its best at certain moments when it comes to a point, as through a burning glass, in the activity and destiny of a single performer out of so many. One ring is always bigger than three. One rider, one aerialist, is always greater than six. In short, a man has to catch the circus unawares to experience its full impact and share its gaudy dream.

4   The ten-minute ride the girl took achieved—as far as I was concerned, who wasn't looking for it, and quite unbeknownst to her, who wasn't even striving for it—the thing that is sought by performers everywhere, on whatever stage, whether struggling in the tidal currents of Shakespeare or bucking the difficult motion of a horse. I somehow got the idea she was just cadging a ride, improving a shining ten minutes in the diligent way all serious artists seize free moments to hone the blade of their talent and keep themselves in trim. Her brief tour included only elementary

postures and tricks, perhaps because they were all she was capable
of, perhaps because her warmup at this hour was unscheduled
and the ring was not rigged for a real practice session. She swung
herself off and on the horse several times, gripping his mane. She
did a few knee-stands—or whatever they are called—dropping to
her knees and quickly bouncing back up on her feet again. Most
of the time she simply rode in a standing position, well aft on
the beast, her hands hanging easily at her sides, her head erect,
her straw-colored ponytail lightly brushing her shoulders, the blood
of exertion showing faintly through the tan of her skin. Twice
she managed a one-foot stance—a sort of ballet pose, with arms
outstretched. At one point the neck strap of her bathing suit
broke and she went twice around the ring in the classic attitude
of a woman making minor repairs to a garment. The fact that
she was standing on the back of a moving horse while doing this
invested the matter with a clownish significance that perfectly
fitted the spirit of the circus—jocund, yet charming. She rolled
the strap into a neat ball and stowed it inside her bodice while
the horse rocked and rolled beneath her in dutiful innocence. The
bathing suit proved as self-reliant as its owner and stood up well
enough without benefit of strap.

5   The richness of the scene was in its plainness, its natural
condition—of horse, of ring, of girl, even to the girl's bare feet
that gripped the bare back of her proud and ridiculous mount.
The enchantment grew not out of anything that happened or was
performed but out of something that seemed to go round and
around and around with the girl, attending her, a steady gleam
in the shape of a circle—a ring of ambition, of happiness, of
youth. (And the positive pleasures of equilibrium under difficulties.)
In a week or two, all would be changed, all (or almost all) lost:
the girl would wear makeup, the horse would wear gold, the ring
would be painted, the bark would be clean for the feet of the
horse, the girl's feet would be clean for the slippers that she'd
wear. All, all would be lost.

6   As I watched with the others, our jaws adroop, our eyes alight,
I became painfully conscious of the element of time. Everything
in the hideous old building seemed to take the shape of a circle,
conforming to the course of the horse. The rider's gaze, as she
peered straight ahead, seemed to be circular, as though bent by

force of circumstances; then time itself began running in circles, and so the beginning was where the end was, and the two were the same, and one thing ran into the next and time went round and around and got nowhere. The girl wasn't so young that she did not know the delicious satisfaction of having a perfectly behaved body and the fun of using it to do a trick most people can't do, but she was too young to know that time does not really move in a circle at all. I thought: "She will never be as beautiful as this again"—a thought that made me acutely unhappy—and in a flash my mind—(which is too much of a busybody to suit me) had projected her twenty-five years ahead, and she was now in the center of the ring, on foot, wearing a conical hat and high-heeled shoes, the image of the older woman, holding the long rein, caught in the treadmill of an afternoon long in the future. "She is at that enviable moment in life [I thought] when she believes she can go once around the ring, make one complete circuit, and at the end be exactly the same age as at the start." Everything in her movements, her expression, told you that for her the ring of time was perfectly formed, changeless, predictable, without beginning or end, like the ring in which she was traveling at this moment with the horse that wallowed under her. And then I slipped back into my trance, and time was circular again— time, pausing quietly with the rest of us, so as not to disturb the balance of a performer.

7   Her ride ended as casually as it had begun. The older woman stopped the horse, and the girl slid to the ground. As she walked toward us to leave, there was a quick, small burst of applause. She smiled broadly, in surprise and pleasure; then her face suddenly regained its gravity and she disappeared through the door.

8   It was been ambitious and plucky of me to attempt to describe what is indescribable, and I have failed, as I knew I would. But I have discharged my duty to my society, and besides, a writer, like an acrobat, must occasionally try a stunt that is too much for him. At any rate, it is worth reporting that long before the circus comes to town, its most notable performances have already been given. Under the bright lights of the finished show, a performer need only reflect the electric candle power that is directed upon him; but in the dark and dirty old training rings and in the makeshift cages, whatever light is generated, whatever

excitement, whatever beauty must come from original sources—
from internal fires of professional hunger and delight, from the
exuberance and gravity of youth. It is the difference between
planetary light and the combustion of stars.

II

9   The South is the land of the sustained sibilant. Everywhere, for the
appreciative visitor, the letter "s" insinuates itself in the scene: in the
sound of sea and sand, in the singing shell, in the heat of sun and sky,
in the sultriness of the gentle hours, in the siesta, in the stir of birds
and insects. In contrast to the softness of its music, the South is also
cruel and hard and prickly. A little striped lizard, flattened along the
sharp green bayonet of a yucca, wears in its tiny face and watchful eye
the pure look of death and violence. And all over the place, hidden at
the bottom of their small sandy craters, the ant lions lie in wait for the
ant that will stumble into their trap. (There are three kinds of lions in
this region: the lions of the circus, the ant lions, and the Lions of the
Tampa Lions Club, who roared their approval of segregation at a meeting the other day—all except one, a Lion named Monty Gurwit, who
declined to roar and thereby got his picture in the paper.)
10   The day starts on a note of despair; the sorrowing dove, alone on
its telephone wire, mourns the loss of night, weeps at the bright
perils of the unfolding day. But soon the mocking bird wakes and
begins an early rehearsal, setting the dove down by force of character,
running through a few slick imitations, and trying a couple of original
numbers into the bargain. The redbird takes it from there. Despair
gives way to good humor. The Southern dawn is a pale affair, usually,
quite different from our northern daybreak. It is a triumph of gradual-
ism; night turns to day imperceptibly, softly, with no theatrics. It is
subtle and undisturbing. As the first light seeps in through the blinds
I lie in bed half awake, despairing with the dove, sounding the A
for the brothers Alsop. All seems lost, all seems sorrowful. Then a
mullet jumps in the bayou outside the bedroom window. It falls
back into the water with a smart smack. I have asked several people

why the mullet incessantly jump and I have received a variety of answers. Some say the mullet jump to shake off a parasite that annoys them. Some say they jump for the love of jumping—as the girl on the horse seemed to ride for the love of riding (although she, too, like all artists, may have been shaking off some parasite that fastens itself to the creative spirit and can be got rid of only by fifty turns around a ring while standing on a horse).

11   In Florida at this time of year, the sun does not take command of the day until a couple of hours after it has appeared in the east. It seems to carry no authority at first. The sun and the lizard keep the same schedule; they bide their time until the morning has advanced a good long way before they come fully forth and strike. The cold lizard waits astride his warming leaf for the perfect moment; the cold sun waits in his nest of clouds for the crucial time.

12   On many days, the dampness of the air pervades all life, all living. Matches refuse to strike. The towel, hung to dry, grows wetter by the hour. The newspaper with its headlines about integration, wilts in your hand and falls limply into the coffee and the egg. Envelopes seal themselves. Postage stamps mate with one another as shamelessly as grasshoppers. But most of the time the days are models of beauty and wonder and comfort, with the kind sea stroking the back of the warm sand. At evening there are great flights of birds over the sea, where the light lingers; the gulls, the pelicans, the terns, the herons stay aloft for half an hour after land birds have gone to roost. They hold their ancient formations, wheel and fish over the Pass, enjoying the last of day like children playing outdoors after suppertime.

13   To a beachcomber from the North, which is my present status, the race problem has no pertinence, no immediacy. Here in Florida I am a guest in two houses—the house of the sun, the house of the State of Florida. As a guest, I mind my manners and do not criticize the customs of my hosts. It gives me a queer feeling though, to be at the center of the greatest social crisis of my time and see hardly a sign of it. Yet the very absence of signs seems to increase one's awareness. Colored people do not come to the public beach to bathe, because they would not be made welcome there; and they don't fritter away their time visiting the circus, because they have other things to do. A few of them turn up at the ballpark, where they occupy a separate but equal section of the left-field bleachers and watch Negro players on the visiting Braves team using the same bases as the white players, instead of separate (but

equal) bases. I have had only two small encounters with "color." A colored woman named Viola, who had been a friend of my wife's sister years ago showed up one day with some laundry of ours that she had consented to do for us and with the bundle she brought a bunch of nasturtiums, as a sort of natural accompaniment to the delivery of clean clothes. The flowers seemed a very acceptable thing and I was touched by them. We asked Viola about her daughter, and she said she was at Kentucky State College, studying voice.

14   The other encounter was when I was explaining to our cook, who is from Finland, the mysteries of bus travel in the American Southland. I showed her the bus stop, armed her with a timetable, and then, as a matter of duty mentioned the customs of the Romans. "When you get on the bus," I said, "I think you'd better sit in one of the front seats—the seats in back are for colored people." A look of great weariness came into her face, as it does when we use too many dishes, and she replied, "Oh, I know—isn't it silly!"

15   Her remark, coming as it did all the way from Finland and landing on this sandbar with a plunk, impressed me. The Supreme Court said nothing about silliness, but I suspect it may play more of a role than one might suppose. People are, if anything, more touchy about being thought silly than they are about being thought unjust. I note that one of the arguments in the recent manifesto of Southern Congressmen in support of the doctrine of "separate but equal" was that it had been founded on "common sense." The sense that is common to one generation is uncommon to the next. Probably the first slave ship, with Negroes lying in chains on its decks, seemed commonsensical to the owners who operated it and to the planters who patronized it. But such a vessel would not be in the realm of common sense today. The only sense that is common, in the long run, is the sense of change—and we all instinctively avoid it, and object to the passage of time, and would rather have none of it.

16   The Supreme Court decision is like the Southern sun, laggard in its early stages, biding its time. It has been the law in Florida for two years now, and the years have been like the hours of the morning before the sun has gathered its strength. I think the decision is as incontrovertible and warming as the sun, and, like the sun, will eventually take charge.

17   But there is certainly a great temptation in Florida to duck the passage of time. Lying in warm comfort by the sea, you receive

gratefully the gift of the sun, the gift of the South. This is true seduction. The day is a circle—morning, afternoon, and night. After a few days I was clearly enjoying the same delusion as the girl on the horse—that I could ride clear around the ring of day, guarded by wind and sun and sea and sand, and be not a moment older.

18   P.S. (April 1962). When I first laid eyes on Fiddler Bayou, it was wild land, populated chiefly by the little crabs that gave it its name, visited by wading birds and by an occasional fisherman. Today, houses ring the bayou, and part of the mangrove shore has been bulkheaded with a concrete wall. Green lawns stretch from patio to water's edge, and sprinklers make rainbows in the light. But despite man's encroachment, Nature manages to hold her own and assert her authority: high tides and high winds in the gulf sometimes send the sea crashing across the sand barrier, depositing its wrack on lawns and ringing everyone's front door bell. The birds and the crabs accommodate themselves quite readily to the changes that have taken place; every day brings herons to hunt around among the roots of the mangroves, and I have discovered that I can approach to within about eight feet of a Little Blue Heron simply by entering the water and swimming slowly toward him. Apparently he has decided that when I'm in the water, I am without guile—possibly even desirable, like a fish.

19   The Ringling circus has quit Sarasota and gone elsewhere for its hibernation. A few circus families still own homes in the town, and every spring the students at the high school put on a circus, to let off steam, work off physical requirements, and provide a promotional spectacle for Sarasota. At the drugstore you can buy a postcard showing the bed John Ringling slept in. Time has not stood still for anybody but the dead, and even the dead must be able to hear the acceleration of little sports cars and know that things have changed.

20   From the all-wise *New York Times*, which has the animal kingdom ever in mind, I have learned that one of the creatures most acutely aware of the passing of time is the fiddler crab himself. Tiny spots on his body enlarge during daytime hours, giving him the same color as the mudbank he explores and thus protecting him from his enemies. At night the spots shrink, his color fades, and he is almost invisible in the light of the moon. These changes are synchronized with the tides, so that each day they occur at a different hour. A

scientist who experimented with the crabs to learn more about the phenomenon discovered that even when they are removed from their natural environment and held in confinement, the rhythm of their bodily change continues uninterrupted, and they mark the passage of time in their laboratory prison, faithful to the tides in their fashion.

Discussion Questions

1. Explain the meaning of the essay's title.
2. In small groups, discuss what White's thesis is. Identify specific passages that lead you to your answer.
3. What responsibilities does White claim because he is a writer? Do most writers have similar responsibilities? Do you? Why or why not?
4. Explain the connection between the circus and White's awareness of time.
5. In paragraph 8, White admits to having failed in his attempt to "describe what is indescribable." How does this confession affect your interest in the essay and your respect of White as a writer?
6. Why does White break his essay into three parts? What links the parts? Comment on the effectiveness of this organization.

Writing Assignments

1. Write a journal entry that describes a moment in which you became "painfully conscious of the element of time."
2. In an essay, recount an incident that exemplifies order arising from disorder, much like White writes of the circus.
3. Write a paper supporting or refuting the idea that a certain species is more aware of the "passing of time" than others.

The View from 80

MALCOLM COWLEY

Malcolm Cowley (1898–1989) drove an ambulance during World War I, graduated from Harvard University in 1920, and returned to France with other American literary expatriates. A poet, literary critic, literary and social historian, and lecturer, Cowley was the editor of the *New Republic* and literary advisor for the Viking Press. Cowley is the author of a collection of poetry entitled *Blue Juniata* (1929), *And I Worked at the Writer's Trade* (1978), and *The Dream of the Golden Mountains: Remembering the 30s* (1980). His most famous works are *Exiles Return* (1934), extensively revised in 1951, which examines the literary scene of the 1920s, and *A Second Flowering: Works and Days of the Lost Generation* (1973), which analyzes the literary works of Hart Crane, e. e. cummings, John Dos Passos, William Faulkner, F. Scott Fitzgerald, Ernest Hemingway, and Thomas Wolfe. Cowley was awarded the Gold Medal of the American Academy of Arts and Letters in 1981. Upon being prompted by *Life* magazine to write an essay on turning eighty, Cowley wrote the following selection, a reflection on aging, which can serve as a "road map and guide" for people of all ages.

1   They gave me a party on my 80th birthday in August 1978. First there were cards, letters, telegrams, even a cable of congratulations or condolence; then there were gifts, mostly bottles; there was catered

food and finally a big cake with, for some reason, two candles (had I gone back to very early childhood?). I blew the candles out a little unsteadily. Amid the applause and clatter I thought about a former custom of the Northern Ojibwas when they lived on the shores of Lake Winnipeg. They were kind to their old people, who remembered and enforced the ancient customs of the tribe, but when an old person became decrepit, it was time for him to go. Sometimes he was simply abandoned, with a little food, on an island in the lake. If he deserved special honor, they held a tribal feast for him. The old man sang a death song and danced, if he could. While he was still singing, his son came from behind and brained him with a tomahawk.

2   That was quick, it was dignified, and I wonder whether it was any more cruel, essentially, than some of our civilized customs or inadvertencies in disposing of the aged. I believe in rites and ceremonies. I believe in big parties for special occasions such as an 80th birthday. It is a sort of belated bar mitzvah, since the 80-year-old, like a Jewish adolescent, is entering a new stage of life; let him (or her) undergo a *rite de passage*, with toasts and a cantor. Seventy-year-olds, or septuas, have the illusion of being middle-aged, even if they have been pushed back on a shelf. The 80-year-old, the octo, looks at the double-dumpling figure and admits that he is old. The last act has begun, and it will be the test of the play.

3   To enter the country of age is a new experience, different from what you supposed it to be. Nobody, man or woman, knows the country until he has lived in it and has taken out his citizenship papers. Here is my own report, submitted as a road map and guide to some of the principal monuments.

4   The new octogenarian feels as strong as ever when he is sitting back in a comfortable chair. He ruminates, he dreams, he remembers. He doesn't want to be disturbed by others. It seems to him that old age is only a costume assumed for those others; the true, the essential self is ageless. In a moment he will rise and go for a ramble in the woods, taking a gun along, or a fishing rod, if it is spring. Then he creaks to his feet, bending forward to keep his balance, and realizes that he will do nothing of the sort. The body and its surroundings have their messages for him, or only one message: "You are old." Here are some of the occasions on which he receives the message:

- when it becomes an achievement to do thoughtfully, step by step, what he once did instinctively
- when his bones ache
- when there are more and more little bottles in the medicine cabinet, with instructions for taking four times a day
- when he fumbles and drops his toothbrush (butterfingers)
- when his face has bumps and wrinkles, so that he cuts himself while shaving (blood on the towel)
- when year by year his feet seem farther from his hands
- when he can't stand on one leg and has trouble pulling on his pants
- when he hesitates on the landing before walking down a flight of stairs
- when he spends more time looking for things misplaced than he spends using them after he (or more often his wife) has found them
- when he falls asleep in the afternoon
- when it becomes harder to bear in mind two things at once
- when a pretty girl passes him in the street and he doesn't turn his head
- when he forgets names, even of people he saw last month ("Now I'm beginning to forget nouns," the poet Conrad Aiken said at 80)
- when he listens hard to jokes and catches everything but the snapper
- when he decides not to drive at night anymore
- when everything takes longer to do—bathing, shaving, getting dressed or undressed—but when time passes quickly, as if he were gathering speed while coasting downhill. The year from 79 to 80 is like a week when he was a boy.

5   Those are some of the intimate messages. "Put cotton in your ears and pebbles in your shoes," said a gerontologist, a member of that new profession dedicated to alleviating all maladies of old people except the passage of years. "Pull on rubber gloves. Smear Vaseline over your glasses, and there you have it: instant aging." Not quite. His formula omits the messages from the social world, which are louder, in most cases, than those from within. We start by growing old in other people's eyes, then slowly we come to share their judgment.

6   I remember a morning many years ago when I was backing
out of the parking lot near the railroad station in Brewster, New
York. There was a near collision. The driver of the other car
jumped out and started to abuse me; he had his fists ready. Then
he looked hard at me and said, "Why, you're an old man." He
got back into his car, slammed the door, and drove away, while
I stood there fuming. "I'm only 65," I thought. "He wasn't
driving carefully. I can still take care of myself in a car, or in a
fight, for that matter."

7   My hair was whiter—it may have been in 1974—when a young
woman rose and offered me her seat in a Madison Avenue bus. That
message was kind and also devastating. "Can't I even stand up?" I
thought as I thanked her and declined the seat. But the same thing
happened twice the following year, and the second time I gratefully
accepted the offer, though with a sense of having diminished myself.
"People are right about me," I thought while wondering why all
those kind gestures were made by women. Do men now regard
themselves as the weaker sex, not called upon to show consideration?
All the same it was a relief to sit down and relax.

8   A few days later I wrote a poem, "The Red Wagon," that belongs
in the record of aging:

> For his birthday they gave him a red express wagon
> with a driver's high seat and a handle that steered.
> His mother pulled him around the yard.
> "Giddyap," he said, but she laughed and went off
> to wash the breakfast dishes.
>
> "I wanta ride too," his sister said,
> and he pulled her to the edge of a hill.
> "Now, sister, go home and wait for me,
> but first give a push to the wagon."
> He climbed again to the high seat,
> this time grasping that handle-that-steered.
> The red wagon rolled slowly down the slope,
> then faster as it passed the schoolhouse
> and faster as it passed the store,
> the road still dropping away.
> Oh, it was fun.

But would it ever stop?
Would the road always go downhill?

The red wagon rolled faster.
Now it was in strange country.
It passed a white house he must have dreamed
about,
deep woods he had never seen,
a graveyard where, something told him, his sister
was buried.

Far below
the sun was sinking into a broad plain.

The red wagon rolled faster.
Now he was clutching the seat, not even trying to
steer.
Sweat clouded his heavy spectacles.
His white hair streamed in the wind.

9   Even before he or she is 80, the aging person may undergo another
identity crisis like that of adolescence. Perhaps there had also been
a middle-aged crisis, the male or the female menopause, but the rest
of adult life he had taken himself for granted, with his capabilities
and failings. Now, when he looks in the mirror, he asks himself, "Is
this really me?"—or he avoids the mirror out of distress at what it
reveals, those bags and wrinkles. In his new makeup he is called upon
to play a new role in a play that must be improvised. André Gide,
that long-lived man of letters, wrote in his journal, "My heart has
remained so young that I have the continual feeling of playing a
part, the part of the 70-year-old that I certainly am; and the infirmities
and weaknesses that reminded me of my age act like a prompter,
reminding me of my lines when I tend to stray. Then, like the good
actor I want to be, I go back into my role, and I pride myself on
playing it well."

10   In his new role the old person will find that he is tempted by new
vices, that he receives new compensations (not so widely known),
and that he may possibly achieve new virtues. Chief among these is
the heroic or merely obstinate refusal to surrender in the face of

time. One admires the ships that go down with all flags flying and the captain on bridge.

11   Among the vices of age are avarice, untidiness, and vanity, which last takes the form of a craving to be loved or simply admired. Avarice is the worst of those three. Why do so many old persons, men and women alike, insist on hoarding money when they have no prospect of using it and even when they have no heirs? They eat the cheapest food, buy no clothes, and live in a single room when they could afford better lodging. It may be that they regard money as a form of power; there is a comfort in watching it accumulate while other powers are dwindling away. How often we read of an old person found dead in a hovel, on a mattress partly stuffed with bankbooks and stock certificates! The bankbook syndrome, we call it in our family, which has never succumbed.

12   Untidiness we call the Langley Collyer syndrome. To explain, Langley Collyer was a former concert pianist who lived alone with his 70-year-old brother in a brownstone house on upper Fifth Avenue. The once fashionable neighborhood had become part of Harlem. Homer, the brother, had been an admiralty lawyer, but was now blind and partly paralyzed; Langley played for him and fed him on buns and oranges, which he thought would restore Homer's sight. He never threw away a daily paper because Homer, he said, might want to read them all. He saved other things as well and the house became filled with rubbish from roof to basement. The halls were lined on both sides with bundled newspapers, leaving narrow passageways in which Langley had devised booby traps to catch intruders.

13   On March 21, 1947, some unnamed person telephoned the police to report that there was a dead body in the Collyer house. The police broke down the front door and found the hall impassable; then they hoisted a ladder to a second-story window. Behind it, Homer was lying on the floor in a bathrobe; he had starved to death. Langley had disappeared. After some delay, the police broke into the basement, chopped a hole in the roof, and began throwing junk out of the house, top and bottom. It was 18 days before they found Langley's body, gnawed by rats. Caught in one of his own booby traps, he had died in a hallway just outside Homer's door. By that time the police had collected, and the Department of Sanitation had hauled away 120 tons of rubbish, including, besides the newspapers, 14 grand pianos and the parts of a dismantled Model T Ford.

14   Why do so many old people accumulate junk, not on the scale of Langley Collyer, but still in a dismaying fashion? Their tables are piled high with it, their bureau drawers are stuffed with it, their closet rods bend with the weight of clothes not worn for years. I suppose that the piling up is partly from lethargy and partly from feeling that everything once useful, including their own bodies, should be preserved. Others, though not so many, have such a fear of becoming Langley Collyers that they strive to be painfully neat. Every tool they own is in its place, though it will never be used again; every scrap of paper is filed away in alphabetical order. At last their immoderate neatness becomes another vice of age, if a milder one.

15   The vanity of older people is an easier weakness to explain, and to condone. With less to look forward to, they yearn for recognition of what they have been: the reigning beauty, the athlete, the soldier, the scholar. It is the beauties who have the hardest time. A portrait of themselves at twenty hangs on the wall, and they try to resemble it by making an extravagant use of creams, powders, and dyes. Being young at heart, they think they are merely revealing their essential persons. The athletes find shelves for their silver trophies, which are polished once a year. Perhaps a letter sweater lies wrapped in a bureau drawer. I remember one evening when a no-longer athlete had guests for dinner and tried to find his sweater. "Oh, that old thing," his wife said, "The moths got into it and I threw it away." The athlete sulked and his guests went home early.

16   But there are also pleasures of the body, or the mind, that are enjoyed by a greater number of older persons. Those pleasures include some that younger people find hard to appreciate. One of them is simply sitting still, like a snake on a sun-warmed stone, with a delicious feeling of indolence that was seldom attained in earlier years. A leaf flutters down; a cloud moves by inches across the horizon. At such moments the older person, completely relaxed, has become a part of nature—and a living part, with blood coursing through his veins. The future does not exist for him. He thinks, if he thinks at all, that life for younger persons is still a battle royal of each against each, but that now he has nothing more to win or lose. He is not so much above as outside the battle, as if he had assumed the uniform of some small neutral country, perhaps Liechtenstein or Andorra. From a distance he notes that some of the combatants, men or women, are jostling ahead—but why do they fight so hard

when the most they can hope for is a longer obituary? He can watch the scrounging and gouging, he can hear the shouts of exultation, the moans of the gravely wounded, and meanwhile he feels secure; nobody will attack him from ambush.

17   Age has other physical compensations besides the nirvana of dozing in the sun. A few of the simplest needs become a pleasure to satisfy. When an old woman in a nursing home was asked what she really liked to do, she answered in one word: "Eat." She might have been speaking for many of her fellows. Meals in a nursing home, however badly cooked, serve as climactic moments of the day. The physical essence of the pensioners is being renewed at an appointed hour; now they can go back to meditating or to watching TV while looking forward to the next meal. They can also look forward to sleep, which has become a definite pleasure, not the mere interruption it once had been.

18   Here I am thinking of old persons under nursing care. Others ferociously guard their independence, and some of them suffer less than one might expect from being lonely and impoverished. They can be rejoiced by visits and meetings, but they also have company inside their heads. Some of them are busiest when their hands are still. What passes through the minds of many is a stream of persons, images, phrases, and familiar tunes. For some that stream has contin- ued since childhood, but now it is deeper; it is their present and their past combined. At times they conduct silent dialogues with a vanished friend, and these are less tiring—often more rewarding— than spoken conversations. If inner resources are lacking, old persons living alone may seek comfort and a kind of companionship in the bottle. I should judge from the gossip of various neighborhoods that the outer suburbs from Boston to San Diego are full of secretly alcoholic widows. One of those widows, an old friend, was moved from her apartment into a retirement home. She left behind her a closet in which the floor was covered wall to wall with whiskey bottles. "Oh, those empty bottles!" she explained. "They were left by a former tenant."

19   Not whiskey or cooking sherry but simply giving up is the greatest temptation of age. It is something different from a stoical acceptance of infirmities, which is something to be admired.

20   The givers-up see no reason for working. Sometimes they lie in bed all day when moving about would still be possible, if difficult.

I had a friend, a distinguished poet, who surrendered in that fashion. The doctors tried to stir him to action, but he refused to leave his room. Another friend, once a successful artist, stopped painting when his eyes began to fail. His doctor make the mistake of telling him that he suffered from a fatal disease. He then lost interest in everything except the splendid Rolls-Royce, acquired in his prosperous days, that stood in the garage. Daily he wiped the dust from its hood. He couldn't drive it on the road any longer, but he used to sit in the driver's seat, start the motor, then back the Rolls out of the garage and drive it in again, back twenty feet and forward twenty feet; that was his only distraction.

21   I haven't the right to blame those who surrender, not being able to put myself inside their minds or bodies. Often they must have compelling reasons, physical or moral. Not only do they suffer from a variety of ailments, but also they are made to feel that they no longer have a function in the community. Their families and neighbors don't ask them for advice, don't really listen when they speak, don't call on them for efforts. One notes that there are not a few recoveries from apparent senility when that situation changes. If it doesn't change, old persons may decide that efforts are useless. I sympathize with their problems, but the men and women I envy are those who accept old age as a series of challenges.

22   For such persons, every new infirmity is an enemy to be outwitted, an obstacle to be overcome by force of will. They enjoy each little victory over themselves, and sometimes they win a major success. Renoir was one of them. He continued painting, and magnificently, for years after he was crippled by arthritis; the brush had to be strapped to his arm. "You don't need your hand to paint," he said. Goya was another of the unvanquished. At 72 he retired as an official painter of the Spanish court and decided to work only for himself. His later years were those of the famous "black paintings" in which he let his imagination run (and also of the lithographs, then a new technique). At 78 he escaped a reign of terror in Spain by fleeing to Bordeaux. He was deaf and his eyes were failing; in order to work he had to wear several pairs of spectacles, one over another, and then use a magnifying glass; but he was producing splendid work in a totally new style. At 80 he drew an ancient man propped on two sticks, with a mass of white hair and beard hiding his face and with the inscription "I am still learning."

23   "Eighty years old!" the great Catholic poet Paul Claudel wrote in his journal. "No eyes left, no ears, no teeth, no legs, no wind! And when all is said and done, how astonishingly well one does without them!"

Discussion Questions

1. Summarize Cowley's feelings about old age.
2. What age do you consider as "old"? What benefits and liabilities do you see of old age? Do you find one outweighing the other? Why?
3. How does Cowley's poem contribute to the essay?
4. Do you agree with Cowley's observation in paragraph 3, "To enter the country of age is a new experience, different from what you supposed it to be. Nobody, man or woman, knows the country until he has lived in it and has taken out his citizenship papers"? Why or why not?
5. What does this essay reveal about Cowley? Identify specific passages that support your response.
6. In small groups, discuss what Cowley's essay can teach young people about aging.
7. How would E. B. White respond to Cowley's essay?

Writing Assignments

1. Interview some elderly people about their lives as older people and write an essay in which you report on their attitudes toward age. From what you have learned from them, summarize what it is like to be an elderly person.
2. Unlike in the United States, people in countries such as Japan and China venerate old age. Write an essay that analyzes why American attitudes toward old age are so different from those of the Far East.
3. Write an essay detailing the problems attached to being young as Cowley addresses the problems of old age.
4. Many young people yearn to be older. Write a journal entry in which you project what your life will be like when you are older.

CLASSIC ESSAYS ON

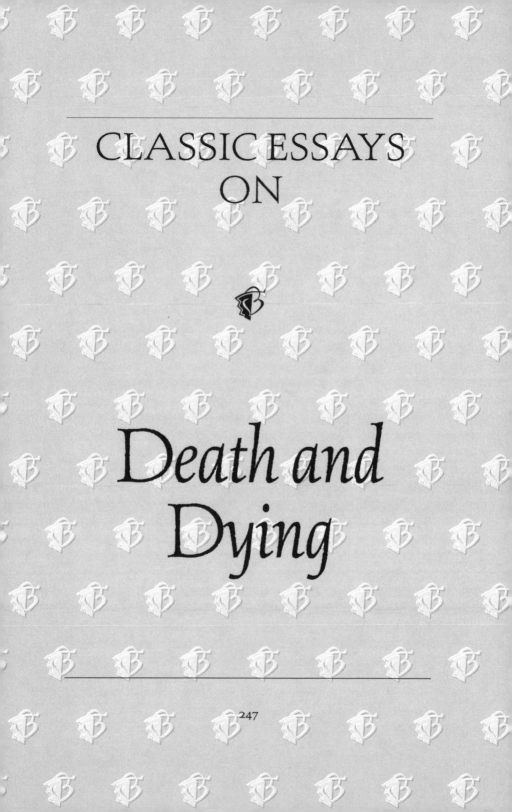

Death and Dying

The Death of a Friend

SAMUEL JOHNSON

Samuel Johnson (1709–1784) was born in Lichfield in Stafford-shire, England. Partial blindness did not prevent Johnson from developing a keen interest in books. As a youth, he spent a lot of time in his father's bookshop. In 1728, Johnson entered Pembroke College, Oxford, but left after only a year when he could no longer afford tuition. After a brief stint at teaching, Johnson moved to London in 1737 and worked for *The Gentle-man's Magazine*. In 1738, *London*, a satire, was published anony-mously to much acclaim. Also a writer of poetry, fiction, drama, biography, and literary criticism, Johnson wrote many works includ-ing *Life of Savage* (1744), *Observations on Macbeth* (1745), *Vision of Theodore* (1748), *The Vanity of Human Wishes* (1749), *Rasselas, Prince of Abyssinia* (1759), *The Fountains* (1766), and the posthu-mous *Prayers and Meditations* (1785). Johnson is famous for compiling the first comprehensive English dictionary, *Dictionary of the English Language*, which remained a standard for a hundred years. He is also heralded for his essays in *The Rambler*, *The Adventurer*, and *The Idler*. (These were among the first periodicals that published essays exclusively. Their popularity helped to estab-lish the essay as a genre.) Johnson was one of the leading figures in English literature's Augustan Age. As an essayist, Johnson offers a serious moral and religious slant to his topics, many of which include sketches of domestic life, character essays, criticism, letters, and "papers of morality." A follower of essayists Richard Steele and Joseph Addison, Johnson wrote classic essays of self-reflective and abstract thinking. The following selection is one such example in which he offers his introspective thoughts concerning a friend's death.

Truditur dies die,
Novæque pergunt interire lunæ;
Tu secanda marmora
Locas sub ipsum funus, et sepulchri
Immemor sturis domos. Horace, *Odes* II, xviii, 15–19

Day presses on the heels of day,
And moons increase to their decay;
But you, with thoughtless pride elate,
Unconscious of impending fate,
Command the pillar'd dome to rise,
When lo! thy tomb forgotten lies. Francis

To the Rambler

SIR,

1   I have lately been called, from a mingled life of business and amusement, to attend the last hours of an old friend; an office which has filled me, if not with melancholy, at least with serious reflections, and turned my thoughts towards the contemplation of those subjects which, though of the utmost importance and of indubitable certainty, are generally secluded from our regard by the jollity of health, the hurry of employment, and even by the calmer diversions of study and speculation; or, if they become accidental topics of conversation and argument, yet rarely sink deep into the heart but give occasion only to some subtleties of reasoning, or elegancies of declamation, which are heard, applauded, and forgotten.

2   It is, indeed, not hard to conceive how a man, accustomed to extend his views through a long concatenation of causes and effects, to trace things from their origin to their period, and compare means with ends, may discover the weakness of human schemes, detect the fallacies by which mortals are deluded, shew the insufficiency of wealth, honours, and power to real happiness, and please himself, and his auditors, with learned lectures on the vanity of life.

3   But though the speculatist may see and shew the folly of terrestrial hopes, fears, and desires, every hour will give proofs that he never felt it. Trace him through the day or year, and you will find him acting upon the principles which he has in common with the illiterate and unenlightened, angry and pleased like the lowest of the vulgar, pursuing, with the same ardour, the same designs, grasping, with all the eagerness of transport, those riches which he knows he cannot keep, and swelling with the applause which he has gained by proving that applause is of no value.

4   The only conviction that rushes upon the soul and takes away from our appetites and passions the power of resistance is to be found, where I have received it, at the bed of a dying friend. To enter this school of wisdom is not the peculiar privilege of geometricians: the most sublime and important precepts require no uncommon opportunities nor laborious preparations; they are enforced without the aid of eloquence and understood without skill in analytic science. Every tongue can utter them and every understanding can conceive them. He that wishes in earnest to obtain just sentiments concerning his condition, and would be intimately acquainted with the world, may find instructions on every side. He that desires to enter behind the scene which every art has been employed to decorate and every passion labours to illuminate, and wishes to see life stripped of those ornaments which make it glitter on the stage and exposed in its natural meanness, impotence, and nakedness, may find all the delusion laid open in the chamber of disease: he will there find vanity divested of her robes, power deprived of her sceptre, and hypocrisy without her mask.

5   The friend whom I have lost was a man eminent for genius, and, like others of the same class, sufficiently pleased with acceptance and applause. Being caressed by those who have preferments and riches in their disposal, he considered himself as in the direct road of

advancement, and had caught the flame of ambition by approaches to its object. But in the midst of his hopes, his projects, and his gaieties, he was seized by a lingering disease, which, from its first stage, he knew to be incurable. Here was an end of all his visions of greatness and happiness; from the first hour that his health declined all his former pleasures grew tasteless. His friends expected to please him by those accounts of the growth of his reputation which were formerly certain of being well received; but they soon found how little he was now affected by compliments, and how vainly they attempted, by flattery, to exhilarate the languor of weakness and relieve the solicitude of approaching death. Whoever would know how much piety and virtue surpass all external goods might here have seen them weighed against each other, where all that gives motion to the active and elevation to the eminent, all that sparkles in the eye of hope and pants in the bosom of suspicion, at once became dust in the balance, without weight and without regard. Riches, authority, and praise lose all their influence when they are considered as riches which tomorrow shall be bestowed upon another, authority which shall this night expire for ever, and praise which, however merited, or however sincere, shall, after a few moments, be heard no more.

6   In those hours of seriousness and wisdom, nothing appeared to raise his spirits or gladden his heart but the recollection of acts of goodness, nor to excite his attention, but some opportunity for the exercise of the duties of religion. Everything that terminated on this side of the grave was received with coldness and indifference and regarded rather in consequence of the habit of valuing it than from any opinion that it deserved value; it had little more prevalence over his mind than a bubble that was now broken, a dream from which he was awake. His whole powers were engrossed by the consideration of another state, and all conversation was tedious that had not some tendency to disengage him from human affairs and open his prospects into futurity.

7   It is now past: we have closed his eyes, and heard him breathe the groan of expiration. At the sight of this last conflict I felt a sensation never known to me before, a confusion of passions, an awful stillness of sorrow, a gloomy terror without a name. The thoughts that entered my soul were too strong to be diverted and too piercing to be endured. But such violence cannot be

lasting: the storm subsided in a short time. I wept, retired, and grew calm.

8   I have from that time frequently revolved in my mind the effects which the observation of death produces in those who are not wholly without the power and use of reflection, for by far the greater part it is wholly unregarded. Their friends and their enemies sink into the grave without raising any uncommon emotion or reminding them that they are themselves on the edge of the precipice, and that they must soon plunge into the gulf of eternity.

9   It seems to me remarkable that death increases our veneration for the good and extenuates our hatred of the bad. Those virtues which once we envied, as Horace* observes, because they eclipsed our own, can now no longer obstruct our reputation, and we have therefore no interest to suppress their praise. That wickedness which we feared for its malignity is now become impotent, and the man whose name filled us with alarm, and rage, and indignation, can at last be considered only with pity or contempt.

10   When a friend is carried to his grave we at once find excuses for every weakness and palliations of every fault; we recollect a thousand endearments which before glided off our minds without impression, a thousand favours unrepaid, a thousand duties unperformed, and wish, vainly wish, for his return, not so much that we may receive, as that we may bestow, happiness, and recompense that kindness which before we never understood.

11   There is not, perhaps, to a mind well-instructed, a more painful occurrence than the death of one whom we have injured without reparation. Our crime seems now irretrievable: it is indelibly recorded, and the stamp of fate is fixed upon it. We consider, with the most afflictive anguish, the pain which we have given and now cannot alleviate, and the losses which we have caused and now cannot repair.

12   Of the same kind are the emotions which the death of an emulator or competitor produces. Whoever had qualities to alarm our jealousy, had excellence to deserve our fondness; and to whatever ardour of opposition interest may inflame us, no man ever outlived an enemy whom he did not then wish to have made a friend. Those who are

*I do not know where Horace says this, if at all.

versed in literary history know that the elder Scaliger was the redoubted antagonist of Cardan and Erasmus: yet at the death of each of his great rivals he relented, and complained that they were snatched away from him before their reconciliation was completed.

> *Tu ne etiam moreris? Ah! quid me linquis, Erasme,*
> *Ante meus quam sit conciliatus amor?*

> Art thou too fallen? ere anger could subside
> And love return, has great Erasmus died?

13   Such are the sentiments with which we finally review the effects of passion but which we sometimes delay till we can no longer rectify our errors. Let us, therefore, make haste to do what we shall certainly at last wish to have done: let us return the caresses of our friends and endeavour by mutual endearments to heighten that tenderness which is the balm of life. Let us be quick to repent of injuries while repentance may not be a barren anguish, and let us open our eyes to every rival excellence, and pay early and willingly those honours which justice will compel us to pay at last.

ATHANATUS

Discussion Questions

1. Explain what Johnson is saying in paragraphs 1 through 4.
2. Why does Johnson wait until paragraph 5 to describe his friend who died?
3. Are the mourners' behaviors that Johnson describes fairly typical? Why or why not?
4. What pleas does Johnson make of mourners in the last paragraph? Identify and explain whatever additions you would make to his plea.
5. Describe the tone of Johnson's essay. Point out specific passages that contribute to the tone.
6. In small groups, discuss what Johnson believes people can learn from mourners and death.

Writing Assignments

1. Write a journal entry that explores what you have learned about death from observing people mourning the loss of others.
2. Write an essay that addresses the following question: What does people's behavior at the death of others reveal about human nature?
3. Write an essay that describes how you think people should react to the death of others.

On the Fear of Death

ELISABETH KÜBLER-ROSS

Elisabeth Kübler-Ross (1917–1995) was born in Zurich, Switzerland, and earned her medical degree at the University of Zurich in 1957. She practiced medicine in Switzerland and was involved with relief work in postwar Europe. After moving to the United States, Kübler-Ross taught at the University of Colorado Medical School. She distinguished herself by her interest, care, and expertise in matters concerning dying. Kübler-Ross was a pioneer in writing openly about the importance of talking about death. She was, arguably, responsible for the topic losing some of its stigma and being addressed by the medical community and Western society. Her books, *On Death and Dying* (1969), *Death: The Final State* (1974), *Working It Through* (1981), and *On Childhood and Death* (1985), are considered classics in the field. At the University of Chicago, she established an innovative interdisciplinary course on the care of the terminally ill. She also served as president of Shanti Milaya (House of Peace), a teaching and therapeutic center devoted to people facing death. In the following essay, originally published in 1969, Kübler-Ross argues the necessity of facing death directly as a way to reduce fear of it.

1   Epidemics have taken a great toll of lives in past generations. Death in infancy and early childhood was frequent and there were few families who didn't lose a member of the family at an early age. Medicine has changed greatly in the last decades. Widespread vaccinations have practically eradicated many illnesses, at least in western Europe and the United States. The use of chemotherapy, especially the antibiotics, has contributed to an ever decreasing number of fatalities in infectious diseases. Better child care and education has effected a low morbidity and mortality among children. The many diseases that have taken an impressive toll among the young and middle-aged have been conquered. The number of old people is on the rise, and with this fact come the number of people with malignancies and chronic diseases associated more with old age.

2   Pediatricians have less work with acute and life-threatening situations as they have an ever increasing number of patients with psychosomatic disturbances and adjustments and behavior problems. Physicians have more people in their waiting rooms with emotional problems than they have ever had before, but they also have more elderly patients who not only try to live with their decreased physical abilities and limitations but who also face loneliness and isolation with all its pains and anguish. The majority of these people are not seen by a psychiatrist. Their needs have to be elicited and gratified by other professional people, for instance, chaplains and social workers. It is for them that I am trying to outline the changes that have taken place in the last few decades, changes that are ultimately responsible for the increased fear of death, the rising number of emotional problems, and the greater need for understanding of and coping with the problems of death and dying.

3   When we look back in time and study old cultures and people, we are impressed that death has always been distasteful to man and will probably always be. From a psychiatrist's point of view this is very understandable and can perhaps best be explained by our basic knowledge that, in our unconscious, death is never possible in regard to ourselves. It is inconceivable for our unconscious to imagine an actual ending of our on life here on earth, and if this life of ours had to end, the ending is always attributed to a malicious intervention from the outside by someone else. In simple terms, in our unconscious mind we can only be killed; it is inconceivable to die of a natural cause or of old age. Therefore death in itself is associated

with a bad act, a frightening happening, something that in itself calls for retribution and punishment.

4   One is wise to remember these fundamental facts as they are essential in understanding some of the most important, otherwise unintelligible communications of our patients.

5   The second fact that we have to comprehend is that in our unconscious mind we cannot distinguish between a wish and a deed. We are all aware of some of our illogical dreams in which two completely opposite statements can exist side by side—very acceptable in our dreams but unthinkable and illogical in our wakening state. Just as our unconscious mind cannot differentiate between the wish to kill somebody in anger and the act of having done so, the young child is unable to make this distinction. The child who angrily wishes his mother to drop dead for not having gratified his needs will be traumatized greatly by the actual death of his mother—even if this event is not linked closely in time with his destructive wishes. He will always take part or the whole blame for the loss of his mother. He will always say to himself—rarely to others—"I did it, I am responsible, I was bad, therefore Mommy left me." It is well to remember that the child will react in the same manner if he loses a parent by divorce, separation, or desertion. Death is often seen by a child as an impermanent thing and has therefore little distinction from a divorce in which he may have an opportunity to see a parent again.

6   Many a parent will remember remarks of their children such as, "I will bury my doggy now and next spring when the flowers come up again, he will get up." Maybe it was the same wish that motivated the ancient Egyptians to supply their dead with food and goods to keep them happy and the old American Indians to bury their relatives with their belongings.

7   When we grow older and begin to realize that our omnipotence is really not so omnipotent, that our strongest wishes are not powerful enough to make the impossible possible, the fear that we have contributed to the death of a loved one diminishes—and with it the guilt. The fear remains diminished, however, only so long as it is not challenged too strongly. Its vestiges can be seen daily in hospital corridors and in people associated with the bereaved.

8   A husband and wife may have been fighting for years, but when the partner dies, the survivor will pull his hair, whine and cry louder,

and beat his chest in regret, fear and anguish, and will hence fear his own death more than before, still believing in the law of talion—an eye for an eye, a tooth for a tooth—"I am responsible for her death. I will have to die a pitiful death in retribution."

9   Maybe this knowledge will help us understand many of the old customs and rituals which have lasted over the centuries and whose purpose is to diminish the anger of the gods or the people as the case may be, thus decreasing the anticipated punishment. I am thinking of the ashes, the torn clothes, the veil, the *Klage Weiber** of the old days—they are all means to ask you to take pity on them, the mourners, and are expressions of sorrow, grief, and shame. If someone grieves, beats his chest, tears his hair, or refuses to eat, it is an attempt at self-punishment to avoid or reduce the anticipated punishment for the blame that he takes on the death of a loved one.

10   This grief, shame, and guilt are not very far removed from feelings of anger and rage. The process of grief always includes some quality of anger. Since none of us likes to admit anger at a deceased person, these emotions are often disguised or repressed and prolong the period of grief or show up in other ways. It is well to remember that it is not up to us to judge such feelings as bad or shameful but to understand their true meaning and origins as something very human. In order to illustrate this I will again use the example of the child and the child in us. The five-year-old who loses his mother is both blaming himself for her disappearance and being angry at her for having deserted him and for no longer gratifying his needs. The dead person then turns into something the child loves and wants very much but also hates with equal intensity for this severe deprivation.

11   The ancient Hebrews regarded the body of a dead person as something unclean and not to be touched. The early American Indians talked about the evil spirits and shot arrows in the air to drive the spirits away. Many other cultures have rituals to take care of the "bad" dead person, and they all originate in this feeling of anger which still exists in all of us, though we dislike admitting it. The tradition of the tombstone may originate in this wish to keep the bad spirits deep down in the ground, and the pebbles that many

*Wailing wives. [ed.]

mourners put on the grave are left-over symbols of the same wish.
Though we call the firing of guns at military funerals a last salute,
it is the same symbolic ritual as the Indian used when he shot his
spears and arrows into the skies.

12   I give these examples to emphasize than man has not basically
changed. Death is still a fearful, frightening happening, and the fear
of death is a universal fear even if we think we have mastered it on
many levels.

13   What has changed is our way of coping and dealing with death
and dying and our dying patients.

14   Having been raised in a country in Europe where science is not
so advanced, where modern techniques have just started to find their
way into medicine, and where people still live as they did in this
country half a century ago, I may have had an opportunity to study
part of the evolution of mankind in a shorter period.

15   I remember as a child the death of a farmer. He fell from a tree and
was not expected to live. He asked simply to die at home, a wish that
was granted without questioning. He called his daughters into the bedroom and spoke with each one of them alone for a few moments. He
arranged his affairs quietly, though he was in great pain, and distributed
his belongings and his land, none of which was to be split until his wife
should follow him in death. He also asked each of his children to share
in the work, duties, and tasks that he had carried on until the time of
the accident. He asked his friends to visit him once more, to bid goodbye to them. Although I was a small child at the time, he did not exclude
me or my siblings. We were allowed to share in the preparations of the
family just as we were permitted to grieve with them until he died.
When he did die, he was left at home, in his own beloved home which
he had built, and among his friends and neighbors who went to take
a last look at him where he lay in the midst of flowers in the place he
had lived in and loved so much. In that country today there is still
no make-believe slumber room, no embalming, no false makeup to
pretend sleep. Only the signs of very disfiguring illnesses are covered
up with bandages and only infectious cases are removed from the home
prior to the burial.

16   Why do I describe such "old-fashioned" customs? I think they
are an indication of our acceptance of a fatal outcome, and they help
the dying patient as well as his family to accept the loss of a loved
one. If a patient is allowed to terminate his life in the familiar and

beloved environment, it requires less adjustment for him. His own family knows him well enough to replace a sedative with a glass of his favorite wine; or the smell of a home-cooked soup may give him the appetite to sip a few spoons of fluid which, I think is still more enjoyable than an infusion. I will not minimize the need for sedatives and infusions and realize full well from my one experience as a country doctor that they are sometimes life-saving and often unavoidable. But I also know that patience and familiar people and foods could replace many a bottle of intravenous fluids given for the simple reason that it fulfills the physiological need without involving too many people and/or individual nursing care.

17 The fact that children are allowed to stay at home where a fatality has stricken and are included in the talk, discussions, and fears gives them the feeling that they are not alone in the grief and gives them the comfort of shared responsibility and shared mourning. It prepares them gradually and helps them view death as part of life, an experience which may help them grow and mature.

18 This is in great contrast to a society in which death is viewed as taboo, discussion of it is regarded as morbid, and children are excluded with the presumption and pretext that it would be "too much" for them. They are then sent off to relatives, often accompanied with some unconvincing lies of "Mother has gone on a long trip" or other unbelievable stories. The child senses that something is wrong, and his distrust in adults will only multiply if other relatives add new variations of the story, avoid his questions or suspicions, or shower him with gifts as a meager substitute for a loss he is not permitted to deal with. Sooner or later the child will become aware of the changed family situation and, depending on the age and personality of the child, will have an unresolved grief and regard this incident as a frightening, mysterious, in any case very traumatic experience with untrustworthy grownups, which he has no way to cope with.

19 It is equally unwise to tell a little child who lost her brother that God loved little boys so much that he took little Johnny to heaven. When this little girl grew up to be a woman she never solved her anger at God, which resulted in a psychotic depression when she lost her own little son three decades later.

20 We would think that our great emancipation, our knowledge of science and of man, has given us better ways and means to prepare ourselves and our families for this inevitable happening. Instead the

days are gone when a man was allowed to die in peace and dignity in his own home.

21   The more we are making advancements in science, the more we seem to fear and deny the reality of death. How is this possible?

22   We use euphemisms, we make the dead look as if they were asleep; we ship the children off to protect them from the anxiety and turmoil around the house if the patient is fortunate enough to die at home, we don't allow children to visit their dying parents in the hospitals, we have long and controversial discussions about whether patients should be told the truth—a question that rarely arises when the dying person is tended by the family physician who has known him from delivery to death and who knows the weaknesses and strengths of each member of the family.

23   I think there are many reasons for this flight away from facing death calmly. One of the most important facts is that dying nowadays is more gruesome in many ways, namely, more lonely, mechanical, and dehumanized; at times it is even difficult to determine technically when the time of death has occurred.

24   Dying becomes lonely and impersonal because the patient is often taken out of his familiar environment and rushed to an emergency room. Whoever has been very sick and has required rest and comfort especially may recall his experience of being put on a stretcher and enduring the noise of the ambulance siren and hectic rush until the hospital gates open. Only those who have lived through this may appreciate the discomfort and cold necessity of such transportation which is only the beginning of a long order—hard to endure when you are well, difficult to express in words when noise, light, pumps, and voices are all too much to put up with. It may well be that we might consider more the patient under the sheets and blankets and perhaps stop our well-meant efficiency and rush in order to hold the patient's hand, to smile, or to listen to a question. I include the trip to the hospital as the first episode in dying, as it is for many. I am putting it exaggeratedly in contrast to the sick man who is left at home—not to say that lives should not be saved if they can be saved by a hospitalization but to keep the focus on the patient's experience, his needs and his reactions.

25   When a patient is severely ill, he is often treated like a person with no right to an opinion. It is often someone else who makes the decision if and when and where a patient should be hospitalized. It would take

so little to remember that the sick person too has feelings, has wishes and opinions, and has—most important of all—the right to be heard.

26 Well, our presumed patient has now reached the emergency room. He will be surrounded by busy nurses, orderlies, interns, residents, a lab technician perhaps who will take some blood, an electrocardiogram technician who takes the cardiogram. He may be moved to X-ray and he will overhear opinions of his condition and discussions and questions to members of the family. He slowly but surely is beginning to be treated like a thing. He is no longer a person. Decisions are made often without his opinion. If he tries to rebel he will be sedated and after hours of waiting and wondering whether he has the strength, he will be wheeled into the operating room or intensive treatment unit and become an object of great concern and great financial investment.

27 He may cry for rest, peace, and dignity, but he will get infusions, transfusions, a heart machine, or tracheotomy if necessary. He may want one single person to stop for one single minute so that he can ask one single question—but he will get a dozen people around the clock, all busily preoccupied with his heart rate, pulse, electrocardiogram or pulmonary functions, his secretions or excretions but not with him as a human being. He may wish to fight it all but it is going to be a useless fight since all this is done in the fight for his life, and if they can save his life they can consider the person afterwards. Those who consider the person first may lose precious time to save his life! At least this seems to be the rationale or justification behind all this—or is it? Is the reason for this increasingly mechanical, depersonalized approach our own defensiveness? Is this approach our own way to cope with and repress the anxieties that a terminally or critically ill patient evokes in us? Is our concentration on equipment, on blood pressure, our desperate attempt to deny the impending death which is so frightening and discomforting to us that we displace all our knowledge onto machines, since they are less close to us than the suffering face of another human being which would remind us once more of our lack of omnipotence, our own limits and failures, and last but not least perhaps our own mortality?

28 Maybe the question has to be raised: Are we becoming less human or more human? . . . [I]t is clear that whatever the answer may be, the patient is suffering more—not physically, perhaps, but emotionally. And his needs have not changed over the centuries, only our ability to gratify them.

Discussion Questions

1. Explain the essay's epigraph and how it complements the essay.
2. Why does Kübler-Ross think it is important to study, remember, and understand old cultures and people?
3. In paragraph 5, Kübler-Ross distinguishes between a wish and a deed. Explain the distinction.
4. In small groups, discuss whether people are more afraid of pain than of dying.
5. What do you think Kübler-Ross saw as the purpose and audience of her essay? Explain.
6. Given the tremendous advances in medical knowledge and practice in the nearly thirty years since this essay was first published, is the essay still relevant today? Why or why not?
7. Identify what you learned from Kübler-Ross's essay.

Writing Assignments

1. In a journal entry, answer the question that Kübler-Ross asks at the end of her essay: "Are we becoming less human or more human?" Provide specific reasons to support your stance.
2. Write a letter to a trusted friend or family member in which you convey your fears about death.
3. In paragraph 27, Kübler-Ross raises a number of questions about the extraordinary measures taken in hospitals to save lives. Write an essay addressing the ethics of life support systems and current medical technology in prolonging life.
4. Write an essay that examines what facing death can teach people about life.
5. Research other cultures' (for example, Native Americans, Asians, Indians) traditions regarding death. Then, in a paper, compare and contrast the different attitudes toward death and dying as demonstrated in their practices.

Death

LU HSUN

Lu Hsun (1881–1936) was born Chou Shu-jen in the Chekiang prov-
ince of China. After graduating from the Nanking Mining Academy
in 1902, he went to Japan and enrolled in Kobun College to study
Japanese. The illness and death of his father spawned Hsun's interest
in studying medicine, which he pursued for two years at Sendai University. The comfort he found in writing made him switch to studying
literature. Hsun taught Chinese literature at Peking University. He is
the author of a collection of short stories, *Battlecry* (1923); a collections of prose-poems, *Wild Grass* (1927); and a memoir, *Morning
Flowers Picked at Dawn* (1928). Hsun's writing centers around the
plights of common people, especially poverty and suffering. Such
themes garnered him praise from the left wing, but left him susceptible
to trouble with the right wing. His rebellious thinking forced him to
take refuge in Amoy and Canton in 1926. He later became a founding
member of the League of Left-Wing Writers. His books were part of
the school curriculum after the Communists overtook the government in 1948. Written just before he died, the following selection, in
which he reflects on death, is representative of Hsun's writing.

1   While preparing a selection of Käthe Kollwitz's works for publication, I asked Miss Agnes Smedley to write a preface. This struck me
as most appropriate because the two of them were good friends.

Soon the preface was ready, I had Mr. Mao Dun translate it, and it
has now appeared in the Chinese edition. One passage in it reads:

> All these years Käthe Kollwitz—who never once
> used any title conferred on her—has made a great
> many sketches, pencil and ink drawings, woodcuts
> and etchings. When we study these, two dominant
> themes are evident: in her younger days her main
> theme was revolt, but in her later years it was moth-
> erly love, the protective maternal instinct, succour
> and death. All her works are pervaded by the idea
> of suffering, of tragedy, and a passionate longing
> to protect the oppressed.
>
> Once I asked her, "Why is it that instead of your
> former theme of revolt you now seem unable to
> shake off the idea of death?" She answered in tones
> of anguish, "It may be because I am growing older
> every day. . . ."

2   At that point I stopped to think. I estimated that it must have
been in about 1910 that she first took death as her theme, when she
was no more than forty-three or -four. I stop to think about it now
because of my own age, of course. But a dozen or so years ago, as
I recall, I did not have such a feeling about death. No doubt our
lives have long been treated so casually as trifles of no consequence
that we treat them lightly ourselves, not seriously as Europeans do.
Some foreigners say that the Chinese are most afraid of death. But
this is not true—actually, most of us die with no clear understanding
of the meaning of death.

3   The general belief in a posthumous existence further strengthens
the casual attitude towards death. As everyone knows, we Chinese
believe in ghosts (more recently called "souls" or "spirits"); and
since there are ghosts, after death we can at least exist as ghosts if
not as men, which is better than nothing. But the imagined duration
of this ghostly existence seems to vary according to one's wealth.
The poor appear to believe that when they die their souls will pass
into another body, an idea derived from Buddhism. Of course, transmigration in Buddhism is a complicated process, by no means so
simple; but the poor are usually ignorant people who do not know

this. That is why criminals condemned to death often show no fear when taken to the execution ground, but shout, "Twenty years from now I shall be a stout fellow again!" Moreover, according to popular belief a ghost wears the clothes he had on at the time of death; and since the poor have no good clothes and cannot therefore cut a fine figure as ghosts, it is far better for them to be reborn at once as naked babies. Did you ever see a new-born infant wearing a beggar's rags or a swimming-suit? No, never. Very well, then, that is a fresh start. Someone may object: If you believe in transmigration, in the next existence you may even be worse off or actually become a beast—what a fearful thought! But the poor don't seem to think that way. They firmly believe that they have not committed sins frightful enough to condemn them to becoming beasts: they have not had the position, power or money to commit such sins.

4   But neither do those men with position, power and money believe that they should become beasts. They either turn Buddhist in order to become saints, or advocate the study of the Confucian classics and a return to ancient ways in order to become Confucian sages. Just as in life they expect to be a privileged class, after death they expect to be exempt from transmigration. As for those who have a little money, though they also believe they should be exempt from transmigration, since they have no high ambitions or lofty plans they just wait placidly. Round about the age of fifty, they look for a burial place, buy a coffin, and burn paper money to open a bank account in the nether regions, expecting their sons and grandsons to sacrifice to them every year. This is surely much pleasanter than life on earth. If I were a ghost now, with filial descendants in the world of men, I should not have to sell my articles one by one, or ask the Beixin Publishing House for payment. I could simply lie at ease in my cedarwood or fir coffin, while at every festival and at New Year a fine feast and a pile of banknotes would be placed before me. That would be the life!

5   Generally speaking, unlike the very rich and great, who are not bound by the laws of the nether regions, the poor would like to be reborn at once, while those comfortably-off would like to remain as ghosts for as long as possible. The comfortably-off are willing to remain ghosts because their life as ghosts (this sounds paradoxical but I can think of no better way of expressing it) is the continuation of their life on earth and they are not yet tired of it. Of course there

are rulers in the nether regions who are extremely strict and just; but they will make allowances for these ghosts and accept presents from them too, just like good officials on earth.

6   Then there are others who are rather casual, who do not think much about death even when they are dying, and I belong to this casual category. Thirty years ago as a medical student I considered the problem of the existence of the soul, but did not know what to conclude. Later I considered whether death was painful or not, and concluded that it varied in different cases. And later still I stopped thinking about the matter and forgot it. During the last ten years I have sometimes written a little about the death of friends, but apparently I never thought of my own. In the last two years I have been ill a great deal and usually for a considerable length of time, which has often reminded me that I am growing older. Of course, I have been constantly reminded of this fact by other writers owing to their friendly or unfriendly concern.

7   Since last year, whenever I lay on my wicker chair recovering from illness, I would consider what to do when I was well, what articles to write, what books to translate or publish. My plans made, I would conclude, "All right—but I must hurry." This sense of urgency, which I never had before, was due to the fact that unconsciously I had remembered my age. But still I never thought directly of "death."

8   Not till my serious illness this year did I start thinking distinctly about death. At first I treated my illness as in the past, relying on my Japanese doctor, S____. Though not a specialist in tuberculosis, he is an elderly man with a rich experience who studied medicine before me, is my senior, and knows me very well—hence he talks frankly. Of course, however well a doctor knows his patient, he still speaks with a certain reserve; but at least he warned me two or three times, though I never paid any attention and did not tell anyone. Perhaps because things had dragged on so long and my last attack was so serious, some friends arranged behind my back to invite an American doctor, D____, to see me. He is the only Western specialist on tuberculosis in Shanghai. After his examination, although he complimented me on my typically Chinese powers of resistance, he also announced that my end was near, adding that had I been a European I would already have been in my grave for five years. This verdict moved my soft-hearted friends to tears. I did not ask him to

prescribe for me, feeling that since he had studied in the West he could hardly have learned how to prescribe for a patient five years dead. But Dr. D____'s diagnosis was in fact extremely accurate. I later had an X-ray photograph made of my chest which very largely bore out his findings.

9   Though I did not pay much attention to his announcement, it has influenced me a little: I spend all the time on my back, with no energy to talk or read and not enough strength to hold a newspaper. Since my heart is not yet "as tranquil as an old well," I am forced to think, and sometimes I think of death too. But instead of thinking that "twenty years from now I shall be a stout fellow again," or wondering how to prolong my stay in a cedarwood coffin, my mind dwells on certain trifles before death. It is only now that I am finally sure that I do not believe that men turn into ghosts. It occurred to me to write a will, and I thought: If I were a great nobleman with a huge fortune, my sons, sons-in-law, and others would have forced me to write a will long ago; whereas nobody has mentioned it to me. Still, I may as well leave one. I seem to have thought out quite a few items for my family, among which were:

1. Don't accept a cent from anyone for the funeral. This does not apply to old friends.
2. Get the whole thing over quickly, have me buried and be done with it.
3. Do nothing in the way of commemoration.
4. Forget me and live your own lives—if you don't, the more fools you.
5. When the child grows up, if he has no gifts let him take some small job to make a living. On no account let him become a writer or artist in name only.
6. Don't take other people's promises seriously.
7. Have nothing to do with people who injure others but who oppose revenge and advocate tolerance.

10   There were other items, too, but I have forgotten them. I remember also how during a fever I recalled that when a European is dying there is usually some sort of ceremony in which he asks pardon of others and pardons them. Now I have a great many enemies, and

what should my answer be if some modernized person asked me my views on this? After some thought I decided: Let them go on hating me. I shall not forgive a single one of them either.

11   No such ceremony took place, however, and I did not draw up a will. I simply lay there in silence, struck sometimes by a more pressing thought: if this is dying, it isn't really painful. It may not be quite like this at the end, of course; but still, since this happens only once in a lifetime, I can take it. . . . Later, however, there came a change for the better. And now I am wondering whether this was really the state just before dying: a man really dying may not have such ideas. What it will be like, though, I still do not know.

September 5, 1936

—*Translated by Yang Xianyi and Gladys Yang*

Discussion Questions

1. Do you agree with Hsun when he states in paragraph 2 that "most of us die with no clear understanding of the meaning of death"? Why or why not?
2. Explain the purpose of Hsun's discussing transmigration in paragraph 3.
3. What is Hsun's attitude toward people with "position, power and money" regarding their feelings about afterlife? What specifically informs your answer?
4. What contributed to Hsun's understanding of death: his illness, his age, or his having been a medical student? Explain.
5. In small groups, discuss the list of seven instructions that Hsun presents. What do the items in the list reveal about Hsun? Which items would you add or delete from the list? Explain.

Writing Assignments

1. Write a journal entry that explores the following question: Is it ever possible to understand the meaning of death? If not, why not? If so, what can contribute to that understanding?

2. In an essay, describe how your understandings of and attitudes toward death have evolved from childhood to the present.
3. Research Buddhist thinking about afterlife. Write a paper that compares Buddist perspectives on life after death with those of the Western world. Which do you find more comforting? Why?
4. Choose other essays from this section of the book and write an essay comparing and contrasting the views of the authors on death and dying. What can people learn from their insights?

On Natural Death

LEWIS THOMAS

Lewis Thomas (1913–1993) was born in New York and earned his B.S. from Princeton University in 1933 and his M.D. from Harvard University in 1937. A physician-writer, Thomas is the author of *The Lives of a Cell: Notes of a Biology Watcher* (1974); *The Medusa and the Snail: More Notes of a Biology Watcher* (1983), in which the following essay appears; *The Youngest Science: Notes of a Medicine Watcher* (1983); *Late Night Thoughts on Listening to Mahler's Ninth Symphony* (1983); and *Et Cetera, Et Cetera: Notes of a Word Watcher* (1991). Many of his essays originally appeared in the *New England Journal of Medicine*. An eminent physician and medical researcher, Thomas was the president of the Memorial Sloan-Kettering Cancer Center in New York City, as well as the recipient of the National Book Award for nonfiction in 1974 and the American Book Award for science in 1981. In ten brief paragraphs, Thomas couples his medical knowledge with personal observation to produce the following thoughtful and reflective essay, which posits that people can learn from seeing the many forms that death, a natural occurrence, takes.

1   There are so many new books about dying that there are now special shelves set aside for them in bookshops, along with the health-diet and home-repair paperbacks and the sex manuals. Some of them are so packed with detailed information and step-by-step instructions

for performing the function that you'd think this was a new sort of skill which all of us are now required to learn. The strongest impression the casual reader gets, leafing through, is that proper dying has become an extraordinary, even an exotic experience, something only the specially trained get to do.

2   Also, you could be led to believe that we are the only creatures capable of the awareness of death, that when all the rest of nature is being cycled through dying, one generation after another, it is a different kind of process, done automatically and trivially, more "natural," as we say.

3   An elm in our backyard caught the blight this summer and dropped stone dead, leafless, almost overnight. One weekend it was a normal-looking elm, maybe a little bare in spots but nothing alarming, and the next weekend it was gone, passed over, departed, taken. Taken is right, for the tree surgeon came by yesterday with his crew of young helpers and their cherry picker, and took it down branch by branch and carted it off in the back of a red truck, everyone singing.

4   The dying of a field mouse, at the jaws of an amiable household cat, is a spectacle I have beheld many times. It used to make me wince. Early in life I gave up throwing sticks at the cat to make him drop the mouse, because the dropped mouse regularly went ahead and died anyway, but I always shouted unaffections at the cat to let him know the sort of animal he had become. Nature, I thought, was an abomination.

5   Recently I've done some thinking about that mouse, and I wonder if his dying is necessarily all that different from the passing of our elm. The main difference, if there is one, would be in the matter of pain. I do not believe that an elm tree has pain receptors, and even so, the blight seems to me a relatively painless way to go even if there were nerve endings in a tree, which there are not. But the mouse dangling tail-down from the teeth of a gray cat is something else again, with pain beyond bearing, you'd think, all over his small body.

6   There are now some plausible reasons for thinking it is not like that at all, and you can make up an entirely different story about the mouse and his dying if you like. At the instant of being trapped and penetrated by teeth, peptide hormones are released by cells in the hypothalamus and the pituitary gland; instantly these substances, called endorphins, are attached to the surface of other cells responsi-

ble for pain perception; the hormones have the pharmacologic prop-
erties of opium; there is no pain. Thus it is that the mouse seems
always to dangle so languidly from the jaws, lies there so quietly
when dropped, dies of his injuries without a struggle. If a mouse
could shrug, he'd shrug.

7   I do not know if this is true or not, nor do I know how to prove
it if it is true. Maybe if you could get in there quickly enough and
administer naloxone, a specific morphine antagonist, you could turn
off the endorphins and observe the restoration of pain, but this is
not something I would care to do or see. I think I will leave it there,
as a good guess about the dying of a cat-chewed mouse, perhaps
about dying in general.

8   Montaigne had a hunch about dying, based on his own close call
in a riding accident. He was so badly injured as to be believed dead
by his companions, and was carried home with lamentations, "all
bloody, stained all over with the blood I had thrown up." He remembers the entire episode, despite having been "dead, for two full
hours," with wonderment:

> It seemed to me that my life was hanging only by
> the tip of my lips. I closed my eyes in order, it
> seemed to me, to help push it out, and took pleasure
> in growing languid and letting myself go. It was an
> idea that was only floating on the surface of my
> soul, as delicate and feeble as all the rest, but in
> truth not only free from distress but mingled with
> that sweet feeling that people have who have let
> themselves slide into sleep. I believe that this is the
> same state in which people find themselves whom
> we see fainting in the agony of death, and I maintain
> that we pity them without cause. . . . In order to
> get used to the idea of death. I find there is nothing
> like coming close to it.

Later, in another essay, Montaigne returns to it:

> If you know not how to die, never trouble yourself;
> Nature will in a moment fully and sufficiently
> instruct you; she will exactly do that business for
> you; take you no care for it.

9   The worst accident I've ever seen was in Okinawa, in the early days of the invasion, when a jeep ran into a troop carrier and was crushed nearly flat. Inside were two young MPs, trapped in bent steel, both mortally hurt, with only their heads and shoulders visible. We had a conversation while people with the right tools were prying them free. Sorry about the accident, they said. No, they said, they felt fine. Is everyone else okay, one of them said. Well, the other one said, no hurry now. And then they died.

10   Pain is useful for avoidance, for getting away when there's time to get away, but when it is end game, and no way back, pain is likely to be turned off, and the mechanisms for this are wonderfully precise and quick. If I had to design an ecosystem in which creatures had to live off each other and in which dying was an indispensable part of living, I could not think of a better way to manage.

Discussion Questions

1. In small groups, discuss why there are growing numbers of books on dying. Who reads them? Are people obsessed with the topic, or is their interest understandable?
2. Do you find Thomas's comparison of the dying of the mouse and of the elm convincing? Why or why not?
3. How does Thomas refrain from morbidity while describing death?
4. What does the Montaigne quote add to Thomas's essay? Explain.
5. What is Thomas's purpose in describing "the worst accident" he had ever seen (paragraph 9)?
6. Do you agree or disagree with Thomas's idea about pain in the last paragraph? Why or why not?

Writing Assignments

1. Medical advancements have dramatically lengthened people's life spans, and it is not uncommon for people to live past the age of one hundred. Do you think most people would like to be centenarians? Would you? Write a journal entry that examines these questions.

2. One of the adages people hear or utter when faced with illness or death is *carpe diem* (seize the day, or live for the moment). Write a letter to a friend in which you express your views on the thinking behind this saying.

3. Write an essay that examines whether death is the final stage of life.

4. On what points regarding dying would Lewis Thomas and Elisabeth Kübler-Ross agree and disagree? Write a paper that compares and contrasts their thinking about death.

The Right to Die

NORMAN COUSINS

Norman Cousins (1915–1990) was born in Union Hill, New Jersey. He attended Columbia University Teacher's College and began his career in journalism in 1934 as the education editor of the *New York Evening Post*. From 1935 to 1940, Cousins worked at *Current History* as a book critic, literary editor, and managing editor. In 1940, he became editor of the *Saturday Review*, a post that lasted for some forty years. Cousins was a lecturer, a diplomat under three presidents, and a social critic. He authored *The Good Inheritance: The Democratic Chance* (1942); *Modern Man Is Obsolete* (1945), which was his response to the bombing of Hiroshima; *The Poetry of Freedom* (1946); *Who Speaks for Man?* (1953); *The Reality of Human Brotherhood* (1954); *Education for the Freedom Years* (1956); *Wanted: Two Billion Angry Men* (1958); *In Place of Folly* (1962); *Present Tense: An American Editor's Odyssey* (1967); *The Celebration of Life: A Dialogue on Immortality and Infinity* (1974); *Human Options* (1981); *Healing and Belief* (1982); *The Healing Heart: Antidotes to Panic and Helplessness* (1983); *The Pathology of Power* (1987); and *Head First, the Biology of Hope* (1989). Cousins is best known, however, for *Anatomy of an Illness as Perceived by the Patient: Reflections on Healing and Regeneration* (1979), in which he chronicles the illness that left him paralyzed. Dissatisfied with traditional medicine, Cousins checked himself out of the hospital and moved into a hotel where he consumed massive amounts of vitamin C, watched comical movies, and read humorous books until he regained his health. His prescription for regaining one's

health soon became famous. The following essay was one of the
first published articles about patients' rights, in which Cousins
argues that people be allowed to die with dignity and that suicide
be a person's own choice.

1   The world of religion and philosophy was shocked recently
when Henry P. Van Dusen and his wife ended their lives by their
own hands. Dr. Van Dusen had been president of Union Theologi-
cal Seminary; for more than a quarter-century he had been one
of the luminous names in Protestant theology. He enjoyed world
status as a spiritual leader. News of the self-inflicted death of the
Van Dusens, therefore, was profoundly disturbing to all those
who attach a moral stigma to suicide and regard it as a violation
of God's laws.

2   Dr. Van Dusen had anticipated this reaction. He and his wife
left behind a letter that may have historic significance. It was very
brief, but the essential point it made is now being widely discussed
by theologians and could represent the beginning of a reconsidera-
tion of traditional religious attitudes toward self-inflicted death.
The letter raised a moral issue: does an individual have the
obligation to go on living even when the beauty and meaning
and power of life are gone?

3   Henry and Elizabeth Van Dusen had lived full lives. In recent
years, they had become increasingly ill, requiring almost continual
medical care. Their infirmities were worsening, and they realized
they would soon become completely dependent for even the most
elementary needs and functions. Under these circumstances, little
dignity would have been left in life. They didn't like the idea of
taking up space in a world with too many mouths and too little
food. They believed it was a misuse of medical science to keep them
technically alive.

4   They therefore believed they had the right to decide when to die.
In making that decision, they weren't turning against life as the
highest value; what they were turning against was the notion that
there were no circumstances under which life should be discontinued.

5   An important aspect of human uniqueness is the power of free will. In his books and lectures, Dr. Van Dusen frequently spoke about the exercise of this uniqueness. The fact that he used his free will to prevent life from becoming a caricature of itself was completely in character. In their letter, the Van Dusens sought to convince family and friends that they were not acting solely out of despair or pain.

6   The use of free will to put an end to one's life finds no sanction in the theology to which Pitney Van Dusen was committed. Suicide symbolizes discontinuity; religion symbolizes continuity, represented at its quintessence by the concept of the immortal soul. Human logic finds it almost impossible to come to terms with the concept of nonexistence. In religion, the human mind finds a larger dimension and is relieved of the ordeal of a confrontation with non-existence.

7   Even without respect to religion, the idea of suicide has been abhorrent throughout history. Some societies have imposed severe penalties on the families of suicides in the hope that the individual who sees no reason to continue his existence may be deterred by the stigma his self-destruction would inflict on loved ones. Other societies have enacted laws prohibiting suicide on the grounds that it is murder. The enforcement of such laws, of course, has been an exercise in futility.

8   Customs and attitudes, like individuals themselves, are largely shaped by the surrounding environment. In today's world, life can be prolonged by science far beyond meaning or sensibility. Under these circumstances, individuals who feel they have nothing more to give to life, or to receive from it, need not be applauded, but they can be spared our condemnation.

9   The general reaction to suicide is bound to change as people come to understand that it may be a denial, not an assertion, of moral or religious ethics to allow life to be extended without regard to decency or pride. What moral or religious purpose is celebrated by the annihilation of the human spirit in the triumphant act of keeping the body alive? Why are so many people more readily appalled by an unnatural form of dying than by an unnatural form of living?

10   "Nowadays," the Van Dusens wrote in their last letter, "it is difficult to die. We feel that this way we are taking will become more usual and acceptable as the years pass.

11   "Of course, the thought of our children and our grandchildren makes us sad, but we still feel that this is the best way and the right way to go. We are both increasingly weak and unwell and who would want to die in a nursing home?

12   "We are not afraid to die. . . ."

13   Pitney Van Dusen was admired and respected in life. He can be admired and respected in death. "Suicide," said Goethe, "is an incident in human life which, however much disputed and discussed, demands the sympathy of every man, and in every age must be dealt with anew."

14   Death is not the greatest loss in life. The greatest loss is what dies inside us while we live. The unbearable tragedy is to live without dignity or sensitivity.

Discussion Questions

1. What is Cousins's attitude toward people ending their own lives?
2. Does Cousins adequately distinguish between his approval of some groups of people ending their lives as opposed to others? Explain your answer.
3. Discuss the effect of Cousins's beginning his essay with a specific example of a husband and wife ending their own lives.
4. Do you agree with Cousins when he states in paragraph 6, "Human logic finds it almost impossible to come to terms with the concept of nonexistence"? Why or why not?
5. In small groups, discuss the extent to which you agree or disagree with the ideas in the last paragraph of Cousins's essay.
6. How would Dr. Jack Kevorkian react to Cousins's essay? What leads you to your answer?

Writing Assignments

1. In a journal, address the following questions: Why do you think society generally does not support euthanasia even for people who are in pain or have terminal diseases? What do people's views on euthanasia reveal about their thoughts on life and death?

2. In a paper, take a stand on people ending their own lives. Are people who attempt suicide (and people who assist them, such as Dr. Jack Kevorkian) cowardly or courageous? Research the medical establishment's position on this topic and include your findings as a way to support your argument.

3. Many people use euphemisms for death, such as "passed away," "went to sleep," and "returned to God." Generate a list of these euphemisms and write an essay in which you discuss whether they are preferable to the word *death*. What do people's word choice say about their attitudes toward death?

4. Dr. Jack Kevorkian has assisted some forty-five people in their deaths. Some people think he is a murderer who should be imprisoned while others feel he is a compassionate physician. Research what has been written about Kevorkian in newspapers and magazines and write a letter to him in which you explain why he is a murderer or a humanitarian.

5. With the increase in teens smoking, engaging in unsafe sex, and eating unhealthy foods, to what extent can the argument be made that they are slowly taking their own lives? Write an essay that examines this observation.

The Brown Wasps

LOREN EISELEY

Loren Eiseley (1907–1977) was born in Lincoln, Nebraska. He earned his B.A. from the University of Nebraska in 1933, his A.M. from the University of Pennsylvania in 1935, and his Ph.D. from the University of Pennsylvania in 1937. He was a professor of anthropology and the history of science for over forty years at such schools as the University of Kansas, Oberlin College, the University of Pennsylvania, Columbia University, and the University of California at Berkeley. A voluminous writer, Eiseley is the author of *The Immense Journey* (1957), *Darwin's Century: Evolution and the Men Who Discovered It* (1958), *Firmament of Time* (1960), *The Unexpected Universe* (1969), *The Invisible Pyramid* (1970), *The Night Country* (1971), and *The Man Who Saw Through Time* (1973). His autobiography is *All the Strange Hours: The Excavation of a Life* (1975), and his poetry volumes include *Notes of an Alchemist* (1972) and *All the Night Wings* (posthumous, 1979). His many articles have appeared in the *Saturday Evening Post, Harper's, Scientific American, Horizon, New York Herald Tribune,* and *The New York Times.* Eiseley's many awards include the Athenaeum of Philadelphia Award for nonfiction in 1958; the Phi Beta Kappa award in science in 1959; the John Burroughs Medal and Pierre Lecomte de Nouy Foundation Award, both in 1961; and the Joseph Wood Krutch Medal from the Humane Society for the United States in 1976 for his "significant contribution to the improvement of life and the environment in this country." Eiseley is especially adept at making difficult topics understandable and interesting to lay readers. The following selection is one such example in which Eiseley reflects on natural life, human beings, and death.

1   There is a corner in the waiting room of one of the great Eastern stations where women never sit. It is always in the shadow and overhung by rows of lockers. It is, however, always frequented—not so much by genuine travelers as by the dying. It is here that a certain element of the abandoned poor seeks a refuge out of the weather, clinging for a few hours longer to the city that has fathered them. In a precisely similar manner I have seen, on a sunny day in midwinter, a few old brown wasps creep slowly over an abandoned wasp nest in a thicket. Numbed and forgetful and frost-blackened, the hum of the spring hive still resounded faintly in their sodden tissues. Then the temperature would fall and they would drop away into the white oblivion of the snow. Here in the station it is in no way different save that the city is busy in its snows. But the old ones cling to their seats as though these were symbolic and could not be given up. Now and then they sleep, their gray old heads resting with painful awkwardness on the backs of the benches.

2   Also they are not at rest. For an hour they may sleep in the gasping exhaustion of the ill-nourished and aged who have to walk in the night. Then a policeman comes by on his round and nudges them upright.

3   "You can't sleep here," he growls.

4   A strange ritual then begins. An old man is difficult to waken. After a muttered conversation the policeman presses a coin into his hand and passes fiercely along the benches prodding and gesturing toward the door. In his wake, like birds rising and settling behind the passage of a farmer through a cornfield, the men totter up, move a few paces and subside once more upon the benches.

5   One man, after a slight, apologetic lurch, does not move at all. Tubercularly thin, he sleeps on steadily. The policeman does not

look back. To him, too, this has become a ritual. He will not have to notice it again officially for another hour.

6   Once in a while one of the sleepers will not awake. Like the brown wasps, he will have had his wish to die in the great droning center of the hive rather than in some lonely room. It is not so bad here with the shuffle of footsteps and the knowledge that there are others who share the bad luck of the world. There are also the whistles and the sounds of everyone, everyone in the world, starting on journeys. Amidst so many journeys somebody is bound to come out all right. Somebody.

7   Maybe it was on a like thought that the brown wasps fell away from the old paper nest in the thicket. You hold till the last, even if it is only to a public seat in a railroad station. You want your place in the hive more than you want a room or a place where the aged can be eased gently out of the way. It is the place that matters, the place at the heart of things. It is life that you want, that bruises your gray old head with the hard chairs; a man has a right to his place.

8   But sometimes the place is lost in the years behind us. Or sometimes it is a thing of air, a kind of vaporous distortion above a heap of rubble. We cling to a time and place because without them man is lost, not only man but life. This is why the voices, real or unreal, which speak from the floating trumpets at spiritualist seances are so unnerving. They are voices out of nowhere whose only reality lies in their ability to stir the memory of a living person with some fragment of the past. Before the medium's cabinet both the dead and the living revolve endlessly about an episode, a place, an event that has already been engulfed by time.

9   This feeling runs deep in life; it brings stray cats running over endless miles, and birds homing from the ends of the earth. It is as though all living creatures, and particularly the more intelligent, can survive only by fixing or transforming a bit of time into space or by securing a bit of space with its objects immortalized and made permanent in time. For example, I once saw, on a flower pot in my own living room, the efforts of a field mouse to build a remembered field. I have lived to see this episode repeated in a thousand guises, and since I have spent a large portion of my life in the shade of a nonexistent tree, I think I am entitled to speak for the field mouse.

10   One day as I cut across the field which at that time extended on one side of our suburban shopping center, I found a giant slug feeding

from a runnel of pink ice cream in an abandoned Dixie cup. I could see his eyes telescope and protrude in a kind of dim, uncertain ecstasy as his dark body bunched and elongated in the curve of the cup. Then, as I stood there at the edge of the concrete, contemplating the slug, I began to realize it was like standing on a shore where a different type of life creeps up and fumbles tentatively among the rocks and sea wrack. It knows its place and will only creep so far until something changes. Little by little as I stood there I began to see more of this shore that surrounds the place of man. I looked with sudden care and attention at things I had been running over thoughtlessly for years. I even waded out a short way into the grass and the wild-rose thickets to see more. A huge black-belted bee went droning by and there were some indistinct scurryings in the underbrush.

11   Then I came to a sign which informed me that this field was to be the site of a new Wanamaker suburban store. Thousands of obscure lives were about to perish, the spores of puffballs would go smoking off to new fields, and the bodies of little white-footed mice would be crunched under the inexorable wheels of the bulldozers. Life disappears or modifies its appearances so fast that everything takes on an aspect of illusion—a momentary fizzing and boiling with smoke rings, like pouring dissident chemicals into a retort. Here man was advancing, but in a few years his plaster and bricks would be disappearing once more into the insatiable maw of the clover. Being of an archaeological cast of mind, I thought of this fact with an obscure sense of satisfaction and waded back through the rose thickets to the concrete parking lot. As I did so, a mouse scurried ahead of me, frightened of my steps if not of that ominous Wanamaker sign. I saw him vanish in the general direction of my apartment house, his little body quivering with fear in the great open sun on the blazing concrete. Blinded and confused, he was running straight away from his field. In another week scores would follow him.

12   I forgot the episode then and went home to the quiet of my living room. It was not until a week later, letting myself into the apartment, that I realized I had a visitor. I am fond of plants and had several ferns standing on the floor in pots to avoid the noon glare by the south window.

13   As I snapped on the light and glanced carelessly around the room, I saw a little heap of earth on the carpet and a scrabble of pebbles that had been kicked merrily over the edge of one of the flower

pots. To my astonishment I discovered a full-fledged burrow delving downward among the fern roots. I waited silently. The creature who had made the burrow did not appear. I remembered the wild field then, and the fight of the mice. No house mouse, no *Mus domesticus*, had kicked up this little heap of earth or sought refuge under a fern root in a flower pot. I thought of the desperate little creature I had seen fleeing from the wild-rose thicket. Through intricacies of pipes and attics, he, or one of his fellows, had climbed to this high green solitary room. I could visualize what had occurred. He had an image in his head, a world of seed pods and quiet, of green sheltering leaves in the dim light among the weed stems. It was the only world he knew and it was gone.

14   Somehow in his fight he had found his way to this room with drawn shades where no one would come till nightfall. And here he had smelled green leaves and run quickly up the flower pot to dabble his paws in common earth. He had even struggled half the afternoon to carry his burrow deeper and had failed. I examined the hole, but no whiskered twitching face appeared. He was gone. I gathered up the earth and refilled the burrow. I did not expect to find traces of him again.

15   Yet for three nights thereafter I came home to the darkened room and my ferns to find the dirt kicked gaily about the rug and the burrow reopened, though I was never able to catch the field mouse within it. I dropped a little food about the mouth of the burrow, but it was never touched. I looked under beds or sat reading with one ear cocked for rustlings in the ferns. It was all in vain; I never saw him. Probably he ended in a trap in some other tenant's room.

16   But before he disappeared I had come to look hopefully for his evening burrow. About my ferns there had begun to linger the insubstantial vapor of an autumn field, the distilled essence, as it were, of a mouse brain in exile from its home. It was a small dream, like our dreams, carried a long and weary journey along pipes and through spider webs, past holes over which loomed the shadows of waiting cats, and finally, desperately, into this room where he had played in the shuttered daylight for an hour among the green ferns on the floor. Every day these invisible dreams pass us on the street, or rise from beneath our feet, or look out upon us from beneath a bush.

17   Some years ago the old elevated railway in Philadelphia was torn down and replaced by a subway system. This ancient El with its

barnlike stations containing nut-vending machines and scattered food scraps had, for generations, been the favorite feeding ground of flocks of pigeons, generally one flock to a station along the route of the El. Hundreds of pigeons were dependent upon the system. They flapped in and out of its stanchions and steel work or gathered in watchful little audiences about the feet of anyone who rattled the peanut-vending machines. They even watched people who jingled change in their hands, and prospected for food under the feet of the crowds who gathered between trains. Probably very few among the waiting people who tossed a crumb to an eager pigeon realized that this El was like a food-bearing river, and that the life which haunted its banks was dependent upon the running of the trains with their human freight.

18   I saw the river stop.

19   The time came when the underground tubes were ready; the traffic was transferred to a realm unreachable by pigeons. It was like a great river subsiding suddenly into desert sands. For a day, for two days, pigeons continued to circle over the El or stand close to the red vending machines. They were patient birds, and surely this great river which had flowed through the lives of unnumbered generations was merely suffering from some momentary drought.

20   They listened for the familiar vibrations that had always heralded an approaching train; they flapped hopefully about the head of an occasional workman walking along the steel runways. They passed from one empty station to another, all the while growing hungrier. Finally they flew away.

21   I thought I had seen the last of them about the El, but there was a revival and it provided a curious instance of the memory of living things for a way of life or a locality that has long been cherished. Some weeks after the El was abandoned workmen began to tear it down. I went to work every morning by one particular station, and the time came when the demolition crews reached this spot. Acetylene torches showered passersby with sparks, pneumatic drills hammered at the base of the structure, and a blind man who, like the pigeons, had clung with his cup to a stairway leading to the change booth, was forced to give up his place.

22   It was then, strangely, momentarily, one morning that I witnessed the return of a little band of the familiar pigeons. I even recognized one or two members of the flock that had lived around this particular

station before they were dispersed into the streets. They flew bravely in and out among the sparks and the hammers and the shouting workmen. They had returned—and they had returned because the hubbub of the wreckers had convinced them that the river was about to flow once more. For several hours they flapped in and out through the empty windows, nodding their heads and watching the fall of girders with attentive little eyes. By the following morning the station was reduced to some burned-off stanchions in the street. My bird friends had gone. It was plain, however, that they retained a memory for an insubstantial structure now compounded of air and time. Even the blind man clung to it. Someone had provided him with a chair, and he sat at the same corner staring sightlessly at an invisible stairway where, so far as he was concerned, the crowds were still ascending to the trains.

23   I have said my life has been passed in the shade of a nonexistent tree, so that such sights do not offend me. Prematurely I am one of the brown wasps and I often sit with them in the great droning hive of the station, dreaming sometimes of a certain tree. It was planted sixty years ago by a boy with a bucket and a toy spade in a little Nebraska town. That boy was myself. It was a cottonwood sapling and the boy remembered it because of some words spoken by his father and because everyone died or moved away who was supposed to wait and grow old under its shade. The boy was passed from hand to hand, but the tree for some intangible reason had taken root in his mind. It was under its branches that he sheltered; it was from this tree that his memories, which are my memories, led away into the world.

24   After sixty years the mood of the brown wasps grows heavier upon one. During a long inward struggle I thought it would do me good to go and look upon that actual tree. I found a rational excuse in which to clothe this madness. I purchased a ticket and at the end of two thousand miles I walked another mile to an address that was still the same. The house had not been altered.

25   I came close to the white picket fence and reluctantly, with great effort, looked down the long vista of the yard. There was nothing there to see. For sixty years that cottonwood had been growing in my mind. Season by season its seeds had been floating farther on the hot prairie winds. We had planted it lovingly there, my father and I, because he had a great hunger for soil and live things growing, and because none of these things had long been ours to protect. We had planted the little sapling and watered it faithfully, and I

remembered that I had run out with my small bucket to drench its roots the day we moved away. And all the years since it had been growing in my mind, a huge tree that somehow stood for my father and the love I bore him. I took a grasp on the picket fence and forced myself to look again.

26   A boy with the hard bird eye of youth pedaled a tricycle slowly up beside me.

27   "What'cha lookin' at?" he asked curiously.

28   "A tree," I said.

29   "What for?" he said.

30   "It isn't there." I said, to myself mostly, and began to walk away at a pace just slow enough not to seem to be running.

31   "What isn't there?" the boy asked. I didn't answer. It was obvious I was attached by a thread to a thing that had never been there, or certainly not for long. Something that had to be held in the air, or sustained in the mind, because it was part of my orientation in the universe and I could not survive without it. There was more than an animal's attachment to a place. There was something else, the attachment of the spirit to a grouping of events in time; it was part of our morality.

32   So I had come home at last, driven by a memory in the brain as surely as the field mouse who had delved long ago into my flower pot or the pigeons flying forever admist the rattle of nut-vending machines. These, the burrow under the greenery in my living room and the red-bellied bowls of peanuts now hovering in midair in the minds of pigeons, were all part of an elusive world that existed nowhere and yet everywhere. I looked once at the real world about me while the persistent boy pedaled at my heels.

33   It was without meaning, though my feet took a remembered path. In sixty years the house and street had rotted out of my mind. But the tree, the tree that no longer was, that had perished in its first season, bloomed on in my individual mind, unblemished as my father's words. "We'll plant a tree here, son, and we're not going to move any more. And when you're an old, old man you can sit under it and think how we planted it here, you and me, together."

34   I began to outpace the boy on the tricycle.

35   "Do you live here, Mister?" he shouted after me suspiciously. I took a firm grasp on airy nothing—to be precise, on the bole of a great tree. "I do," I said. I spoke for myself, one field mouse, and

several pigeons. We were all out of touch but somehow permanent. It was the world that had changed.

Discussion Questions

1. What is Eiseley's thesis in this essay?
2. In small groups, discuss what Eiseley means when he observes in paragraph 8, "We cling to a time and place because without them man is lost, not only man but life."
3. Describe the tone of Eiseley's essay and identify specific passages that contribute to it.
4. What is your reaction to Eiseley's equating people to wasps? How does this analogy strengthen or weaken his essay?
5. How convincing is the ending of Eiseley's essay? Explain.

Writing Assignments

1. Write a journal that explores what humans can learn from animals.
2. Write an essay in which you describe "a time and place" that serve as important anchors in your life.
3. Do you think Eiseley's essay is an example of the expression "You can't go home again"? Write a paper that supports your answer.

Acknowledgments

Ascher, Barbara Lazear. "Middle Age: Becoming the Person You Always Were," from *Playing After Dark* by Barbara Lazear Ascher. Copyright © 1982, 1983, 1984, 1985, 1986 by Barbara Lazear Ascher. Used by permission of Doubleday, a division of Bantam Doubleday Dell Publishing Group, Inc.

Baldwin, James. "The Discovery of What It Means to Be an American" by James Baldwin was originally published in *The New York Times Book Review*. © 1959 by James Baldwin. Copyright renewed. Collected in Nobody Knows My Name, published by Vintage Books. Reprinted by arrangement with the James Baldwin Estate.

Conroy, Frank. "Think about It" by Frank Conroy. Copyright © 1988 by *Harper's Magazine*. All rights reserved. Reproduced from the November issue by special permission.

Cousins, Norman. "The Right to Die" by Norman Cousins, *The Saturday Review*, June 14, 1975. Reprinted by permission of The Saturday Review, © 1975, SR Publications, Ltd.

Cowley, Malcolm. "The View From 80," from *The View From 80* by Malcolm Cowley. Copyright © 1976, 1978, 1980 by Malcolm Cowley. Used by permission of Viking Penguin, a division of Penguin Books USA Inc.

Didion, Joan. "Goodbye to All That" from "Seven Places of the Mind" from *Slouching Towards Bethlehem* by Joan Didion. Copyright © 1968 and copyright renewed © 1996 by Joan Didion. Reprinted by permission of Farrar, Straus & Giroux, Inc.

Eiseley, Loren. "The Brown Wasps" by Loren Eiseley. Reprinted with the permission of Scribner, a Division of Simon & Schuster from *The Night Country* by Loren Eiseley. Copyright © 1971 by Loren Eiseley.

Fisher, M. F .K. "Moment of Wisdom" by M. F. K. Fisher. From *Sister Age* by M. F. K. Fisher. Copyright © 1983 by M. F. K. Fisher. Reprinted by permission of Alfred A. Knopf, Inc.

Hellman, Lillian. From *An Unfinished Woman* by Lillian Hellman. Copyright © 1969 by Lillian Hellman. By permission of Little, Brown and Company.

Hsun, Lu. "Death" from *Selected Stories of Lu Hsun* by Lu Hsun, translated by Yang Xianyi and Gladys Yang, 1960. Reprinted by permission of Foreign Languages Press.

Klass, Perri. "Conclusion—Baby Doctor" by Perri Klass. Reprinted by permission of The Putnam Publishing Group from *A Not Entirely Benign Procedure* by Perri Klass. Copyright © 1987 by Perri Klass.

Kübler-Ross, Elisabeth. "On the Fear of Death" by Elisabeth Kübler-Ross. Reprinted with the permission of Simon & Schuster from *On Death and Dying* by Elisabeth Kübler-Ross. Copyright © 1969 by Elisabeth Kübler-Ross.

Mairs, Nancy. "On Being a Cripple" by Nancy Mairs. From *Plaintext* by Nancy Mairs. Copyright © 1986 by University of Arizona Press. Reprinted by permission of the publisher.

Mead, Margaret. "Adolescents" from *Family* by Margaret Mead. Reprinted with courtesy of the Institute of Intercultural Studies, Inc.

Momaday, N. Scott. "My Horse and I" from *The Names* by N. Scott Momaday. Copyright © 1987 by N. Scott Momaday. Reprinted by permission of the author.

Montaigne, trans. by Donald M. Frame. "Of Age" by Montaigne. Reprinted from *The Complete Essays of Montaigne* translated by Donald M.

Frame with the permission of the publishers, Stanford University Press. © 1958 by the Board of Trustees of the Leland Stanford Junior University.

Rodriguez, Richard. From *Hunger of Memory* by Richard Rodriguez. Reprinted by permission of David R. Godine, Publisher, Inc. Copyright © 1982 by Richard Rodriguez.

Sarton, May. "The Rewards of Living a Solitary Life" by May Sarton, *The New York Times,* April 8, 1974. Copyright © 1974 by The New York Times Co. Reprinted by permission.

Steele, Shelby. Copyright © 1990 by Shelby Steele from *The Content of Our Character: A New Vision of Race in America* by Shelby Steele. Reprinted by permission of St. Martin's Press Incorporated.

Thomas, Lewis. "On Natural Death," copyright © 1979 by Lewis Thomas, from *The Medusa and the Snail* by Lewis Thomas. Used by permission of Viking Penguin, a division of Penguin Books USA Inc.

Thurber, James. "University Days" from *My Life and Hard Times* by James Thurber. Copyright © 1933 by James Thurber. Copyright © 1961 Helen Thurber and Rosemary A. Thurber. Reprinted by permission of Barbara Hogenson Agency, Inc.

Walker, Alice. "Beauty: When the Other Dancer Is the Self" from *In Search of Our Mothers' Gardens: Womanist Prose,* copyright © 1983 by Alice Walker, reprinted by permission of Harcourt Brace & Company.

Welty, Eudora. "The Little Store" from *The Eye of the Story: Selected Essays & Reviews* by Eudora Welty. Copyright © 1975 by Eudora Welty. Reprinted by permission of Random House, Inc.

White, E. B. "The Ring of Time" from *The Points of My Compass* by E. B. White. Copyright © 1956 by E. B. White. Originally appeared in The New Yorker. Reprinted by permission of HarperCollins Publishers, Inc.

Index of Authors and Titles